A CALL TO MERCY

MOTHER TERESA

A CALL TO MERCY

Hearts to Love, Hands to Serve

edited and with a preface and introduction by

BRIAN KOLODIEJCHUK, MC

IMAGE

NEW YORK

IMAGE   Mother Teresa Center

Copyright © 2016 by The Mother Teresa Center, exclusive
licensee throughout the world of the Missionaries of Charity
for the works of Mother Teresa.
Published in the United States by Image, an imprint of the
Crown Publishing Group, a division of Penguin Random
House LLC, New York.
crownpublishing.com

IMAGE is a registered trademark and the "I" colophon is a
trademark of Penguin Random House LLC.

Nihil Obstat: Donald F. Haggerty, S.T.D., Censor Librorum

Imprimatur: Timothy Michael Cardinal Dolan, D.D.,
Archbishop of New York

The *Nihil Obstat* and *Imprimatur* are official declarations
that a book or pamphlet is free of doctrinal or moral errors.
No implication is contained therein that those who have
granted the *Nihil Obstat* and *Imprimatur* agree with the
content, opinions, or statements expressed.

Library of Congress Cataloging-in-Publication Data is
available upon request.

ISBN 978-0-451-49820-5
eBook ISBN 978-0-451-49821-2

Printed in the United States of America

Jacket design by Jessie Bright

10 9 8 7 6 5 4 3 2 1

First Edition

To the poorest of the poor,

all those who are unwanted, unloved, rejected, and

forgotten, that through the tender and merciful love shown

to them by Mother Teresa and those inspired by her, they be

certain how precious they are in God's eyes.

Contents

Preface

The Holy Father's inspiration to proclaim the Extraordinary Jubilee of Mercy came as a quite unexpected but most welcome surprise. In *Misericordiae Vultus* (MV), the document (a bull of indiction) that established the Extraordinary Jubilee of Mercy, as well as on the many occasions he has spoken on this theme, Pope Francis not only invites us to enter more deeply into the "mystery of mercy" (MV 2), a gift God always longs to give us, but also seeks to make us aware of our responsibility to extend this gift to others. He presents Jesus as the "face of the Father's mercy," indeed, the expression of the Father's mercy par excellence.

The joyful occasion of Mother Teresa's canonization, which the Holy Father wished to take place during the Jubilee, is a providential opportunity to once again bring her example and message of God's tender and merciful love to the attention of Christians and all those who look to her as a model of what it is to be a "carrier" of that love. *A Call to Mercy* is an attempt to do precisely that.

Although every saint could, in some way at least, be called a "saint of mercy," it still may be asked why God's Providence would have Mother Teresa canonized during this special time. What message does this particular "saint of tender and merciful love" offer to the universal church—and even beyond—on the theme of mercy, which is, as we know, the leitmotif of the Holy Father's teaching and example. There is a particular resonance between Pope Francis's special attention and love for those on the "peripheries of human existence" and Mother Teresa's preferential choice to serve the poorest of the poor. Tenderness and compassion are the outstanding qualities of the charity that she understood Jesus wanted her to "carry"—to make known and experienced—to the poorest of the poor. For example, she urged her followers to "go to the poor with tenderness and serve the poor with tender and compassionate love." This is "carrying" the love of Jesus, who, she was absolutely convinced, "loves each one of us tenderly with mercy and compassion."

In keeping with the Holy Father's invitation in *Misericordiae Vultus* for us to "rediscover these corporal works of mercy" and not to "forget the spiritual works of mercy" (MV 15), the canonization of Mother Teresa is an opportune occasion to present both her teaching related to merciful love and her way of putting those teachings into practice through her daily action.

It is frequently said that "actions speak louder than words"; this is a book primarily about Mother Teresa's actions. Through her own words, and through the lens of direct witnesses, she emerges as an icon of tender and merciful love, a reflection of God's mercy for today, especially for the poorest of the poor.

It is my hope that the example of this "Saint of Mercy" as presented in this book will encourage us to deepen our own relationship with the God of tender and merciful love and to extend this love to our brothers and sisters, especially to those most in need, the materially or spiritually poorest of the poor.

Fr. Brian Kolodiejchuk, MC
Postulator

Introduction

In Mother Teresa's life (1910–1997), as in the lives of many other saints, we are offered a lived theology. We do not find in her writings or speeches any elaborate explanation on the meaning of mercy. However, we do find a rich heritage of a spirituality of mercy and compassion, as she experienced it personally and lived it out in her service of others. The numerous and very concrete ways of being merciful lived out by Mother Teresa and her followers caught the attention even of the secular world.

Interestingly, *mercy* is not a word that Mother Teresa employed frequently in her spoken or written word. Nonetheless, she understood herself to be someone in constant need of God's mercy, not just in a general way as a sinner in need of redemption, but also specifically as a weak and sinful human being who depended entirely on God's love, strength, and compassion each day. In fact, Jesus Himself had told her when inviting her to found the Missionaries of Charity: *"You are I know the most incapable person, weak and sinful, but just because you are that I want to use you, for My Glory!"* This was Mother Teresa's existential experience, one so deeply rooted in her heart that it shone forth in her face and in her attitude to others. She considered the poor, just like herself, to be in need of God's love and compassion, of God's care and tenderness. She easily identified with every other human being: "my sister, my brother." Her experience of being "in need" in front of God led to her vision of herself as one of the poor.

Pope Francis tells us that the etymological meaning of the Latin word for mercy—*misericordia*—"is *miseris cor dare,* to 'give the heart to the wretched,' those in need, those who are suffering. That is what Jesus did: He opened His heart to the wretchedness of man."[1]

Thus mercy involves both the interior and the exterior: the inner movement of the heart—the feeling of compassion—and then, as Mother Teresa liked to say, "putting love in living action."

In *Misericordiae Vultus* (the official document establishing the Extraordinary Jubilee of Mercy), Pope Francis says that mercy is "the fundamental law that dwells in the heart of every person who looks sincerely into the eyes of his brothers and sisters on the path of life."[2] He says that his desire for the coming year is that it "be steeped in mercy, so that we can go out to every man and woman, bringing the goodness and tenderness of God."[3]

This idea implies that our attitude is not from "above downward," as it were, where we think ourselves superior to those we serve, but rather that we recognize ourselves for who we are: *one of* the poor, *identified with* them in some way, being in some way in the same condition. And this must come from the heart, since understanding involves our very selves. Mother Teresa is a wonderful example of this principle.

Pope Emeritus Benedict indicates the source of this attitude in *Deus Caritas Est:* "Practical activity will always be insufficient, unless it visibly expresses a love for man, a love nourished by an encounter with Christ."[4] It was indeed an encounter with Christ that made Mother Teresa embark on a new mission, outside her secure convent routine. Jesus Himself was calling her to be His love and compassion to the poorest of the poor, to be His "face of mercy." She recounted: "I heard the call to give up all and follow Him into the slums—to serve Him in the poorest of the poor. . . . I knew it was His will and that I had to follow Him. There was no doubt that it was going to be His work." Pope Benedict continues: "My deep personal sharing in the needs and sufferings of others becomes a sharing of my very self with them: if my gift is not to prove a source of humiliation, I must give to others not only something that is my own, but my very self; I must be personally present in my gift."[5]

Mother Teresa epitomizes this act of giving.

"Her heart," said Sister Nirmala, Mother Teresa's immediate successor, "was big like the Heart of God Himself, filled with love, affection, compassion, and mercy. Rich and poor, young and old, strong and weak, learned and ignorant, saints and sinners of all nations, cultures, and religions found a loving welcome in her heart, because in each of them she saw the face of her Beloved—Jesus."

The canonization of Mother Teresa is, then, most appropriate during this Jubilee of Mercy because she epitomized so well what it means to accept Pope Francis's invitation to the Church: that we "enter more deeply into the heart of the Gospel where the poor have a special experience of God's mercy."[6] In meeting her, the poor indeed had the opportunity to meet God's mercy. They met a person who loved, who cared, who had compassion and the ability to understand their pain and their sufferings. In her wrinkled face, the poor—and all those who met her—had a chance to "see" the tender and compassionate face of the Father's love for us. They knew that she understood them, that she was one with them. An entry in her diary on December 21, 1948—the first day she went into the slums of Calcutta[7] to begin her mission to the poorest—reads:

> *At Agamuddin Street I had a number of children with bad sores—There an old woman came very close to me—"You Mother, you big Mother has become one of us—for us—how wonderful—what sacrifice." I told her that I was very happy to be one of them—and I really am. To see the sad suffering faces of some of them lit up with joy—because Mother has come—well, it is worth [it] after all.*[8]

The concrete expressions of mercy, as revealed in the Gospel, are referred to as the corporal and spiritual works of mercy. As Pope Francis says in MV,

> *Jesus introduces us to these works of mercy in his preaching so that we can know whether or not we are living as his disciples. Let us rediscover these* corporal works of mercy: *to feed the hungry, give drink to the thirsty, clothe the naked, welcome the*

stranger, heal the sick, visit the imprisoned, and
bury the dead. And let us not forget the spiritual
works of mercy: *to counsel the doubtful, instruct the*
ignorant, admonish sinners, comfort the afflicted,
forgive offenses, bear patiently those who do us ill,
and pray for the living and the dead.[9]

In response to the Holy Father's "burning desire that,
during this Jubilee, the Christian people may reflect on the
corporal and spiritual works of mercy,"[10] *A Call to Mercy*
presents Mother Teresa's teaching on and practice of the
works of mercy. My hope is that her example may, according to the Holy Father's wishes, "reawaken our conscience,
too often grown dull in the face of poverty."[11] She lived almost fifty years of her life completely dedicated to the care
of the poor and the marginalized. Astonishingly, for those
nearly fifty years she identified completely with the poor
she served by her own experience of being seemingly unwanted and unloved by God. In a mystical way—through
this painful interior "darkness"—she tasted their greatest
poverty of being "unwanted, unloved, and uncared for."
By this experience she did not see any significant difference
between herself and the poor she cared for: "The physical
situation of my poor left in the streets unwanted, unloved,
unclaimed—[is] the true picture of my own spiritual life,
of my love for Jesus, and yet this terrible pain has never
made me desire to have it different."

The following pages present some of Mother Teresa's
thoughts and writings on how she understood mercy and
the works of mercy. Just as important, they present a selection of testimonies that illustrate how she practiced the

corporal and spiritual works of mercy. These anecdotes reveal Mother Teresa as seen through the eyes of those closest to her; they reveal the face of mercy.

How This Book Came About and Its Structure

When the thought of presenting Mother Teresa as an "icon of tender and merciful love" first arose, the most suitable approach seemed to be to show her "in action." Thus the need to depict her more as an example than as just a teacher was evident from the outset. Her words, characterized by her distinctive simplicity and depth, are given their due importance; yet at the same time, revealing the coherence of her example with that teaching was deemed crucial to the project. The authenticity of her teaching is brought to the fore by the authenticity of her living; thus her teachings are words of wisdom that can serve as matter for prayer and contemplation as well as an impetus to action, a call to imitation.

A Call to Mercy shows Mother Teresa's daily living, her doing "ordinary things with extraordinary love," from the unique perspective of those closest to her. Testimony given by witnesses at Mother Teresa's process of canonization was chosen so as to provide powerful examples that would give even greater effect to her teaching. For the sake of authenticity, the anecdotes and stories recounted are given with minimum editing, even though it is evident that English is not the first language of some of the witnesses, so as to preserve the remarkable influence she had on the eyewitnesses.

The book treats separately each of the seven corporal and seven spiritual works of mercy. For each of these works, a short introduction gives Mother Teresa's understanding of these spiritual and corporal acts, followed by a selection of quotes from her writings (letters to the sisters, other members of her religious family, Co-Workers, friends; exhortations/instructions to her sisters; public addresses and speeches; as well as interviews). There is also a rich selection of the testimonies given by those closest to her, those who collaborated with her for many years, either in daily contact "under the same roof" like her sisters, or other members of her religious family, or otherwise close collaborators, Co-Workers, volunteers, or friends. These eyewitnesses were in a privileged position to see her dealings with the poor and with many others who came in contact with her. Some stories are firsthand accounts of how she dealt with the person relating the story, while others witness how she interacted with some other person or group.

Finally, a short section of questions for reflection and a prayer are meant to prompt us to be more open to God's mercy in our own life, and also, following the example of Mother Teresa, to be more open and willing to extend that mercy to our brothers and sisters. The questions are intended "to reawaken our conscience, too often grown dull in the face of poverty"[12] as Pope Francis bid us to do. It is my hope that each one of us may respond to this call with humility, docility, and generosity.

In order to respect the privacy of those concerned, a short general description of the witness is provided rather than the person's name. These descriptions are found in the notes at the end of the book. In this way, the required confidentiality is maintained, while at the same time we are able to present the text clearly and share the rich heritage of Mother Teresa's words and example with a larger public.

Fr. Brian Kolodiejchuk, MC
Postulator

ONE

FEED THE HUNGRY

"I saw the children—their eyes shining with hunger—I don't know if you have ever seen hunger. But I have seen it very often." As these words make it plain, Mother Teresa's sensibility to the hungry is evident in the way she was moved by her direct contact with them. She was stirred in the depths of her heart by her encounter with those suffering real physical hunger, as is clear especially in the way she recounted the stories of her experiences with the hungry. These experiences began when she was a child. Her mother had accustomed her and her siblings to serve and look after people from the street. When she witnessed hunger (or any other need of the poor), her reaction was "We have to do something about it." She then did anything possible (and at times also the nearly impossible) in order to bring food to the hungry. At times she tried to literally "move the world" to provide food for those who were starving.

Hunger may be something that is remote from our

experience or from our immediate surroundings. Maybe we "meet" the poor who suffer hunger only through the disturbing reports about some faraway disaster. However, if we "open our eyes to see," as Mother Teresa challenges us to do, we might encounter many more people suffering from having their basic need for sustenance unmet.

Mother Teresa is known not for setting up great programs that resolve world hunger (worthy and necessary as they are) but for "feeding the hungry," one by one, one at a time. Yet in doing so she made a great difference first in the lives of these individuals, and ultimately in the world.

There is another type of hunger that Mother Teresa began to speak of, especially after opening her houses in the West. She often repeated that people are "not only hungry for bread but hungry for love." Though suffering from this need is not commonly referred to as poverty, she realized that this type of poverty was "so much more difficult to remove." Thus it was also this "hunger for love" that she wanted to alleviate. She challenged her sisters, "You are meant to be that love and compassion to the people here [in the West]."

> When I pick up a person from the street, hungry, I give him a plate of rice, a piece of bread, I have satisfied, I have removed that hunger. But a person that is shut out, that feels unwanted, unloved, terrified, the person that has been thrown out from society—that poverty is so hurtful and so much, and I find that very difficult. Our sisters are working amongst that kind of people in the West.

Finally, Mother Teresa found another type of hunger, in countries both poor and rich, among people of all classes and religious backgrounds. "People are hungry for God," she used to say. This reality of "spiritual hunger," which she experienced deeply and encountered wherever she went, she addressed in a simple and timely manner. She wanted to be "God's love, His compassion, His presence" wherever she went, so that people looking at her might come to know the God whom she wished to reflect.

HER WORDS

It's Because He Loved

Before [Jesus] taught the people, He had pity on the multitude, and He fed them. He made a miracle. He blessed the bread, and He fed five thousand people. It's because He loved the people. He had pity on them. He saw the hunger in their faces and He fed them. And only then He taught them.[1]

✳

More than ever people want to see love in action through our humble works—how necessary it is for us to be in love with Jesus—to be able to feed Him in the hungry and the lonely. How pure our eyes and hearts must be to see Him in the poor. How clean our hands must be to touch Him in the poor with love and compassion. How clean our words must be to be able to proclaim the Good News to the poor.[2]

The Pain of Hunger

Some time ago one woman came with her child to me and said, "Mother, I went to two, three places to beg some food, for we have not eaten for three days but they told me that I am young and I must work and eat. No one gave me anything." I went to get some food and by the time I returned the baby in her hand had died of hunger. I hope it was not our convents that refused her.[3]

✳

We all speak of the terrible hunger. What I have seen in Ethiopia, what I have seen in other places, especially these days in places like Ethiopia, the people in hundreds and thousands are facing death just for [lack of] a piece of bread, for [lack of] a glass of water. People have died in my own hands. And yet we forget, why they and not we? Let us love again, so let us share, let us pray that this terrible suffering be removed from our people.[4]

✳

The pain of hunger is terrible and that is where you and I must come and give until it hurts. *I want you to give until it hurts*. And this giving is love of God in action. Hunger is not only for bread, hunger is for love.[5]

✳

The other day I picked up a child in Calcutta. From her dark eyes I saw she was hungry. And I gave her some bread and she was eating crumb by crumb. I told her, "Eat the bread, you are hungry."[6] I asked her why she eats so slowly. She replied: "I am afraid to eat faster. When I finish this piece, soon I will be hungry again." I told her: "Eat faster then I will give you more." That *small child* already knows the pain of hunger. "I am afraid." See—*we* don't know. As you can see we do not know what hunger is. We do not know how it is to feel pain because of hunger. I have seen small children dying for [lack of] a cup of milk. I have seen mothers in awful pain because children were dying in their own hands out of hunger. Don't forget! I am not asking for money. I want you to give of your sacrifice. I want you to sacrifice something you like, something you would like to have for yourself. . . . One day a very poor lady came to our house. She said: "Mother, I want to help but I am very poor. I am going from house to house to wash other people's clothes every day. I need to feed my children, but I want to do something. Please, let me come every Saturday to wash your children's clothes for a half an hour." This woman gave me more than thousands of rupees because she has given me her heart completely.[7]

✳

This morning I went to see the cardinal of Marseille, who is in charge of *Cor Unum,* to ask [them] to send food for our people in Africa. There is great poverty in Africa. The other day our sisters wrote that the people

just come in front of our gate for food and many of them
died of hunger. If the situation continues like now, many
are in danger of death; children are dying in the arms
of their mothers—what a terrible suffering. So I went
to this cardinal to ask if he could send some food to our
sisters. He was very nice; he told me that until our sisters
went, they were not aware of the presence of the poor.[8]

Love, to Be True, Has to Hurt

I had the most extraordinary experience of love of
neighbor with a Hindu family. A gentleman came to
our house and said, "Mother Teresa, there is a family
who has not eaten for so long. Do something." So I
took some rice and went there immediately. And I saw
the children—their eyes shining with hunger. I don't
know if you have ever seen hunger, but I have seen it
very often. And the mother of the family took the rice I
gave her and went out. When she came back I asked her,
"Where did you go; what did you do?" And she gave
me a very simple answer: "They [a Muslim family] are
hungry also." What struck me most was that she knew,
and who are they? A Muslim family. And she knew.
And I did not bring any more rice that evening because
I wanted them—Hindus and Muslims—to enjoy the joy
of sharing. But there were those children radiating joy,
sharing their joy and peace with their mother because
she had the love to give until it hurts, and you see this is
where love begins—at home in the family.[9]

Love, to be true, has to hurt and this woman who was hungry—she knew that her neighbor was also hungry, and that family happened to be a Mohammedan family. So it was so touching, so real. This is where we are most unjust to our poor—we don't know them. We don't know them—how great they are, how lovable they are, how hungry they are for that understanding love.[10]

✺

We have another word, *free*. I cannot charge anything for the work I do. People criticize us and say ugly things because of this word, *free*. The other day I read in one article, written by [a priest], that charity is like a drug for the poor—that when we give the people things free, it is like giving them drugs. I've decided that I will write to him and ask him: "Why did Jesus have pity on the people?" He must have drugged them also when He fed them by the multiplication of the loaves and fishes. He came to give Good News to the people but when He saw that they were hungry and tired, He fed them first. One more question that I'm going to ask him, "Did you ever feel the hunger of the poor?"[11]

✺

You know we cook for thousands of people in Calcutta. It happened one day that a sister came to me and said, "Mother, we have nothing to cook." It had never happened before. Then, at nine o'clock a truck arrived, full of bread. The government had closed the schools for the day and sent us the bread. See again, God's concern. He even closed the schools, but He would not

let the hungry ones die—that tenderness and concern
of God.[12]

We Want to Serve

The other day a Gujarati family came to Dum Dum[13]
where we have crippled people and undernourished
children and TB patients. This family, the whole family,
came with cooked food. Once upon a time, people
would never think of going near to these people. When
they came, I told the sisters to go and help them in the
serving. [To] my surprise they said, "Mother, we want to
serve by ourselves." For them it is a great thing, for they
become unclean. This is our privilege. Some of them
were even old. Nothing prevented them; unbelievable for
a Hindu family to say and to do such things.[14]

Together, We Can Do Something Beautiful for God

Love is for today; programs are for the future. We are
for today; when tomorrow will come, we shall see what
we can do. Somebody is thirsty for water for today,
hungry for food for today. Tomorrow we will not have
them if we don't feed them today. So be concerned with
what you can do today.[15]

✳

I never get mixed up in what governments should or
should not do. Instead of spending time [on] those
questions, I say, "Let me do [something] now."
Tomorrow may never come—our people may be dead

by tomorrow. So today they need a slice of bread and a
cup of tea; I give it to them today. Somebody was finding
fault with the work and said, "Why do you always give
them the fish to eat? Why don't you give them the rod to
catch the fish?" So I said, "Our people, they cannot even
stand properly on account of hunger and disease, still
less would they be able to hold a rod to catch the fish.
But I will keep on giving them the fish to eat and when
they are strong enough and they can stand on their feet,
I will hand them over to you and you give them the rod
to catch the fish." And I think this is the sharing. This
is where we need each other. It's where what *we* can do,
you may not be able to do. But what *you* can do, *we*
cannot do. But if we put these two works together, there
can be something beautiful for God.[16]

*

The other day again, a group of Hindu schoolchildren
came from very far. All the first and second prize-
winners went and asked the headmistress to give the
money instead of the prizes. So she put all the money in
an envelope and gave it to them. Then they all asked:
"Now take us to Mother Teresa: we want to give the
money to her poor people." Now see how wonderful
it was that they did not use that money for themselves.
Because we have created this awareness, the whole world
wants to share with the poor. Whenever I accept money
or an award or anything, I always take it in the name of
the poor, whom they recognize in me. I think I am right,
because after all what am I? I am nothing. It is the poor
whom they recognize in me that they want to give to,

because they see what we do. Today people in the world want to see.[17]

Tremendous Hunger for Love

In Ethiopia and in India, hundreds of people are coming and dying just there for [lack of] a piece of bread. In Rome and London and places like that people die of loneliness and bitterness.[18]

※

You see, we have a wrong idea that only hunger for bread is hunger. There is much greater hunger and much more painful hunger: hunger for love, for the feeling of being wanted, to be somebody to somebody. A feeling of being unwanted, unloved, rejected. I think that's a very great hunger and very great poverty.[19]

※

We have houses all over Europe and the United States and other places where there is no hunger for a piece of bread. But there's a tremendous hunger for love, a feeling of being unwanted, unloved, shut in, rejected, forgotten. There are people who have forgotten what is a human smile, what is a human touch. I think that is very, very great poverty. . . . And it is very difficult to remove that poverty while [satisfying that] hunger for a piece of bread, or nakedness for a piece of cloth, for a home made of bricks . . . , I think that's the much greater poverty, much greater disease, much greater painful situation of today.[20]

✳

Another time I was walking through the streets of
London in a poor area where our sisters also work.
I saw a man in a truly terrible condition sitting there
looking so sad and alone. So I walked up to him and
took him by the hand and asked him how he was. When
I did this, he looked up at me and said, "Oh, after such
a long time, I feel the warmth of a human hand. After
such a long time, someone is touching me." And then his
eyes brightened, and he started to sit up straight. Such
a tiny attention had brought Jesus into his life. He had
been waiting so long for a show of human love, but it
was actually a show of God's love. These are beautiful
examples of the hunger I see in these people, the poorest
of the poor, the ignorant and unwanted, the unloved, the
rejected, and the forgotten. They are hungry for God.
This is something you priests must meet continually;
not only a hunger in people suffering physically, but
also a great hunger in people suffering spiritually and
emotionally—people suffering in their hearts and souls,
especially young people.[21]

Terrible Hunger for the Word of God

"Where is that hunger in our country?" Yes, there is
hunger. Maybe not the hunger for a piece of bread, but
there is a terrible hunger for love. There is a terrible
hunger for the word of God. I will never forget when
we went to Mexico, and we went visiting very poor
families. And those people we saw had scarcely anything

in their homes, and yet nobody asked for anything. They all asked us: "Teach us the word of God. Give us the word of God." They were hungry for the word of God. Here too in the whole world there is a hunger for God, among the young especially. And it is there that we must find Jesus and satisfy that hunger.[22]

HER EXAMPLE: The Testimonies[*]

We Carried Food on Our Heads and Waded Through the Water

In 1968 there was a big flood in Calcutta. We went in our truck at night to give food to the people affected by the flood in Tiljala. We carried food on our heads and waded through the water. At one moment the flood current almost carried Sister Agnes away and so we sent her back to the truck. We were drenched to the skin and freezing. When we returned home at three a.m. Mother was waiting for us at the gate. She had kept hot water for all of us to bathe and a nice strong cup of hot coffee to make us warm. We were very touched by Mother's tender loving care for us her children.[23]

---

[*] As noted in the introduction, to maintain privacy as well as a meditative quality to the text that follows, a short description of the witnesses who contributed their thoughts and memories in each section entitled "HER EXAMPLE: The Testimonies" is provided in the notes.

Filling the Measuring Container Full and Pressing

Mother joined us to make Christmas hampers for the poor. How I lifted up my mind to God seeing Mother filling the measuring container full and pressing. You could hear voices, "Mother, we have yet so many hampers to make." "God will send" was the reply. Piles of hampers, we were not short. Mother's faith and trust in God was something living, had become part of herself, one could sense it; yes, one could see Mother had a close Friend, powerful and faithful, working with her all the time. Mother's principle: give what He takes and take what He gives with a big smile. No doubt it was hard for me, yet when done generously it became a touch of God's love.[24]

Others Hesitated—but Not Mother

I was deeply touched, when millions of [refugees from Bangladesh] poured into India and for her numbers did not matter [i.e., did not discourage her]. She would somehow or other do it. She just said, "We will do what we can," while moving everything possible to get every possible priest, sister, to help her in this work. "Why, this is God's work. These children are suffering, they are dying. We have to do something about it." She went out there and she was concerned about getting enough bread, getting the food. She would call the sisters aside, find out, try to get medical aid especially when the chicken-pox epidemic broke out at the Salt Lake camp. There were two hundred thousand there at the time. She immediately had to find somebody to assist them. She was just thirsty, impatient to find out other ways to get more people to come and assist them. To me, I think this was another example of her deep love—that she could embrace the whole world like the good "Mother" she was. At the time when the whole world was aghast at the influx of millions of refugees into India—this little woman, so weak—just went ahead to spur us on to help them. Her whole attitude being: if it is for Him, it can't fail. Others hesitated—but not Mother.[25]

A Messenger of Peace in Beirut

In August 1982 the violence in Beirut was at its height. Mother arrived on August 15, at a time when the bombing and shelling were at their worst. She had often told others, "Let us not use bombs and guns to overcome the world but let us radiate the peace of God and extinguish all hatred and love of power in the world and in the hearts of all men." . . . Mother found the sisters safe in Mar Takla in East Beirut. Mother came to know through the Red Cross that there were children mentally and physically ill in an asylum in West Beirut. Bombs had damaged the home and the children suffered from dire neglect. Upon hearing this news and despite repeated reminders from Church leaders as to how unsafe the situation was, Mother was determined to take the children out of danger. . . . However, because there was open firing, she could not cross the Green Line into West Beirut to do so. In her great faith she prayed for a cease-fire. And it happened! With an unexpected cease-fire in place, Mother traveled (carrying the Blessed Sacrament on her person) with four Red Cross vehicles and rescued the thirty-eight severely mentally retarded and crippled children. She helped the Red Cross and hospital workers to carry them one by one to the vehicles and then set off from there to Mar Takla convent. Two days later, Mother again crossed the Green Line to evacuate another twenty-seven children. . . . Clothes, food, and other supplies came from neighboring people. . . . Twelve-year-olds were so malnourished that they looked like five-year-olds. They were like little animals, eating whatever they could reach (e.g., nappies and bedding). They even tried to eat each other. To cure their diarrhea and at the same time prevent them from eating up the rubber bedding, I hung pieces of toasted bread around their cot sides. There was no water or electricity but slowly help started to arrive. . . . By November the children had improved so much. . . .

A sad ending for all of us was the day when the children had to be returned to the same hospital from where Mother had rescued them. . . . God's love once again had been blocked by man's greed for money, the government money grant provided for these children. It was a big disappointment to Mother. Her hands were tied and she had to abandon them into God's mercy. As Mother said, "Do not allow yourself to be disheartened by any failure as long as you have done your best."

I experienced from this situation in Beirut an example of how Mother was often the first to reach areas devastated by natural causes or human conflict. The need that arose spurred her on to take immediate action even at the risk of her own safety. This first of all brings out to me her heroic charity in such dangerous and impossible missions. Her trust in God was so great that there seemed to be nothing human that could come as an obstacle between His call and the fulfillment of it. The belief that God wanted her there seemed to enable a tremendous power to enter into her and so she arrived in Beirut and accomplished her mission against all "the prudent advice" given her.[26]

She Asked Not for Personal Needs

When she came to Delhi, we were driving to the airport and the commander of the Indian Air Force had asked if it was possible for Mother to visit and bless him in his office, and she agreed to do this. And she [said] in the car, "What can the Air Force do for us?" One of us said, "Mother, there is nothing the Air Force can do. Maybe you can ask him if when there is a need, will he provide a helicopter for you to go to some rescue or on some humanitarian cause." So she said, "Helicopter?" We went in, met with the chief. She said, "By the way, can your army men"—and it was the Air Force; she didn't make the connection—"plant trees?" And he said, "Yes, Mother. Well, could you elaborate?" "Somebody has given us a property to develop a home for the needy. It will be wonderful if we have fruit trees where these people can have fruit, because fruit will be good for them." He said, "We will look into it." Later we prompted her on what she did ask! Well, it was Divine Providence, because the next day the Air Force sent some people. But there was no water in this place and there was no way of getting water. The Air Force ended up drilling three tube wells to irrigate the soil to plant the trees, and today there is an orchard there. Yes, she asked, but not for personal needs. Nobody would have thought of asking the Air Force commander to plant trees! But she kept herself open to the prompting of the Holy Spirit.[27]

Collect Leftover Food

Mother asked for [the leftover] food not only in planes but also in hotels. That request was not for any show. Truly, with that extra food, a food fund for Mother's girls was formed. Part of the evening and morning meal at Dum Dum is given from Calcutta airport and extra food. The leftovers from "Flurys Bakery" is given to "Shanti Dan" as tiffin for one or two days in a week. Besides these, I have seen in Delhi that the extra food from the planes is used for the patients in their homes. The sisters collect all these things regularly. Sometimes the people from the airport also [deliver] the food to these centers.[28]

The Expense of the Dinner, a Gift for the Poor

Sister Agnes and I went with Mother to Oslo and witnessed her Nobel Prize speech. . . . Through all the ceremony and applause, Mother sat there quietly as if it was all for someone else. She accepted nothing but water at the reception after the ceremony. The banquet that usually followed had been canceled at Mother's request, and the expense of the dinner was given to Mother as a gift for the poor. . . . "I am myself unworthy of the prize. I do not want it, personally. But by this award the Norwegian people have recognized the existence of the poor. It is on their behalf that I have come."[29]

Love, to Be True, Has to Cost

Mother used to love to tell of the sacrifices the poor made to her work "to share the joy of loving" through the sisters' works of charity. She told us about the Buddhist monks who

visited her at Mother House and afterward imitated the
Missionaries of Charity (MC) First Friday fast that Mother
and the sisters make for the poor each first Friday of the
month. The monks imitated the MC custom to sacrifice one
meal and use the money to buy food for the poor. Those
monks on their own decided not to eat their lunch one day
and they saved that cost of the meal and brought the money
to Mother, asking her to use it to buy food for the poor.
Mother loved to share those stories, which reflected unexpected goodness and generosity, because she believed in that
goodness within each individual. She just invited people to
find it within themselves, and to share it with others. The
benefactors who made a real sacrifice to give, Mother used
to lift up as beautiful examples of love, because "Love, in
order to be true, has to cost." Surely many good people gave
her large donations for the poor, but Mother only told of the
little people who make a real sacrifice in order to share—
just as Jesus Himself gave praise for the donation of a widow's few pennies to support the temple. One of Mother's
favorite examples was of a beggar man out on the streets in
front of Mother House who came up to her and pulled three
rupees from under his rags and offered it as his contribution
to Mother's work. She knew it was probably all he had, but
she said she had to accept it in order to respect his sacrifice
for others.[30]

※

When Mother came to visit us in Nairobi, some rich people brought very expensive cakes. Mother said, "Send
it all to the patients and children." We sent all to them.
Many times I have seen in her that courage to give up, to

sacrifice. Mother was happy to give up, to sacrifice for love of Jesus.[31]

Do It Happily

I used to go out on apostolate with Mother. We used to walk a great distance to take care of a crippled boy with tuberculosis named Nicholas. . . . He had two big bedsores; Mother used to clean and dress his wounds. . . . The family was very poor, so Mother used to carry daily food for them. I used to be so tired and felt like crying every day, but Mother used to say, "We have to save souls and we must do it happily." I knew Mother was also tired, but she did not show it in any way. This we did for several years.[32]

With Due Dignity, Love, and Tender Care

The way she fed people in the home for the dying was so edifying and so exemplary that she clearly did not treat them like recipients of her mercy, but rather she approached them with due dignity, love, and tender care. . . . Although there were so many people, she dealt with each one individually. She used to say that just as the priest handles the Body of Christ at the altar, so we who receive the Body of Jesus so respectfully must also treat the broken bodies of the poor with the same respect and reverence.[33]

Have Faith in God

I remember during the Indochina War, in Darjeeling all the roads to the plains were cut off. I did not know where I would get food for sixty children, fifty old people, the poor people who came for food, and the sisters. I phoned Mother and asked, "What shall we do?" Mother asked me, "Did you say the Our Father?" I said, "Yes"; then she told me, "Have faith in God." That was the last phone call I was able to make or needed to make. Suddenly people from the hills around knew that we had so many people to feed, brought us food, milk, and so many other things, that till the war was over, we had enough.[34]

As God Loves Them

For Mother, charity meant to love all people as God loves them. With Mother this was so outstanding, this love of neighbor. If they were in need of bodily care, she would do this first, clean them and feed them. And then she would take care of their souls. As Mother said, "On an empty stomach one can hardly think of God. Jesus fed the people." In Nirmal Hriday (Mother Teresa's Home for the Dying), Mother did just this. And seeing these acts of charity, the sick felt that Mother, in her love for them, Mother was [like] God.[35]

Don't Talk, Do Something About It

There was a conference on World Hunger in India in 1987 and Mother was invited to speak. When we arrived at the side entrance of the building . . . there was a man on the ground. He was hungry and wanting something to eat. She said to me, "I'm going to take him home." We had a stretcher in the van, and I said I would take him, but she said no, that she was going to do it. She did this, which meant we

got to the conference an hour and a half later. She said nothing about that at the time, didn't use this as an example, but
here we are, it was a conference to eradicate hunger, and
hunger was at the front door.

Her attitude was always do one thing, one thing, one
thing. At this conference I was assuring her, "You go in and
I will look after him," because there were a million people
on the roads in India, but that was the type of person she
was; she had to look after this one person herself. She would
say, "Don't talk, do something about it." There were lots of
criticisms that she didn't speak to politicians. She said, "I'm
a religious. I'm here to give Christ to that person."[36]

Mother Herself Would Go

On one occasion, while I was in Calcutta as a first-year novice, there was a big flood in Calcutta and we could not go
out to the poor families because the land was flooded above
the knee. We went with Mother to distribute bread to the
hungry and the poor. People could not pass the street because of the water, but Mother in her great and tender love
for God and His poor went down into the water and started
giving bread to the hungry; because for her it was Jesus who
was hungry. And Mother didn't allow us novices to go down
into the water. But Mother did that heroic act of love of God
until it hurt.[37]

※

At times a poor person came and they would say to Mother,
"Mother, I have not eaten today." Mother would sit them
down in the parlor and call me to bring food. If I was not

there, Mother herself would go to the cupboard and get food. She was always concerned about the poor people.[38]

Never Send Away a Hungry Person

She taught us never to send away a hungry person even if you have nothing. Mother said, "Give them your smile and a word of comfort." . . . Wherever Mother opened a house, people, both rich and poor, came flocking from every denomination and asked if they could help the poor. Mother never ordered them nor demanded any help. All she said was "Give whatever you can, and if you have nothing, do not worry; give your hands to serve and hearts to love. By helping others, you will be rewarded with peace and joy."[39]

People Were More Hungry for God

The first foundation in Albania was made in Tirana on March 2, 1991. Mother immediately found out that the country was empty of everything. People were not only hungry for material things, but more hungry for God. It was a state of emergency—work must start immediately. Mother got back many churches that had been used as cinema halls, stadiums, storehouses, etc., from the government. She went to the central mosque where sick and homeless people were sheltered, opened the gate, and took them to our second house in Tirana, and handed the mosque over to the Muslim imam.[40]

REFLECTION

"I was hungry and you gave Me food." (Mt 25:35)

"Today they are hungry—tomorrow it may be too late."[41]

"Today, the poor are hungry—for bread and rice—and for love and the living word of God."[42]

Am I able to recognize a "hungry" person in my family, community, parish, neighborhood, city (or even farther away) and find a way to offer some relief of that hunger (material help, a simple gesture of my love and kindness, God's word)? Could I fast in solidarity with those who suffer hunger or join a volunteer program at a local charity?

I will express my gratitude to God for the food I receive through His Providence by praying before and after meals. Also I will not waste food, remembering those who go without.

PRAYER

Make us worthy, Lord, to serve our fellow men throughout the world, who live and die in poverty and hunger. Give them through our hands, this day, their daily bread, and by our understanding love, give peace and joy.

—Blessed Pope Paul VI

TWO

GIVE DRINK TO THE THIRSTY

"Giving drink to the thirsty." This act of mercy had a special resonance in Mother Teresa's life. Jesus's words from the Cross, "I thirst" (Jn 19:28), succinctly summed up her call to quench the infinite thirst of Jesus on the Cross for love and souls. Encounter with the thirsty was then a reminder of that call and an always fresh invitation to respond first to the immediate need of the poor person in front of her, but also in a mystical way to satiate the thirst of Jesus, who was through this person—in the "distressing disguise of the poor"—asking her to "give me to drink" (Jn 4:7).

Always attentive to the needs of the poor, especially their basic physical needs, Mother Teresa took practical and necessary steps to help them. Supplying drinking water with the help of civic authorities or charitable associations wherever there was a shortage was one of her many efforts among the poor.

Yet she did not remain focused only there. She took the experience of thirst a step further, realizing that many people were thirsting "for kindness, for compassion, for delicate love." She endeavored to offer some tangible expression of kindness, compassion, and love to meet this basic human need and encouraged her followers to do the same.

Whatever the concrete reason that someone experiences either real physical thirst (a lack of water, the scarcity of means to reach it, an inability to take it, or the destitution of those dying on the streets) or the human thirst for love, giving drink to the thirsty, as a work of mercy, definitely demands our attention. Following Mother Teresa's example, we are challenged to recognize the thirsty around us, and to do all in our power to satiate their thirst, endeavoring like her to give drink to those who thirst for water but "not only for water, but for knowledge, peace, truth, justice, and love."

HER WORDS

Jesus Is Thirsting for Our Love

When Jesus was dying on the Cross, He cried, "I thirst." [We are] to quench the thirst of Jesus for souls, for love, for kindness, for compassion, for delicate love. By each action done to the sick and the dying, I quench the thirst of Jesus for love of that person—by my giving God's love in me to that particular person, by caring for the unwanted, the unloved, [the] lonely, and . . . all the poor people. This is how I quench the thirst of Jesus for others by giving His love in action to them.[1]

*

When He was dying on the Cross, Jesus said, "I thirst." Jesus is thirsting for our love, and this is the test of everyone, poor and rich alike. We all thirst for the love of others—that they go out of their way to avoid harming us and do good to us. This is the meaning of true love—to give until it hurts.[2]

*

When He said, "I thirst," they thought that He was thirsty for water. So they gave Him vinegar and He didn't take it. But His thirst was there . . . His thirst for love, for souls. And today He's saying the same thing to you and to me: "I thirst" for love, for souls. And how will we satiate that thirst of Jesus? Now, right here, each one of us, by working for the salvation and sanctification of souls. That is His thirst, that terrible thirst of Jesus, that was so painful for Him on the Cross, that He knew He was going through so much suffering and yet so many will not accept Him.[3]

*

We must be able to choose to be poor even in little things. Thousands of people are without light. In prison, people are dying. They get one bucket of water to wash and drink from it. I choose to use one bucket of water,

not because I have to, but because I love to. You will be
a true MC when you know poverty and how to share.
This is the simple way that Our Lady and Our Lord
used when on earth.[4]

What Does He Thirst For?

He sends us to the poor in particular. The cup of water
you give to the poor, to the sick, the way you lift a dying
man, the way you feed a baby, the way in which you
teach an ignorant child, the way you give medicine to a
leper . . . your attitude and manners toward them—all
this is God's love in the world today. "God still loves the
world!" I want this to be imprinted in your minds: God
still loves through you and through me today. Let me see
this love of God in your eyes, in your actions, in the way
you move about.[5]

*

I have seen terrible bodily suffering, terrible, and to see
those people in Ethiopia, just when you open the gate
in the morning, they're just in front of our gate, just
gasping for a glass of water; they have not touched food;
they come all the way just to get a little bit of tender love
and care and some food.[6]

Where Are We?

Many people in the street . . . unwanted, unloved,
uncared for, people hungry for love. They had three,

four bottles near them but they drink that because there is nobody to give them something else. Where are you? Where am I? . . . We have so many people like that right in New York, right in London, in these big European cities. Just a piece of newspaper, lying there. Our sisters go at night from 10:00 p.m. to 1:00 a.m. in the streets of Rome and they bring sandwiches, they bring something hot to drink. In London, I've seen people standing against the factory wall to warm themselves. How? Why? Where are we?[7]

Thirst for Understanding

Not only hungry for bread and rice but hungry for love, to be wanted, to be known that I'm somebody to you, to be called by name, to have that deep compassion, hunger. Today in the world there is a tremendous hunger for that love. Thirsting for understanding.[8]

✳

He is saying: "I am hungry. I am thirsty. I have no place. I have nobody. You did it unto Me." I am always saying that we are not social workers, but contemplatives in the heart of the world. In the heart of the world we are feeding Jesus who is hungry. We are giving the water of mercy and joy to our people, to Jesus.[9]

HER EXAMPLE: The Testimonies

Ethiopia—an Open Calvary

After the visit to Alamata, Ethiopia, Sister called Mother and informed her of what she had seen. Mother said in anguish, "Sister, do something before they die." Sister said, "Mother we need food, medicine, clothing, and most of all water." Mother said, "I will call you back." . . . Mother [phoned] President [Reagan]: "I had a call from Ethiopia just now saying thousands are dying of hunger and thirst. Please do something. They need food, water, clothing, and medicines." The president was moved and said to Mother that he would call her back.

Within a day the USA was involved, and through CRS (Catholic Relief Services) [large] amounts of food were arranged for the MCs in Ethiopia. After sending cargo planes and ships loaded with food, clothing, and medicines, Mother reached Ethiopia with four sisters. She carried with her blankets, biscuits, and clothing. Everyone was waiting to meet Mother. She met a pop singer in the airport. He [greeted] Mother and exclaimed, "Ethiopia is an open hell." Mother looked into his eyes and said, "Ethiopia is an open Calvary, not an open hell. You and I can do our little part and then life will be saved."

The next day, with a burning fever, she was ready to fly to the relief places. The president of Ethiopia gave her his plane for the trips. She saw hundreds of dying skeleton patients, eyes deep down, the stomach stuck into the spines, with a fearful look in their faces; thousands sitting patiently waiting for the cooked food, which was served from seven a.m. to seven p.m. The sisters also managed to give a glass of water to each person. Mother went around and blessed everyone, feeling his or her pain. She took a bucket of water and went around giving it to them to drink. With a big smile she said to the sisters, "I envy all of you because Jesus said if you give a cup of cold water, you will receive the reward in heaven. You are privileged because you are quenching the thirst of Jesus in the poor. Jesus said, 'You did it to Me.' Jesus is true and Jesus cannot cheat us." Seeing the joy of the sisters, Mother said to the regional [superior], "Look at them. So little they have and yet they are so happy and healthy. Yes, we can live without many things. The secret of joy is our poverty and wholehearted and free service to the poorest of the poor." And Mother blessed us and left for Makale. . . .

We went straight from the airport to the camps where the famine victims were kept. The very sick were lying in the tents. Suddenly Mother noticed a little shed made with the jungle wood, and there were many corpses waiting for their turn to be buried. . . . The people said, "Lack of water is killing thousands, Mother. Give us water." Though Mother went to bed early, she did not sleep much. . . . She was waiting for the dawn to return to Addis Ababa. From time to time the sisters could hear Mother say, "How terrible it is to live without water, the terrible thirst." She tossed and turned in her bed.[10]

※

During the big famine, there was no water at all [in Alamata, Ethiopia]. Mother came to visit. There was no water at all, even to drink. At lunchtime we all had one glass of water. But Mother did not drink her water; it was very hot on that day and we all were thirsty. Mother took her water and gave it to a dying lady.[11]

Practical and Concrete

Toward the sick, the suffering, Mother showed an extraordinary love. It was as much an evangelization to see her at Kalighat (a hospice Mother Teresa founded in 1952, also known as Nirmal Hriday), see her go from bed to bed, see her touch the people, see her practical concern, because Mother expressed love. She was a practical woman and she expressed it in a concrete way, whether it was water for the thirsty or chocolates for the fathers, and that was always more of a revelation of love than if she gave us an exhortation. . . . And she would always invite us to sacrifice, then get a move on because of their needs. It was always directly or indirectly to give that wholehearted service, and if she found someone needed something, she would almost divide a sister in half to try to attend to both these needs. That love she showed to them was extraordinary.[12]

Jesus Is Thirsty in the Most Distressing Disguise

One of the main characteristics of Mother's spirituality was seeing Christ in the poorest of the poor, in the most distressing disguise. This expression "distressing disguise" is something very special. It was not just the poorest of the poor, but seeing Jesus in distressing disguise in the form that was very difficult, very hard to discover, but believing that Jesus is there, that Jesus is thirsty, trying to be with Him. You cannot enter into that faith in the distressing disguise unless you have contact through meditation, through prayer, especially through the Eucharist. And then she would say, "The Jesus whom I receive in the Eucharist is the same Jesus whom I serve. It is not a different Jesus." . . . I think the whole spirituality in the Missionaries of Charity is centered on that presence. . . . "I want to serve and love Jesus in the poor. I want to live like Saint Francis of Assisi, a poor life, and serve Him."[13]

REFLECTION

"I was thirsty and you gave Me drink." (Mt 25:35)

"Were you there to give Him the water of compassion, of forgiveness, in His Thirst, through your sister [or brother]?"[14]

"Thirsty for kindness He begs of you. . . . Will you be that 'one' to Him?"[15]

Are there small acts of charity that we could practice without drawing attention to them and that would satisfy not only the thirst for water, but the thirst for love and attention of those nearest to us? Can I render some small service to my family or community member, in an effort to be the first one to serve, rather than to expect to be served? Can I help in a project that provides water for those who do not have it? How can I avoid wasting water, in solidarity with those who suffer a shortage of it?

PRAYER

Mary, Mother of Jesus, you were the first one to hear Jesus cry, "I thirst." You know how real, how deep is His longing for me and for the poor. I am yours— Teach me, bring me face-to-face with the love in the Heart of Jesus Crucified.

With your help, Mother Mary, I will listen to Jesus's thirst and it will be for me a WORD OF LIFE. Standing near you, I will give Him my love, and I will give Him the chance to love me and so be the cause of your joy. And so I will satiate the thirst of Jesus. Amen.

—Mother Teresa

THREE

CLOTHE THE NAKED

Mother Teresa never got used to poverty; after her visits to different communities of her sisters, she often remarked, "Our poor people are suffering so much." "The poverty in New York, London, Rome . . . go at night in the streets of Rome you see people sleeping on a newspaper," she sadly noted. At times it seemed that the poor were getting poorer and poorer. She had eyes to see that many people did not have sufficient clothing. Some had no change of clothes nor a chance to have a shower, and while living on the streets, they had to put up with the scornful looks that their poor appearance or bad smell provoked. They too would have liked to wear decent and nice clothes, as everyone else does.

Whether the poor were ill clad or not, Mother Teresa's reaction to their need was not only to give them proper clothing, but also to show them all the respect she could. She would cover the bodies of those lying naked on the streets, put a warm blanket over those shivering with cold, or shield from shame those lying with maggots and humiliating wounds so that others might not turn with repugnance from their poverty. When she spoke of "clothing the naked not only with clothes, but also with human dignity," she was emphasizing the need to treat people suffering from want with great respect and to restore to them their dignity as sons and daughters of God.

Profound knowledge of herself allowed Mother Teresa to go beyond appearances and see herself as neither different from nor better than others. She was able to do so because she knew in the depths of her heart that she was one of the poorest of the poor. This also helped her to have a profound and tender compassion for the person in front of her, at the same time as she recognized his or her human dignity. Further, she knew that "the poor people are very great people. They can teach us so many beautiful things. . . . These are people who maybe have nothing to eat, maybe they have not a home where they can live, but they are great people."

Yet do we realize how little worth is accorded to human dignity in our modern world? Are individuals not often considered mere objects of exploitation? In so many circumstances in which human dignity is so little respected, and when individuals are considered mere objects to be exploited, the love and respect with which Mother Teresa treated every human being is an even more timely reminder. Treating someone with kindness, respect, and reverence can indeed restore to that person his or her innate dignity.

HER WORDS

He Chose to Be Like Us
The poor are great people and we owe them deep
gratitude, for if they did not accept us, then we would
not exist as MCs. To be able to understand this, we look
at Jesus. To be able to become man, He "being rich,
became poor" [2 Cor 8:9]. He could have chosen the
king's palace, but to be able to be equal to us He chose
to be like us in all things except sin. We, to be equal
to the poor, choose to be poor like them in everything
except destitution.[1]

✳

I am very sure that all those people who have died with
us [are] in heaven, they are really saints; they are in the
presence of God. It may be that they were not wanted on
this earth, but they are very beloved children of God.[2]

Jesus Died for That Naked Person
Jesus died on the Cross to show that greater love, and
He died for you and for me and for that leper, and for
that man dying of hunger, and that naked person lying in
the street, not only of Calcutta, but of Africa, and New
York, and London, and Oslo—and insisted that we love
one another as He loves each one of us. We read that in
the Gospel very clearly, "Love as I have loved you; as I
love you; as the Father has loved Me, I love you."[3]

And He says, "I was hungry and you gave Me to eat, I was naked and you clothed Me, I was sick and you took care of Me, I was homeless and you took Me in, I was lonely and you smiled at Me. . . . Whatever you do to the least of My brethren, you have done it to Me." And this is what Jesus again and again told us: to love one another as He has loved us.[4]

So this is what all of us must take the trouble [to find out], where are these places [in which the poorest of the poor live] and guide the other Co-Workers to go to these places. Say two can go, never go alone. You should never go alone, take another person and go to that place. That is Christ in the distressing disguise, and for us this is the hungry Christ, the naked Christ, and the homeless Christ. . . . Just to do that humble work . . . We have determined to remain with the humble work and . . . it is not a waste of time just to feed and to wash and to scrub and to love and to take care and to do these little things. Because it is directly done to the hungry Christ, the naked Christ. He cannot deceive us; it is that touching Him twenty-four hours. So that's why it is so beautiful that we can pray twenty-four hours when we are in their presence, when we are touching them.[5]

Do you really love Jesus? Do you really often feel
that thirst of Jesus? Do you hear Him saying to you,
"Do you love Me in the poorest of the poor?" Sisters,
listen to Mother, are you able to hear the cry of Jesus
in the hungry one? The naked one? The unloved and
unwanted one? In the leprosy patient with that big
wound full of maggots? Those AIDS patients? With
what dignity do you treat them? Do you find the
suffering Christ in each one? If you are very close to
Jesus, with the help of Our Lady you can say I will
quench the thirst of Jesus by sharing their suffering.
It is the same way in our community, with our own
sisters, our superiors. Now don't forget: "You did it
to Me."[6]

How Clean Your Hands Must Be

How clean your hands must be to join in prayer, to
clothe the naked Christ.[7]

※

Today a group of schoolchildren came to see me. They
had selected a boy and a girl from each class to bring
the money and the food after the puja offerings to us, to
our Shishu Bhavan (Home for Children), and then they
came here to see me. Now how do they know about us,
I do not know. See, sisters, this is the wonderful part of
our vocation, that as MCs we have created an awareness
of the poor in the whole world. Twenty years ago if
you said there is a hungry man or a naked man around,
nobody would believe you. Today the whole world

knows our poor because of our work. Because they
know, they want to share.[8]

✳

Mr. Kennedy came to visit the place. Sister Agnes was
washing the dirty clothes and he insisted on shaking
hands with her. Sister was hiding her hands but he
insisted, "I want . . . These hands are doing the humble
works for the love of Christ."[9]

✳

I remember last time when I was in Beirut and I
brought those children—in terrible condition—hospital
bombed—workers had run away—those thirty-seven
children completely naked, one on top of another,
nobody feeding them, taking care of them—they were
like sucking each other. We brought these children
and put them on nice clean beds. See the difference
these sisters have made for these children. "Thank you,
Mother"—doctors came and everyone said, "Every
single child will die within one week." The most
wonderful thing is that not one single child died, and the
smile on their faces was beautiful.[10]

✳

Let us not make the mistake that here in Europe and
other places we do not have hungry people, we don't
have naked people. There is not only hunger for bread,
there is hunger for love. [Maybe here] there is no
nakedness for [lack of] a piece of clothing but there
is nakedness [for lack] of human dignity; there is no

homelessness for a room made of bricks but there is that rejection of being unwanted, unloved, uncared for. That is why we need to pray. Prayer will give us a clean heart, and with a clean heart we can see God. And if we see God, we will love one another as God loves each one of us.[11]

Nakedness Is the Loss of That Human Dignity

That is why we say, the unwanted, the unloved, the uncared for, the forgotten, the lonely—this is much greater poverty. Because material poverty you can always satisfy with material things: if we pick up a man hungry for bread, we give him the bread and we have already satisfied his hunger. But if we find a man terribly lonely, rejected, a throwaway of society, material help will not help him. Because to remove that loneliness, to remove that terrible hurt, needs prayer, needs sacrifice, needs tenderness and love. And that is very often more difficult to give than to give material things. That is why there is hunger not only for bread, but there is hunger for love.[12]

❋

Every human being is created in the image and likeness of God, and Christ, by His incarnation, is united with each human person. In the beginning when I first started the work, some people passed remarks that the Church is not made of rubbish. That meant the poor, the sick, the dying, the crippled, the homeless, etc. Now everyone seems to have turned toward what was considered rubbish. Yes, the poor are worthy of respect and human dignity. Human beings cannot become conscious of their own dignity unless they have experienced love. It reminds me of the man who died in Nirmal Hriday. "I have lived like an animal in the street, but I will die like an angel, loved and cared for."[13]

❋

There are many people who have died in very cold countries, they are frozen to death. But nakedness is also the terrible loss of human dignity, that loss of [that] beautiful virtue—that purity, a virgin body, a virgin heart, a pure heart—that purity that is pure, that chastity that is chaste, that virginity that is virgin, loss of that beautiful gift of God.[14]

❋

Nakedness is for the loss of that human dignity, the loss of that respect, the loss of that purity that was so beautiful, so great, the loss of that virginity that was the most beautiful thing that a young man and a young woman can give each other because they love each other, the loss of that presence, of what is beautiful, of what is great; this is nakedness.[15]

❋

There is nakedness for that human dignity, for that respect of the Divine that is in each one of us. Because God has created us for greater things, to love and to be

loved. And so when we take away the dignity of that
human being, we are destroying in him that divinity that
is in him.[16]

HER EXAMPLE: The Testimonies

He Was Stark Naked with Many Wounds

Once when an English young man was running wildly on
the road to avoid the stoning from an angry mob, Mother
stopped the ambulance in which we were traveling and took
him in. He was stark naked with many wounds. Mother
took him to the Mother House, gave him water for bathing,
treated his wounds, gave him clothes to put on and a warm
meal.[17]

We Are Going to Take Every Child from Here

When we first went . . . into this orphanage [in Romania],
we found sixty-three children in an unspeakable state. . . .
Mother had permission to take forty of the children. We
went and found them naked, two and three to a bed, many
sitting or lying in urine. Mother said to me, "We are going
to take every child from here." I said, "Mother, we only have
documents for forty." Mother stopped me and said, "I will
not leave without taking every child." Later I found Mother
outside and she kept repeating, "I don't want to judge" (she
was visibly shaken). "I don't want to judge them, but these

people (the caretakers of the children) they are standing there, they are not feeling shy, not feeling embarrassed, how is that possible?" Then again, "I don't want to judge them." Mother did not lose her composure with the caretakers, but she saw to it that we took the children, all sixty-three.[18]

Mother Did Not Send the Lady Away

I was so struck to see Mother's trust in Divine Providence. One day a lady came with torn clothes, so Mother asked the sister in charge to bring a sari. There was no sari to give her, though. Still, Mother did not send the lady away, and in a few minutes a man came and brought many new saris. That lady was so happy.[19]

She Had the Power of God's Love

Albania in 1991 was totally empty of everything: no foodstuffs in the stores, no clothes, no medicines. Mother begged, especially from Italy, for clothes, food, and medicines. Things began to pour in but it was difficult to distribute them. People were undisciplined and hostile. We told Mother about it, but Mother told us to distribute the clothes and food when she was with us. We went and gave out tickets to the people, but even this was impossible. The day for distribution came and Mother was there, ready, with her apron on. Police were also there outside. The crowd outside was enormous in number, beyond police control. Mother went out to the crowd and spoke to them. We were afraid for Mother, as she was suffering from heart disease. She was courageous and determined. She calmed the crowd and that day we gave the people clothes. Mother could do this because she had the power of God's love. After finishing, Mother exclaimed, "Albanian people were not like this." Mother remembered her past. Yes, the whole nation was destroyed in fifty years. If God was legally banished from the country, what could one expect a man to be—a man without dignity. One Albanian said to us: "Communism has taken fifty years to destroy the conscience of people, but to rebuild the conscience of Albanians it will take a hundred years."[20]

The Best Medicine to Stop the Cough

Mother would keep close to her bed whoever was sick so that she could keep an eye on us. If any sister would cough in the chapel, Mother would bring her out and wrap her with her own warm clothing. And if any sister would cough at night in the dormitory, Mother would go to the sister and say gently and lovingly, "Sister, is Mother going to hear your cough all night?" Then that was the end. The best medicine to stop the cough was Mother's great love and concern for us! In our dormitory, every night before Mother went to bed she went around from bed to bed and saw to it that everybody was all right and nicely covered us with a blanket. If our legs were out, she would put them inside the mosquito net and tuck our blankets nicely—even if Mother had lots of letters to write and was very busy. How much I missed Mother, who was so much like my very own mother.[21]

How Much the Poor Must Have to Suffer

I was in the dormitory. It was winter, and with all the doors and windows open I was shivering in my bed. Two blankets were not enough, but again it was around midnight, so I tried to warm myself with what I had. Just then I felt somebody covering me with a blanket. I thought I was imagining, yet I opened my eyes and who was there? Of course, Mother. Once again very lovingly she covered me, tucked the blankets under my mattress, blessed me, and pressed her warm hands on my face and said, "Sleep." Only in the morning did I realize that she had sacrificed her own blanket and given it to me. Was she able to sleep in the cold without a blanket? Only heaven knows. In the morning, Mother told me, "How much the poor must have to suffer sleeping on a bare cold floor without any blanket. Our sufferings are nothing compared to the suffering of the poor."[22]

All My Clothes Are Wet

One day it was raining and all my clothes were wet, and I went to tell Mother, "Mother, I have nothing to put on, all my clothes are wet." And Mother told me to go and take Mother's nightgown from under her pillow and wear that. I did that.[23]

REFLECTION

"I was naked and you clothed Me." (Mt 25:36)

"Naked for loyalty He hopes of you. . . . Will you be that 'one' to Him?"[24]

"The poor are naked—for clothes, for human dignity and compassion."[25]

Do I look down on people whose clothes are shabby or dirty? Do I realize that they might be dressed like that because they have no change of clothes? Do I realize that because of their poor clothing they may seek isolation? And do I contribute to their wretchedness by my condescending look or by pretending I do not see them? Do I realize that they may be suffering because of want and because they are despised by others on account of it? What can I do so that they need not be shunned by others because of the rags they wear?

Do I have eyes to see that the people I encounter on the street need clothes? Do I have a heart ready to share some of my clothing with them? Would a piece of clothing that I do not need help someone? Approaching a needy person might be difficult and challenging, but it may also be rewarding. Try to find a person in need and give something with your own hands, in a way that restores that person's dignity, that makes him or her feel honored and respected. Can I offer someone a warm and friendly greeting, acknowledging that person's innate dignity by the way I interact with him or her?

PRAYER

Dear Jesus, help me to spread Your fragrance
wherever I go.
Flood my soul with Your Spirit and life.
Penetrate and possess my whole being so utterly,
that my life may only be a radiance of Yours.
Shine through me, and be so in me
that every soul I come in contact with
may feel Your presence in my soul.
Let them look up, and see no longer me, but only Jesus!
Stay with me and then I will begin to shine as You shine,
so to shine as to be a light to others.
The light, O Jesus, will be all from You;
none of it will be mine.
It will be You, shining on others through me.
Let me thus praise You in the way which You love best,
by shining on those around me.
Let me preach You without preaching,
not by words but by my example,
by the catching force,
the sympathetic influence of what I do,
the evident fullness of the love my heart bears to You.
Amen.

—Inspired by John Henry Cardinal Newman's own prayer,
prayed by Mother Teresa daily after Holy Communion

FOUR

SHELTER THE HOMELESS

Homelessness is unfortunately becoming ever more common, even in developed countries. When Mother Teresa spoke about the homeless, she was rightly concerned about the poor who had inadequate housing, but even more about the poor living on the streets, "under the heavens," day after day, month after month, and frequently year after year. Their situation was all the more desperate since a different future was not realistically in sight. Realizing the gravity of the problem, she sought appropriate places where she could open shelters or residences for the homeless. These centers were meant to be real homes, where the poor would be welcomed, loved, cared for, and especially where they would "feel at home," as she used to insist.

Yet, however desperate the fact of being homeless is, Mother Teresa saw a deeper problem than just the mere lack of housing. She spoke of "the physical situation of my poor left in the streets unwanted, unloved, unclaimed."

This feeling of being rejected, abandoned, let down, of not belonging anywhere, or not having a reference point or a safe haven while passing through life's struggles was a real suffering that she wanted to remedy along with providing physical shelter.

This deep understanding of "homelessness" came also from her deep mystical experience. In a letter to one of her spiritual directors, she claimed that the condition of the poor in the streets, rejected by all and abandoned to their suffering, was "the true picture of my own spiritual life." This interior and excruciating pain of feeling unwanted, unloved, unclaimed by the God whom she loved with her whole heart, enabled her to grasp what the homeless felt in their daily life. She completely identified with their misery, loneliness, and rejection. And the poor felt this deep compassion of hers, merciful and nonjudgmental; they felt welcomed, loved, and understood.[1]

Familiar with this pain, she used to encourage her sisters to give "shelter to the homeless—not only a shelter made of bricks but a heart that understands, that covers, that loves."[2] She endeavored to create a true home where everyone could feel welcomed, loved, and protected. She did not want just a cold, lifeless institution lacking love and affection, but places of peace and rest, where the homeless could experience God's love and those who were dying could "die in peace with God," knowing that they were loved and cared for.

HER WORDS

Jesus Is Reliving His Passion in Our Poor People
"I was homeless, and you took Me in." I am sure you in
Assisi do not know what is hunger for bread, but there is
hunger for love. . . . You do not find people lying in the
streets maybe, homeless; but they are homeless because
they are rejected, [lacking] that human dignity, that
human love. Do you know the poor of Assisi? We have
homes for the homeless people that we pick up from the
streets of Rome. In Carlo Cattaneo,[3] we have a home
for the people who have no one, who have nothing, who
are hungry. I am sure if we pray we will find that maybe
right there in your own city, in your own place, you will
find the poor.[4]

❋

Jesus is reliving His Passion in our poor people. The
poor people are really going through the Passion of
Christ. We must serve them with respect. We should not
send them from door to door—from Shishu Bhavan to
Mother House. They have already so much to suffer.
We should treat them with dignity. These poor people
are Jesus suffering today. We must find ways and means
of helping them in a better way; don't add to their
sufferings. Poor people are Jesus's Calvary today.[5]

❋

In Calcutta, we have picked up 52,000 people from the
streets—throwaways of society, unwanted, unloved,

having no one to love them. Maybe you have never experienced that, it is a terrible pain, terrible pain.[6]

✴

It may be if you go to the station and it may be if you visit some of the very poor areas, you will find people who are sleeping just in the park or you will see them sleep in the street. I have seen people in London, I have seen people in New York, I have seen people in Rome sleeping out in the street, in the park, and this is not the only kind of homelessness—that is terrible, terrible to see in the cold night, a man, a woman sleeping on a piece of newspaper in the street. But there is much greater homelessness—being rejected, being unwanted, being unloved.[7]

But Mother, How Did You See Him?

When I was in Delhi, I was traveling by car, along one of the big streets. There was a man lying half on the road and half on the pavement. Cars were passing by but no one stopped to see if he was all right. When I stopped the car and picked up the man, the sisters were surprised. They asked me: "But Mother, how did you see him?" No one had seen him, not even the sisters.[8]

Suddenly He Realized God Loves Me

Homeless is not only for [want of] a home made of bricks, though we have many homes for the sick and the dying, many homes for the homeless all over the world,

but it's not only for a home made of bricks, but that
terrible feeling of being unwanted, unloved, uncared
for, a throwaway of society. Like we have at present, we
have so many people who are suffering with AIDS, just
throwaways of society, and yet they are our brothers,
our sisters. It has made such a great difference in their
life and in the life of many volunteers when we opened
the home, the Gift of Love, in New York, and the Gift of
Peace, in Washington, where we gather all these people
suffering with AIDS, that they can die loved and cared
for—and so experience a beautiful death. This is the
fruit of love that you and I can share with them. That
is the protection of life—that those people have been
created for greater things, to love and to be loved.[9]

※

In Australia, we have a home for the alcoholics, and the
sisters picked up a man from the street who had been an
alcoholic for many years. He had ruined his own life and
the life of his children and family and everything. And
[thanks to] the way the sisters [treated him], suddenly
one day he realized "God loves me." When, how? . . .
The way the sisters talked to him, the way they touched
him, the way they loved him. They didn't do anything
special, but the way they dealt with him, with so much
love, so much compassion, so much understanding and
not a bit surprised that he was a drunkard, that he was
so helpless, that he was so hopeless. Then suddenly this
"God loves me," and from that day he never touched
anything. He went back home, went back to his family

and back to his job and everything. Then when he got
the first salary, he took the money and he went to the
place where we are building a rehabilitation center for
the homeless alcoholics, especially for the old people
who are kept in prison just because if they let them out
they have no place to go [and] so they would [go to]
drink. We want to take these people from the jail and
give them a home and make them feel loved and cared
for. He went and brought that salary there and said,
"God has been so wonderful to me. In the sisters and
through the sisters, I have come to know that God loves
me. This has brought me back to life and I want to share
that life with others." These are very small things the
sisters do, they do very little. We can do very little for
these people, but at least they know that we love them
and that we care for them and we are at their disposal.[10]

※

I will never forget the suffering of that little boy at
that hour of the night. He said, "I went to my father."
He went to his father and mother and neither of them
wanted him. And at that hour of the night that little
child had the courage to come to our place. Isn't that
beautiful? I took him home because I took him in. He
was a beautiful child.[11]

※

One day a sister picked up a man from the street, from
the footpath. And as she lifted him up, the whole of his
back—skin and flesh—remained on the floor, on the

footpath. There were big bundles of worms that had eaten his flesh. And she took him to our house. They were all over his body. Sister washed him, she loved him; and then after three hours he died with the most beautiful smile. When I came to the place and Sister told me what had happened, I said to her, "What did you feel? What did you feel inside your heart, what did you feel when you were touching that body?" And that young sister gave me a beautiful answer: "I have never felt that presence, and I knew I was touching the Body of Christ."[12]

No Place for Them in Anyone's Heart

The homeless aren't only those without homes made from bricks or wood, but also those who have found no place for themselves in anyone's heart, the rejected and unloved.[13]

✳

Yesterday the archbishop took me to see [the] Taj Mahal. I felt so bad looking at the big marble building empty of life when beside these cold riches, the lepers and the dying destitute live in utter suffering and want. It hurt me right through—but also it strengthened my resolution to do more for Christ in His distressing disguise.[14]

✳

To find the lost Jesus in the youth and bring Him home—as Mary did—when she found Jesus she brought

Him home. You . . . and many others must go in search
with Mary, in search of Jesus in the distressing disguise
of the youth—by your love and holiness and bring him
home—and at the breaking of bread they will know and
see Jesus in their father and mother, [their] brother and
sister, and their neighbor.[15]

Find a Family for the Unwanted Child

We must bring the child back to the center of our care
and concern. This is the only way that our world can
survive because our children are the only hope of the
future. As other people are called to God, only their
children can take their place. But what does God say to
us? It [Scripture] says, "Even if a mother could forget
her child, I will not forget you, I have carved you in the
palm of My Hand" (Is 49:15–16). We are carved in
the palm of His Hand. That unborn child has been
carved in the Hand of God from conception and is
called by God to love and to be loved not only now in
this life, but forever—God can never forget us. I will tell
you something beautiful. We are fighting abortion by
adoption. By care of the mother and adoption for their
baby, we have saved thousands of lives. We have sent
word to the clinics, hospitals, and police stations, please
don't destroy the child, we will take care, [we will] take
the child, so always have someone tell the mothers in
trouble, "Come, we will take care of you. We will get
a home for your child." And we have a tremendous
demand from couples who cannot have a child, but I
never give a child to a couple who have done something

not to have a child. Jesus said, "Anyone who receives a child in My name, receives Me" (Mt 18:5). By adopting a child, these couples receive Jesus, but by aborting a child, a couple refuses to receive Jesus. Please don't kill the child. I want the child. Please give me the child. I am willing to accept any child who would be aborted and to give that child to a married couple who will love the child and be loved by the child. From our children's home in Calcutta alone, we have saved over three thousand children from abortion. These children have brought such love and joy to their adopted parents and have grown up so full of love.[16]

✳

Pray especially in these days for the refugees, who are suffering so much. They are crowded together everywhere, so let us ask Our Lady to be the mother of refugees so that we can help them to accept this suffering and make use of it for peace in the world.[17]

✳

May God bless all your efforts to help refugees and displaced persons. May you bring God's love, hope, and strength to the homeless and destitute. Remember the words of Jesus, "I was a stranger and you took care of Me."[18]

Humble Works of Love

Because people in the world have been so deeply touched by our humble works of love in action that bring God's

tender love and concern to the unloved, the uncared
for, the destitutes, this has created in the hearts of so
many the deep desire to share; some do so out of their
abundance, but many, and maybe the greater number,
by depriving themselves of something they would have
liked to give themselves, so as to be able to share
with their less privileged brothers and sisters. It is so
beautiful to see the spirit of sacrifice finding its way
into many lives, for this not only benefits the poor who
receive, but the giver is also being enriched with the love
of God.[19]

The Greatest Development of a Human Life

We take care of the sick and the dying; we pick up
people from the street. In Calcutta alone, we have
picked up nearly 31,000 people of whom more than
14,000 have died a very beautiful death. For me, the
greatest development of a human life is to die in peace
with God.[20]

✳

And you and I have been created for the same purpose,
to love and to spread that compassion as Mary did
everywhere she went. . . . I think this is that beautiful
compassion of a woman's heart to feel the hurt of others
and to do something as she did. You and I in our hearts
have that compassion. Do we really use it? Do we have
the eyes of Mary to see the needs of others? Maybe in
our home, do we know the needs of our parents, of our
husband, of our children? Do the children come home

with us as Jesus went with Mary? Do we have a home
for our children?[21]

Maybe Christ Is Homeless in Your Own Heart

They may be homeless for [want of] a shelter of bricks
or lonely, unwanted, uncared for, unloved and so
homeless for want of a home made of love in your heart;
and since love begins at home, maybe Christ is hungry,
naked, sick, homeless, in your own heart, in your family,
in your neighbor, in the country in which you live, in the
world.[22]

※

"I was the one," Jesus said, "that had knocked at your
door. I was the one that was lying in the street. I was the
one that died, frozen in that broken home."[23]

※

Homeless for shelter in your heart, He asks of you . . .
Will you be that "one" to Him?[24]

※

Jesus must love your home so much. I always think
of Him not finding a place in Jerusalem—walking
all the way to Bethany—to Mary and Martha and
Lazarus. They loved Him—they wanted Him. I
think now too He is not wanted in Jerusalem. I am
sure your home is His Bethany. Keep it always all
for Him.[25]

HER EXAMPLE: The Testimonies

We Cannot Leave Him on the Street

Mother had heard that there were many homeless men sleeping on the streets of London, and she asked to be taken to see them. So one night, Ann Blaikie and I accompanied Mother. Noticing one man in particular, Mother got out of the car and went to him. At first, he took no notice of her presence, but when she took his hand, he looked up and said, "It has been a long time since I felt the warmth of a human hand." Mother returned to the car and told us, "This is a sick man. We cannot leave him on the street like this." Ann Blaikie replied, "You are right, Mother, but where can we take him at this hour of the night?" It was about eleven p.m. Mother said, "Let us take him to the cardinal's house." So, much to the chagrin of the driver and Mrs. Blaikie, we took the man and off we went to the cardinal's house in the middle of the night. When we reached there, of course all the gates were locked. We had almost despaired of entering, when a priest coming from outside unlocked a small gate to let himself in. With that, our driver ran and explained to him that Mother Teresa was in the car and needed housing for a homeless man. The priest very kindly told us to wait, phoned the Salvation Army, and arranged everything. Then we took [the man] to the Salvation Army.[26]

Mother Noticed the Suffering of the Homeless

For a long time, Mother had noticed the suffering of the homeless in and around Sealdah station—the jobless seeking petty jobs in the city, the beggars and all those who have no place to stay at night. Mother met the general manager of the railways and the inspector general of police, who gave her their full support. A police contingent from Barrackpore arrived to put up tarpaulin and bamboo shelters on the two pavements of the road. The sisters on their visits to the station picked up patients from the platform. They were given bread and milk and a blanket by the two sisters who came each evening at 9:30 p.m. Volunteers would also help. Many [of the homeless] would leave in the morning to look for some job. The sick, the helpless, and the children stayed back. Those who were in a dying condition were taken to Nirmal Hriday (Home for the Dying). The sick were treated or sent to the hospital, and the children were taught till noon.

A more permanent structure with asbestos roofing was put up and a formal opening took place. On this occasion, Mrs. Dias remarked that Mother Teresa had in her the golden touch of King Midas, gold price was very high, but what Mother Teresa gave was much more precious—the gold of love and affection. A mobile clinic, a relief center, a Bengali and Hindi medium school, a sewing class for women were also started. In the evenings, the children would help keep the streets clean and clear around the station by collecting the dab shells (of coconuts). These were piled high in one corner of the night-shelter for lack of space, waiting to be disposed of in the dirt-bins. One day on her visit, Mother inquired from the sister-in-charge: "What are you collect-ing these dabs for?" And Mother got a simple reply: "We have absolutely no particular purpose." Suddenly Mother said: "Send them all to Prem Dan. Let us start something from this rubbish." So regularly once a week a lorry-load of dab shells was sent to give small jobs to our jobless poor—making coir for rope and doormats, mattresses, etc.[27]

Would You Refuse Shelter to Our Lady and Saint Joseph?

We had a mentally ill family in Shishu Bhavan (Home for Children): a mother with her children. The eldest child was crippled and retarded. This woman used to abuse us so much that one day I refused to go to Shishu Bhavan and gave up the keys, saying that if this mother remains there, I will not go back to Shishu Bhavan. Mother came and told the woman to take her things and children and leave Shishu Bhavan. The woman got up and left. It was a rainy day; it was drizzling and it was also evening. I was happy to be free of her, but not Mother. Toward five p.m. (about an hour after they left), Mother came back to Shishu Bhavan and told me that she was going out to look for them. I had such remorse that I followed Mother. She was worried for them as they had no home and it was drizzling. My heart began to melt. We found them at St. Teresa's Church. We brought them back to Shishu Bhavan. It was a lesson that I never forgot. Mother said: "Always remember how Our Lady and Saint Joseph were refused a shelter in Bethlehem. Would you refuse them a shelter?"[28]

At Once Mother Got Up

Once on Mother's Feastday, Mother House Sisters had prepared a big drama for Mother's feast. The rain poured that day, suddenly so much that the water in Kalighat was rising higher and higher, and there were so many sick people outside. I could not manage to keep them inside because there was not enough room for them. So I told Mother this problem and at once, in the middle of the drama, Mother got up and went with me to Kalighat and quickly solved the problem. The sick people were kept inside without much difficulty by Mother, who arranged everything in such a way that there was a place for everybody. I couldn't imagine how Mother did it so skillfully, and everybody was so happy. It was true that Mother never refused anybody who came to the door. So I too decided to do the same, to make a place for anyone, as Mother said that it is Jesus knocking at the door in the disguise of the poor. So never to refuse, even if there's no place at all. Somehow we managed by God's help.[29]

I Never Refused to Meet Anybody

Everybody who came she welcomed, and she never refused to meet anybody. By her own words she said, "I never refuse to meet anybody," because she had a great openness to everyone, regardless of who they were. And her service of people was tireless, without any considerations of caste or creed or anything like that. She very much had this virtue that she could see everybody equally before God.[30]

Suddenly Mother Left the Crowd

Mother was surrounded by all "Big Sisters," Co-Workers, many people. I was waiting close to the cars with other postulants. Close to me came one poor old man. He could not see properly and he was asking us when Mother was coming. We indicated the crowd close to the gate. We could not see Mother. I felt the pain, because this man could not have the chance to see Mother close—also because the sisters made signs not to come too close. Suddenly, I don't know how, I could not believe, Mother left the "crowd" and came to this man. He put down his hat and asked Mother to bless his eyes, and she spoke to him in English, blessed his eyes, and gave a beautiful smile. The man cried. Personally, I was struck very much, because it was "impossible" for me that Mother could come to us [where we were standing].[31]

Mother's Help and Encouragement

Boys Town started about twenty years ago when the boys that we had in our homes were getting older and needed to be kept separate. Mother approached Archbishop Henry for help and before long they opened this Boys Town for them where they had their schooling. Later she arranged for a Bata Project (a pilot program run by a shoe company in India to help train boys to earn a living) for them for making shoes so that they could earn their livelihood. By and by, as the boys were getting married and wanted to settle down, a project was set up to obtain aid for the boys to build a home and have some land. This materialized and today more than eighty little families are growing up there. At the beginning there was a lot of trouble caused by the boys. There were serious misunderstandings with the priests, and the boys behaved badly. One priest who had been there for a few years was finding it very difficult and wanted to give up his vocation. Mother helped him and brought him back to Boys Town herself to continue his mission. With Mother's help and encouragement, he remained many more years there and did very well.[32]

They Were So Low on the Ladder

The house in Rome was founded to care for aged prostitutes who because of disease acquired in the course of their work were no longer able to take care of themselves. And those were specifically the people Mother was taking care of here—her nuns were taking care of them—who were so low on the ladder that I hadn't even considered that someone would even want to take care of them.[33]

The Friend of the Little Ones

Mother came across abandoned children, sometimes very young babies, at the point of death, lying where they had been thrown on the rubbish dumps. Mother opened the children's home called Shishu Bhavan in 1955. It was to be the first of many homes. Many babies and young children came, brought by the police, social workers, and the sisters themselves. All received care and love, and many malnourished babies made a miraculous recovery. Mother had a wonderful and tender touch with children. They would feel at home in her presence and in no time she had them smiling

and playing with her. Those who were very sick found her
a comforting, compassionate, and calm presence. Looking
at Mother with the children, anyone would be reminded of
Jesus, "the friend of the little ones."[34]

Mother Picked Up the Baby at 10 p.m.

Once in my division in Calcutta a deserted child of seven days
old was picked up by some officers of a police station. . . .
This deserted child could not be accepted anywhere. At
about 9:30 p.m. the officers rang me up for advice. . . . I immediately rang up Mother Teresa, and luckily I found her
and told her about our predicament. She simply asked me
which police station it was, and learning the same, she only
said that she would pick up the child within half an hour. It
was then near about 10 p.m.[35]

One Person Looked After Us: Our Dearest Mother

I am an orphan girl from Darjeeling Shishu Bhavan. Our
parents died when we were very small. We don't remember
our parents, and we only know one person who cared for
us, looked after us, and found a foster home for us; she is
none other than our dearest Mother. I know Mother from
my childhood. I still remember when we were very small,
sometimes Mother used to visit us. She used to come from
Calcutta by train up to Siliguri, and from there she used
to travel by bus, and after getting down at Darjeeling railway station she used to walk up to our house (Shishu Bhavan). Seeing her coming, we used to shout for joy saying,
"Mother," and she used to smile and wave her hand. We

used to run down and carry her bag and hold her hands. Seeing her, we really used to be extremely happy. . . . Being orphans we were abandoned, but our dearest Mother gave us a foster home, looked after us, showed us the way to live, and helped us to stand on our own feet. My husband and I, we are both working and we are happy with our small family. The cause of success is no one else but our loving Mother and the Missionaries of Charity.[36]

I Was the Naughtiest Boy of Shishu Bhavan

Mother had picked me up from the streets of Calcutta at the age of four years approximately. She brought me up, gave me education. I was always close to her, as she was our Mummy. She loved me very much, as I was the naughtiest boy of Nirmala Shishu Bhavan (Home for Children). First she had given me a bath and cleaned my boils, as my whole body was full of boils. She gave medicines and she gave me to eat bread and milk. . . . When she was among us, we found that an "Angel of God" was with us.[37]

Is It Not a Miracle?

A baby girl named Agnes, picked up as a newborn from near a dustbin, had developed some skin infection. I took her home when she was a couple of months old, had her treated by a doctor relative, and returned her to Shishu Bhavan. During the next seven months, I used to take her home to live with my family quite often, after which she left to join her adopting parents in Spain. The adopting parents had a son elder to Agnes and were blessed with another bonny son after Agnes joined them. They had a beautiful home and were very nice to us. . . . Whenever we think of poor little Agnes getting a beautiful home with a sweet elder and younger brother, we wonder, "Is it not a miracle?"[38]

Touch the Leper with Your Compassion

In 1957 five lepers who had been thrown out of their jobs came to Mother. Mother was ever sensitive to the needs of the present moment and so began the work of service to the lepers. Straightaway she used the mobile clinic for them and soon opened five centers in Calcutta. . . .

With the growing numbers of leprosy patients, a home was set up for them that included outdoor as well as indoor departments. The Marian Society joined to support this center in Titagarh. From this work started the slogan, so well known today, "Touch the leper with your compassion." Mother took so much trouble to talk to the lepers who were having treatment and who were deformed. She instilled hope and dignity into them by telling them that they could still do work. This work eventually grew into a township to rehabilitate thousands of lepers who had come from all over India.[39]

* * *

The government would provide a place for the leper families to live. Their lepers lived outside of the city in caves. The whole area was given to Mother for care of the lepers. She had done some amazing work and had been recognized by the government for forming small communities where leper families could live. When [my husband] and I first knew Mother, she told us it cost $150 to build a very small hut, where the family could live and have a little place for a garden to grow their own vegetables. Many people gave memorials for these homes. The person in the family who was a leper was treated and the rest of the family members were treated prophylactically. She called them villages of peace.[40]

Mother Lost No Time

As the refugees were pouring into West Bengal all along the border of Bangladesh (in 1971), Mother lost no time in organizing a group of us to go to the big refugee camps. After the first day, Mother had a good idea [of] what was needed, so she returned the next day to Calcutta alone and without delay sent another batch of sisters and brothers with mats, clothing, and foodstuffs. . . . Every day, Mother went to Salt Lake and made sure as many as possible of our young sisters were fully involved. They would leave early in the morning and return by evening. One of the biggest difficulties in the camp was keeping the large groups of women occupied after having fed and clothed them and catered to their needs in the medical line.

Mother took over a center in Green Park for child refugees near death from starvation and disease. Our sisters cared for the children day and night. There were also two other centers there, one for the sick elderly ladies and another for pregnant mothers. She arranged to make accommodations for them with bamboo and tents. Around this time an impressive booklet was published and distributed worldwide, which featured an appeal by Mother: "We have millions of children suffering from malnutrition and starvation. Unless the world comes in with food and proteins, these children will die and the world will have to answer for their death." The world did indeed respond. Mother did everything possible for the refugees, even though it looked like a drop in the ocean compared to the devastating situation. She was so selfless and tireless. She did not spare herself or the sisters in spite of the many calls she had on her time from her growing Society, which needed her guidance and direction.[41]

Mother Saw That What Was Needed Was Done

I remember one afternoon when I came to Mother House, I saw an old man and woman from a very poor family, crying. Their only daughter had been thrown out of the house because she was an epileptic. That girl was taken into one of Mother's homes and consoled. The woman asked if she could be looked after by a doctor. My husband (a doctor) was there. She had been refused by many hospitals. Mother, with her frail body, waited there till she was settled. She had the tremendous power to see that what was needed was done.[42]

Next to the Minister

One day a minister happened to be in the car with Mother. She saw a very old man sitting by the roadside. Mother picked him up and made him sit next to the minister and drove him to one of our homes. At that moment that poor person was more important than the minister.[43]

We All Forget How Terrible It Is to Live on the Street

I was at the house, and someone had come to see Mother. She was in another room. I answered the door, and there was this poor woman just distraught at the door. She was a street person. She looked mentally ill, in tattered clothes. She said, "I have to go to the bathroom," and she came rushing in. Right in front of the door were the stairs that went up to the bedroom straight ahead. A beautiful American sister just then walked in and said, "Margaret, come in, dear," and Margaret went tearing upstairs to the bathroom without shutting the door. Sister said to me, "Poor Margaret, that's one of the hardest things about living on the street, that there is no privacy to go to the bathroom." So apparently Margaret came there several times a day. Then when she came back downstairs, she was very agitated and said to Sister, "May I go in and speak to Jesus?" Sister said, "Of course you can," so she went to the door of the chapel and took off her worn-out old shoes. Sister and I went in with her and knelt down, and I still remember that she had so many holes in her socks that her feet were almost bare, and I thought, "That poor woman." She wasn't very old, probably in her thirties. We came back out, and she thanked Sister and me, and she went on her way. It was such a moment. The thing that was so lovely was Sister's attitude. The kindness in her voice. I think we all forget how terrible it is to live on the street. They have no place where you'd be welcome to use a bathroom.[44]

How Can I Lie Under a Fan When People Die on the Pavement?

I was in Mother's room. "Doctor, are you feeling hot, warm?" "Yes, Mother, I am feeling warm and sweating." I was looking at the ceiling for a fan, [but] it was not there and I said, "Why don't you use a fan?" The thing that moved me and that I still remember from that day was her saying: "How can I lie under a fan when most of the people in the city are dying on the pavement?" It really moved me.[45]

Two Feet Sticking Out

The brothers were waiting for me and Mother to come out of the convent. We walked out the back door and there was a big trash Dumpster. As we walked past, we saw these two feet sticking out. One foot had a red sock. The other foot was bare, and Mother said, "Oh, someone needs us." . . . Here was this poor man sound asleep. First we thought he was dead. He was just lifeless. She bent over him and said, "Are you all right, sir?" And then he opened his eyes and he was very, very drunk. There was no question about his drunkenness. He looked like he hadn't had a bath in weeks. We helped him to his feet. She said, "Would you like to come with us?" He said, "Yes, I would." She said, "My brothers will help you. They can get you some clean clothes, something to eat." Her whole focus was on this poor man.

The brothers sat in the back of the station wagon, and Mother and the man and I sat in the center row of the wagon. She had a conversation with him between the convent and their house. She treated him with such respect. She asked him if he had a family and he said, "Well, not that I have seen in at least twenty-five years, but I did have a family at one time." She said, "Would you like us to try to get in touch with them for you?" He said he wouldn't have any idea how to do that because he hadn't talked to anyone for so long.

It was that she really cared. She wasn't being magnanimous. This was a person in great need, but she never said to me that he was drunk, or so dirty, or his face hadn't been washed for so long and he had a terrible smell. He was someone. We took him right with us to the house. The brothers took him upstairs that same day. He had a shower and a nap, and a nice meal. The next day, this person that we hardly recognized appeared to thank us. The brothers said to Mother that today was the day the checks come, so he would go over to the post office to collect his social security check. He would go directly to the grocery store and spend it all on wine or something. But anyway, he came in with great dignity and told Mother that he had some business downtown. He would have to leave, and he thanked her for her help and he thanked the brothers. They knew him. He had been there many times. After he left, she was not critical. Other people would not have wanted to go near that man. It never occurred to her not to. If he would have said, "No, I think that I will just lie here," she would not have persuaded him not to. It was so beautiful. I loved how she treated him. He wanted to extend the same to Mother Teresa that she was extending to him. It was a beautiful moment. I never saw her when she wouldn't respond immediately to whatever the need was.[46]

She Rushed to All Places

After the funeral of Indira Gandhi, we and others told Mother about the riots in Delhi claiming thousands of lives. Mother could not sleep, she turned and twisted in her bed. Then straight after Mass she asked the priest who came for Mass to tell her how the people are. . . . Mother hurriedly had breakfast, took some of us to the nearby government school. Oh, it was in a real mess and confusion. . . . Thousands of them crowded in a school for safety because their houses had been burnt. They were like mad people—screaming, shouting, crying—no food, no water. The police were trying to control the crowds inside and outside. . . . Humanly speaking, one would never know what to do about it. The noise was terrible.

Mother silently entered in with a few of us. People recognized her and fell on her, crying. Mother calmly [kept on walking among them while] speaking Bengali and broken Hindi saying, "It will be all right. It will be all right, have courage." She went around a bit and then gave us orders to go and get the brooms. We gathered all the brooms we could and rushed back. She took the brooms and started sweeping the classrooms and telling them in each class as she swept, "Settle family by family." We all did the same, and many men and women joined us. After sweeping we thought all was over, but Mother went to the toilets. They were filthy. Mother was the first to put her hand to clean. We too helped, but in the meantime I noticed the restless people were becoming calm. Screaming, shouting was less as families were trying themselves to obey Mother and settle together. After the laborious work of cleaning the toilets, Mother went to contact the municipality to get drinking water. When it came, she made sure all were in line to collect the water. She again contacted the collector and ministers and organized to get some food for them and personally saw to it that all got the food. I felt as if I was with Jesus on the day He fed the multitude. Thus there was peace in that camp.

By evening Mother reached other camps and started doing the same. She called a meeting with the archbishop and all religious, priests, brothers, and volunteers. Soon more than sixty camps were organized. People with generous hearts donated many things, and Mother saw to it that [everything] was distributed equally and justly to the needy in the camps. Thus because of Mother's initiative and concern for the suffering people, Delhi was saved from a great destruction. Mother also got together government officials, ministers, etc.—[people of all parties]—to work together. Whenever she could squeeze in time, she would bandage the wounds of those hurt or burnt. She never stopped saying little kind words, a pat, a smile, a look of love to those needy people. Mother did miracles, which were beyond human understanding in the camps. Mother left after five days of organizing, but soon returned again. Peace came in the camp by the broom.[47]

※

The flood-relief work in Bangladesh, the refugee camps in the 1970s in the north of West Bengal, the earthquake in Guatemala in 1976, the earthquake in Armenia in 1988, the earthquake in Maharashtra in 1993 . . . She rushed to all these places and did all that she could, as well as helping with many other natural disasters. She worked day in and day out, constantly making inquiries so that she could best discern how to bring effective help. She claimed every sort of person whom nobody else wanted. She told people in government to contact her if there were unwanted persons. . . . She always worked alongside the civil and ecclesiastical authorities, although she always retained her independence and autonomy. She used all her gifts of nature and grace to transform the world into a better place, more human and purer. She was confronted with dirt and misery on every side. But she did not waste her time looking for those responsible to blame them. Instead, she used all her time and energy to relieve the sufferings. She was willing to undergo any sort of humiliations, ill treatment, false accusations, etc., in the name of the poor.[48]

REFLECTION

"I was a stranger and you welcomed Me." (Mt 25:35)

"Give shelter to the homeless—not only a shelter made of bricks but a heart that understands, that covers, that loves."[49]

When I meet a homeless person on the street, do I just cross to the other side to avoid an unpleasant experience? Can I acknowledge that person? Can I greet him or her with a smile and a listening ear? Or do I feel superior and have sentiments of self-righteousness as I reject, or worse, despise the person on the street?

In what way can I open my heart to someone in my own

home, my family, my community, my workplace, or my neighborhood? What small act of kindness can make my home a place where my family members, relatives, friends, or co-workers feel accepted, appreciated, loved, and welcomed? Having a welcoming smile that makes those who approach you feel accepted might be an excellent way to practice hospitality.

PRAYER

Mary, our dearest Mother, give us your heart so beautiful, so pure, so immaculate, your heart so full of love and humility, that we may be able to receive Jesus in the Bread of Life, love Him as you loved Him, and serve Him in the distressing disguise of the poorest of the poor.

—*Mother Teresa*

FIVE

VISIT THE SICK

The sick always had a special place in Mother Teresa's heart. Every human being experiences sickness to some degree at one time or another, and when someone is sick they are most vulnerable and in need. One's own limitations and weakness are highlighted, and dependence on others becomes more pronounced. When she encountered someone in this condition, Mother Teresa offered that person all the care and love she could. She spared herself no effort in order to help, at the same time striving to make no one feel that they were a burden or an annoyance.

In particular, the chronically ill and the dying were an object of her delicate care. In the numerous homes that she opened throughout the world, she insisted that the sick be given proper medical help, but also that they be surrounded with tender loving care. She urged her sisters to be very kind and wholehearted in "nursing the sick and dying not only of the body, but also of mind and spirit." She sought to provide for the well-being of each person in her care, and to find a remedy for her patients' diseases. At the beginning of her work for the poor, she was very much dedicated to the care of those suffering from leprosy (a disease usually contagious at the time), but later faced other equally challenging situations. For example, she was the first to open a hospice for AIDS patients in the United States. Even if it meant danger to herself, she did everything she could to help a sick person.

Mother Teresa's profound compassion for the sick had its origins in her childhood, when she learned to look after the sick from the example of her mother, who occasionally brought a sick woman to their house to enable her to recover. Her two daughters were instructed to assist the woman and look after her children while the mother rested and recuperated.

Mother Teresa's compassion for the sick also had its roots in the fact that she too was not spared from physical illnesses. Though she had good health until she developed a heart condition in her seventies, there were many apparently minor but trying sicknesses that she had to face. One of her doctors reveals a significant detail: "She also had chronic headaches, . . . which she always minimized, but the very fact that she had them all the time meant that they were real and probably unremitting. . . . I'm sure she offered it up as a gift to God. One other interesting thing, she referred to her headaches as this 'crown of thorns.' It was her way of being one with Jesus."[1] As she did with other trials, so with this physical suffering she offered them to the Lord for the good of souls. She could affirm with Saint Paul, "Now I rejoice in what I am suffering for you, and I

fill up in my flesh what is still lacking in regard to Christ's
afflictions, for the sake of his body, which is the Church"
(Col 1:24).

Knowing the value of suffering if taken in the right
spirit, Mother Teresa taught others to appreciate and accept suffering in the same way. With her characteristic
resourcefulness in making the best use of everything,
including suffering, she created a movement of Sick and
Suffering Co-Workers, who would offer their prayers and
sufferings for the fruitfulness of the apostolate among
the poor. "Love demands sacrifice. . . . Suffering in itself
is nothing; but suffering shared with Christ's Passion is a
wonderful gift," she explained. "I am very happy that you
are willing to join the suffering members of the Missionaries of Charity. . . . Everyone and anyone who wishes to become a Missionary of Charity—a carrier of God's love—is
welcome, but I want especially the paralyzed, the crippled,
the incurables to join, for I know they will bring to the feet
of Jesus many souls."

This markedly different understanding of suffering
is an alternative to the mind-set of the dominant secular
culture of the West, which proposes death under many
forms as a way to avoid suffering. By her tender and compassionate love for the sick and by her acceptance of un-
avoidable suffering while elevating it to a spiritual level,
Mother Teresa upholds the importance, value, and dignity
of each human life—unborn, newborn, young, old, sick,
disabled—and the need to respect and protect it.

Though our first reaction might be to ignore and pass
by those "wounded on the road," as did the priest and the

Levite in the parable of the Good Samaritan (Lk 10:33–34), Mother Teresa's example challenges us to be "filled with compassion" and "come near" those needing "a heart to love and hands to serve"[2] them in their need.

HER WORDS

I Was Sick and You Visited Me

Your work with the sick is a beautiful means to help satiate their thirst for Jesus and His love. I think this is our Blessed Mother's most beautiful gift to you.[3]

Jesus Had Become Like a Leper

We know what happened to Our Lady—the wonderful compassionate Mother full of love. She was not ashamed to claim Jesus as her Son. Everybody left Him, she was alone with Him. She was not ashamed that Jesus was scourged, was spat upon, that He had become like a leper, unwanted, unloved, hated by all, that He was her Son, Jesus. There too that deep compassion of her heart. Do we stand by our own people when they suffer? When they are humiliated? When the husband loses his job? What am I to him then? Am I full of compassion to him? Do I understand his pain? And [when] the children are led away and misled—do I have that deep compassion to search for them, to find them, to stand by them, to welcome them home, to love them with a deep loving

heart? Am I like Mary to my sisters in my community?
Do I recognize their pain, their suffering? If I'm a priest,
the priest has the heart of Mary, that compassion to be
the forgiveness, to bring that forgiveness of God to the
suffering sinner in front of him, that deep compassion
of Mary. She was not ashamed. She claimed Jesus as her
own Son.[4]

＊

At the Crucifixion, we see her standing—the Mother
of God standing. What tremendous faith she must have
had because of her living love for her Son—to stand
there, see Him disowned by everybody, unloved by
everybody, unwanted by everybody, one of the worst,
and she stood. And she owned Him as her Son. She
owned Him as one who belonged to her and to whom
she belonged. She was not afraid to own Him. Do we
own our people when they suffer, when they are thrown
out, our people, our own people, our own family, do
we know them, [do we know] that they suffer? Do we
recognize their hunger for Jesus? This is the hunger of
understanding love. This is why Our Lady is so great,
because she had an understanding love and you and
I, being women, we have that tremendous thing in us,
that understanding love. I see that so beautifully in our
people, in our poor women who day after day and every
day meet suffering, accept suffering for the sake of their
children. I have seen a parent—mother—going without
so many things, so many things, even begging so that
the child may have. I have seen a parent holding to the

handicapped child because that child is her child, she had an understanding love for the suffering of her child.[5]

Jesus Brings Joy and Peace

When I see what God is doing with our sisters in the world . . . When [we were in Russia], one evening each week a priest came. We had Holy Mass in our little chapel, and he gave us Jesus. It changed the whole atmosphere of the hospital; the whole place looked quite different. After a week, the doctor came to me and said, "Mother Teresa, what's happening in my hospital?" I said, "I don't know, Doctor. What is happening?" He said, "Something is happening. The nurses and the doctors are much more kind, much more loving with their patients. The patients aren't screaming with pain the way they were before. What's happening? What are the sisters doing?" I looked at him and said, "Doctor, you know what is happening. After seventy years, Jesus came to this hospital. Jesus is in this place now. There, in that little chapel, He is living, He is loving. He has brought this joy and peace." . . . He said, "Oh!" and he didn't say one more word; he just walked away. He did not want to discuss such a great change! He couldn't believe that great change came with us and the Blessed Sacrament![6]

So Many Just Long for a Visit

"I was sick and you visited Me" were the words of Jesus. So many of our poor just long for a visit from someone.

When you talk to them, put all your love and sweetness into your words—or rather ask Jesus to speak through you. [The proof] that Christ was divine, that He was the expected Messiah, [is] that the Gospel is preached to the poor—the proof that this work is God's work is that the Gospel is preached to the poor. Pray and thank God for having chosen you to live this life and do this work.[7]

So Small That We Have No Time for Them

Yesterday, I was talking to our sisters in the place where they are. They visit a place where they have all these old people, people who have no one, people who are wanted by no one. They are just there. And they look forward and they count the time when Sunday will come, that the sisters may come and do simple things for them. Maybe just smile at them, maybe just straighten the sheet a little bit, maybe just lift them up a little bit, brush their hair, cut their nails, small things, so small that we have no time for them and yet these people, these are our people, our brothers and sisters.[8]

✳

In India, for example, we have more and more Hindus, Muslims, Buddhists getting involved in the work. And what for? Why are they coming? Because they feel that presence. They want to serve God in their own way, and they've found that by sacrifice, by prayer, they can do that and they come with the poorest of the poor. For India especially, to touch lepers, to touch the dying is something very, very, very difficult. And yet [we] see these young people coming there and doing what they are doing—because in our Society we have only those humble works—just feeding Him in the hungry, clothing Him in the naked, giving Him a home in the homeless, taking care of Him in the sick, in the imprisoned.[9]

✳

We are taking care of 53,000 lepers, and we have the best of medicine, very expensive, and we can cure the people. We can make the highly positive case [of leprosy] into a negative case [without leprosy] with this expensive medicine. So, where there is medicine, there is hope. We can bring back life and love and joy into the lives of our lepers. Everywhere the government has given us land. There is new life in their lives. But it is so different when it is that loneliness, that being unwanted, unloved.[10]

✳

In our Nirmal Hriday and Shishu Bhavan, I want you to have morning and evening prayer. Begin the leprosy and medical work with a prayer and put in a little more gentleness, a little more compassion with the sick. It will help you to remember that you are touching the Body of Christ. He is hungry for that touch. Will you not give it?[11]

✳

Cling to the humble works of the Society for the poorest of the poor. Our "homes" must be kept clean and tidy, but simple and humble. Our poor, sick, and dying patients must be given tender care; the old, disabled, or mentally sick inmates must be treated with dignity and respect, always keeping in mind Jesus's words: "Whatever you do to the least of my brethren, you do it to Me."[12]

※

When serving the sick Christ in the poor, let us give wholehearted service—let us pay great attention to each sick person, and let no other preoccupation or occupation prevent us from touching and serving the Body of Christ.[13]

※

Some sisters are being driven by the moving forces of development and are slowly bypassing the sick, the dying, the crippled, the lepers, the unwanted. They will soon not have time or place for such as these. Our consecration to God is to the poorest of the poor—the unwanted.[14]

I Need Souls Like Yours

Suffering by itself is nothing, but suffering shared with Christ's Passion is a wonderful gift to human life. It is the most beautiful gift that we can share in the Passion of Christ.

I hope you are better—very often I think of you and I unite the work with your sufferings—and so

I have you close to me. Today I am going to tell you
something which I am sure will make you very happy.
You have been longing and are still deep in your heart a
Missionary. Why not become spiritually bound to our
Society—which you love so dearly? While we work in
the slums, etc., you share in the merit, the prayers, and
the work with your suffering and prayers. The work is
tremendous and I need workers, it is true, but I need
souls like yours to pray and suffer for the work. Would
you like to become my spiritual sister and become a
Missionary of Charity in Belgium, not in body, but
in soul—in India, in the world, where there are souls
longing for Our Lord, but for want of someone to pay
the debt for them, they cannot move toward Him? You
be a true Missionary of Charity and you pay their debt,
while the sisters—your sisters—help them to come to
God in body. You pray over this and let me know what
is your desire. I need many people like you, who would
join the Society like this; for I want to have (1) a glorious
Society in heaven, (2) the Suffering Society—on earth—
the spiritual children, and (3) the Militant Society—the
sisters on the battlefield. I am sure you would be very
happy to see the sisters fighting the devil in the field of
souls. They count nothing as too hard when there is a
question of souls. . . .

How are you? Are you still on your back? How long
will you have to be like that? How Our Lord must love
you to give you so much a part in His suffering. You are
the happy one. For you are His chosen one. Be brave and
cheerful and offer much for me—that I may bring many

souls to God. Once you come in touch with souls, the
thirst grows daily.[15]

＊

I am very happy that you are willing to join the suffering
members of the Missionaries of Charity—you see what I
mean—you and the others who will join will share in all
our prayers, works, and whatever we do for souls, and
you do the same for us with your prayers and sufferings.
You see the aim of our Society is to satiate the thirst of
Jesus on the Cross for love of souls by working for the
salvation and sanctification of the poor in the slums.
Who could do this better than you and the others who
suffer like you? Your suffering and prayers will be the
chalice in which we, the working members, will pour the
love of souls we gather round. Therefore, you are just as
important and necessary for the fulfillment of our aim.
To satiate this thirst, we must have a chalice and you
and the others—men, women, children, old and young,
poor and rich—are all welcome to make the chalice.
In reality you can do much more, while on your bed of
pain, than I running on my feet, but you and I together
can do all things in Him who strengthens us.[16]

We could get a few prayers we say, for you to say them
also, so as to increase the family spirit, but one thing
we must have in common—the spirit of our Society:
total surrender to God, loving trust, and perfect
cheerfulness. By this you will be known as a Missionary
of Charity. Everyone and anyone who wishes to become

a Missionary of Charity, a carrier of God's love, is
welcome, but I want especially the paralyzed, the
crippled, the incurables to join, for I know they will
bring to the feet of Jesus many souls. In our turn, the
sisters will each one have a sister who prays, suffers,
thinks, unites to her, and so on—a second self. You see,
my dear sister, our work is a most difficult one. If you
are with us, praying and suffering for us and the work,
we shall be able to do great things for love of Him—
because of you.[17]

Personally I feel very happy, and a new strength has
come in my soul at the thought of you and others joining
the Society spiritually. Now with you and others doing
the work with us, what would we not do? What can't we
do for Him?[18]

Prayer and Patience

I am glad to hear you are offering your prayers and
sacrifices and the suffering of your illness for the
Missionaries of Charity. Accept your illness as a gift
of God's special love for you. It is a sign that you have
come so close to Him that He can draw you to Himself
on the Cross. It is no longer you suffering, but Christ
suffering in you. So continue to offer up your illness in
prayer and patience and so make it fruitful for souls.[19]

HER EXAMPLE: The Testimonies

You Have a Chance to Carry the Dying Jesus

One day Mother came to visit the families of those who were sick in bed. Mother called a rickshaw and made me sit in it. With the help of a sister, Mother brought a very sick man of about forty-five years old. This man had tuberculosis, as he was coughing and vomiting blood. His clothes were so dirty; he must have been lying in the gutter. Mother told the rickshaw man where to go to the TB hospital. Mother was walking before us along with a sister. I can never, never in my life forget that incident and my terrible reaction to a man so sick, vomiting blood. Then Mother told me, "You have a chance to carry the dying Jesus. Take Him and care for Him. Don't be frightened. I am arranging for his admission in the hospital." I was struggling so much, thinking, "If my father or my relatives would meet me on the road, with a young man, sick and dying on my lap, what would be the result?" . . . I just said a prayer in my heart to Our Lady.

Right after this prayer, that dying man looked at me with such a painful gaze, with tears in his eyes. In one second a flash of light came in my heart, and in my eyes I saw, "It is Jesus who was taken into the arms of Mary from the Cross." The words of Mother—"This is your chance to carry Jesus dying. Carry Him with love. Don't let Him get hurt. Ask Our Lady to help you"—became such a reality to me; my initial repugnance turned into a supernatural love. This experience of Jesus in reality, present in the sick and dying, in such a disguise, will never leave me. The faith that was implanted in my soul, this reality of Jesus in such a distressing disguise, is something rooted by Mother within me from that day.[20]

We Go and Start the Work

So there was this global concern that she operated, and of course this was the simple way where she and her sisters would act. I would often say, "How do you know what to do? Let us say, there was a cyclone or a fire, how do you know what to do?" She would say, "We have plenty of practice, no? So we go and start the work. Everybody joins us. Everybody gives help and then the work gets done." On one level she makes it sound very simple. At another level I think she came to realize that since she and her sisters stood for a kind of dispassionate goodness, it attracted the goodness of ordinary human beings—and we have all some goodness in us—to join the effort and the work would get done.[21]

Mother's Request Was Not to Cut My Leg

Once I [an orphan boy, brought up by Mother Teresa] had an accident at school. I fell down from the roof of the school while I was flying a kite. My leg was broken. The school authority arranged my treatment at a hospital [in Calcutta] and informed Mother. As she got the news, she came to see me along with my sponsors. After one month of treatment at the hospital, she took me to another hospital as she was not satisfied with the treatment. [An orthopedic doctor] told Mother that my leg had to be amputated due to gangrene.

Mother's request was not to cut my leg but to try the best for me. Mother and my sponsor used to come to see me in the hospital. It was a miracle to me that after having three operations, it was fully cured, although it took time, nearly one and a half years in the hospital.[22]

Mother's Generosity Surpassed Everyone Else's

I remember once arriving in Tijuana with her and having a celebration. And she and everyone were tired. It was late and the sun was going down. Somebody just came in from the barrio [neighborhood] and said: "Mother, there is somebody in the hospital and they need a priest." Mother said, "Father, let's go." I must confess I was tired. We had just landed, and I began to make excuses which were reasonable, but not generous: "Mother, when you come into a diocese, you can't just go in. You have to get permission and things like that." And Mother cut me off. "Oh, sure," she said, "we'll get permission," and we got into the car. We went over to this hospital and to the parish next door. She went into the parish and met the parish priest. "Father, could we visit someone in the hospital." He said, "Fine" and she visited this person whom she did not know. That person was beyond her immediate responsibility.[23]

The Biggest Job That She Had in the World

If one would go to Kalighat [a hospice in Calcutta] and see the dying man on one of the beds, with the big hole that maggots have dug into his body, and you see the maggots moving around inside him, the average person couldn't even go close. But for Mother Teresa, one of her fondest memories was when she talked about how the work began. She would never cease to tell people how she sat with this man, with his head on her lap, and pulled out maggots from his body totally oblivious to the stink, the smell, where for her the biggest job that she had in the world was to take those maggots out of his body, knowing fully well that taking those maggots out of that body was not going to stop this man from dying. The natural human thing would be, well, he is going to die, so let us forget about it. We just clean him up and cover him up, and we can give him a dignified burial; but no, she sat there, did something for hours, taking out those maggots. When I used to hear those stories, it didn't mean as much as when I actually went to Kalighat and saw a situation similar to that. Seeing maggots moving inside a person, your whole being, your hair stands up. You don't want to be around. You are afraid. Everything in you says, "Don't be here." And yet hour upon hour, she would be doing that because she saw in him Jesus, and she wanted to love Jesus in him.[24]

He Needs Help

I remember one day walking out of Mother House with Mother. We were going to an event where she was being given a water tanker for water for some of the areas. As we walked out of Mother House, lying right in the little alley was a man in a very critical condition. You could see he really needed attention. She immediately forgot about the fact that she was going to this function where she was going to be the chief guest, to be honored and given the tanker. She knelt right down beside him, picked him up, and said, "We need to look after him. He needs help. He needs to be taken to the hospital." And her whole attention was on him. Her whole position, her not being on time, not being there to receive the water tanker, totally disappeared, because for her, her neighbor who was lying on the street needed her attention. We finally convinced her to go, that we would look after him, we would get him to the hospital. Very reluctantly she left, and kept looking back to see if we would fulfill what we had promised to do. Because for her, that was more important than that she go for the water tanker.[25]

Even the Police Were Really Frightened of Him

We have a home for the AIDS patients in New York, and Mother used to go and visit these people. . . . There was a man brought there. His name was D. He was a criminal, and even the police were really frightened of him. He was converted from his ways, and he loved Mother so much. He was very sick, and we took him to the hospital. Those days Mother came to visit. This man sent word that he wanted to see his friend, that is, Mother. So Mother went to see him. Then this man said, "I want to see you alone." So we all went out and he was alone with Mother. Then he said, "You know, Mother, I have terrible pain in my head; I unite it with the crown of thorns of Jesus. I have terrible pain in my hand. I unite it with the wounded hands of Jesus. I have terrible pain in my leg. I unite it with the wounded feet of Jesus." For every part of his body, he was expressing how he was uniting it with the pain of Jesus. Then he said to Mother,

"Mother, I have one desire." And Mother said, "What?" He said, "Take me to the home of the sisters. I want to die there." And Mother brought him home. And Mother told us, as soon as she came, "I went to the chapel and looked at Jesus, and the man was there for a few minutes. He was speaking to Jesus on the Cross." And afterward Mother told us with a big smile, "You know, I told Jesus, 'See, Jesus, this D., he loves You so much.'" So I tell this story, how these people who had been far away from God had come very, very close to God because of Mother's love for Jesus, which Mother put into living action by sharing this love with the people.[26]

Mother Rushed to Help Him

In 1969 I was traveling with Mother. We were at the train station in Bangalore, walking along the platform to our train. Mother was on my right and the train tracks were on my left. As we walked I was speaking to Mother, leaning toward her so she could hear me in the noise around us. Periodically I would look down, watching our steps as we walked among the baggage lying around. Once I turned back to Mother, but she had disappeared. I began to look around, but I couldn't see her. There was a crowd gathering at the edge of the platform near the track. Suddenly Mother appeared in the middle of the crowd. I rushed over to her. A one-legged beggar with a crutch had been crossing the train tracks. An electric train was coming down that track rapidly, and the beggar would not have made it safely across. Mother saw him and rushed to help him. Leaning down, she

had given him her hand and was trying to pull him up, but Mother was being pulled down. People on the platform saw what was happening and rushed to help, pulling them both to safety up on the platform. I was amazed that Mother had seen that beggar through the crowd, while talking to me and picking her way through the baggage. I think her gift of self was so complete, her charity so deep, that she was a magnet of love that attracted the chance to serve God in others.[27]

I Will Never Forget This Tender Love

I personally have a beautiful experience of Mother's tender love and care for me when I was suffering from very bad asthma. . . . I went to Mother for a special blessing and asked her to pray for me. Mother looked at me with so much love and told me to come to her for nine days daily with Lourdes water and a spoon. Mother would put her hands on me and we prayed together one Memorare. Then she would make me drink one spoonful of Lourdes water. I will never forget this tender love of Mother toward me.[28]

Mother Went into Action

I introduced . . . a woman from my home diocese who was the mother of twelve children. Mother said to her, "Give me one to help serve the poor!" As the two of them were speaking about the children, a woman nearby fell over and went into an epileptic fit, which brought on convulsions. Mother quickly went into action and put her arms under the woman to have her stretch out on the ground. She sent her sisters

for blankets and something warm for the woman to drink. Then Mother kneeling there began to pray. She invited me to join her, and she took a Miraculous Medal from her pocket and asked me to hold it on the woman's forehead. We said the Hail Mary together. In but a few moments the woman calmed down, sat up, and smiled at both of us with a sense of peace. Mother looked at me with a smile and said, "See, Father, you always work miracles!"[29]

If Mother Teresa Came to Visit You . . .

I was a hospital chaplain then and arranged for Mother to visit some patients in the hospital. After she had spoken in St. Christopher's Cathedral to the largest crowd ever in that church, she did visit three patients. One man was to have a heart transplant and said he didn't know if he could bring himself to make peace with God. I had visited him several times and in the end I said, "Look, if Mother Teresa came to visit you, would that be enough for you to come back to God?" He said, "That would never happen." Well, when Mother came and visited him, he sat up in bed, took the medal from Mother, who said a simple prayer, and afterward he made his confession. He went on to have his transplant and survived for some years.[30]

A Coming of Jesus Himself

I had open-heart surgery in a hospital, in Calcutta. On the third day after the operation, I had just been brought back from the intensive care, when suddenly from my bed I heard

a nurse calling out: "Mother Teresa is coming. . . . Mother Teresa is here!" And there was at once running outside in the corridor. I remember wondering, "Why does Mother come here?" But a moment later she was there by my side, bending over me! . . . I was overwhelmed, so much so that I could hardly answer her. . . . I was possessed by an intense feeling that her coming was in some way a coming of Jesus Himself, a sign of His personal love! . . . One thing struck me at that time, in a few moments in a room filled with people: the director of the Heart Center was there, the chief surgeon, who had operated on me, had come running from the operation theater in his surgical gown and many other doctors, nurses, and even patients. They were all looking at Mother and smiling affectionately, reverently. One felt how happy they were to have her among them! A small incident? Yes, but wherever Mother went, the same thing happened, the same outburst of spontaneous reverence and love. People longed to see her, to speak to her, to be blessed by her. I myself have seen it on quite a few occasions.[31]

Nothing Could Be Done for Him

On another day, there was a young man, recently wed, who was totally paralyzed because of an accident in the mine. Nothing could be done for him. The family, in desperation, brought the man on the bed to be placed in front of the altar during Mass. Mother became immediately concerned about him and asked me to bless him. Mother then arranged for the sisters to get him medical attention in Tirana [Albania]. This is one more example of Mother's concern that made sure something concrete be done to help someone in need. When she or her own sisters could not actually do the needful, she would try to get others to do what they could do.[32]

The Joy of My Life

In August 1979, we walked with our Mother in the poor areas of Port-au-Prince, Haiti. Mother saw how the sick and dying people were just left there to die. I saw how rats were eating their flesh. One poor man had diarrhea and was put near the drain outside. After seeing this, Mother said Haiti is poorer than Calcutta. Mother decided to open a house. There were two rooms with cemented floors and a roof. Mother herself was cleaning hard and painting the house. . . . There was no water, no electricity, no transport. But God's Providence was there: the CRS [Catholic Relief Services] director came to see Mother. Mother told him, "Please, I need a car for the transport of the sick and dying people." It worked out at once and by the 5th of August, seventy sick and dying people were brought to our house from the General Hospital of Port-au-Prince. . . .

But something happened; the local people were unhappy to see all the sick people arriving, and so they dug a ditch in front of our gate so that no car was able to enter. In the midst of this problem, our Mother arrived. Mother did not say a single word. Mother joined her hands and her silent prayer worked wonders: the same people filled the ditch again and there was peace; the house could be opened. At the end of the official opening, Mother recited Gandhi's

words: "He who serves the poor, serves God." Mother continued, "I spent hours and hours serving the poor, the sick,
and the dying, the unloved, the unwanted, the lepers, the
mentally handicapped because I love God and I believe His
word: 'You did it to Me.' This is the only reason and the joy
of my life, to love and serve Him in the distressing disguises
of the poor, the homeless, the unwanted, the hungry, the
thirsty, the naked, and naturally, in doing it, I proclaim His
love and compassion for each one of my suffering brothers
and sisters."[33]

The First to See and to Get Up

The shrine is a huge church and it was packed with people.
So many people, of course, were attending in order to see
Mother. A lot of sisters were there from other houses, also
all of the people from our home for the elderly and sick,
and those with AIDS. It was Communion time and José,
one of the men from our home, who is unsteady on his feet,
got up and was going for Communion. José fell and hit his
head on the marble steps and it was bleeding. Though there
were many people there, it was Mother who immediately
got up and went right to José (who is at least twice Mother's
size) and walked with him, took him over to one of the side
altars in the church. Mother was rubbing his face and head
and wouldn't leave him. It struck me so much that it was
Mother who was the first to see what had happened and to
get up, and she insisted on staying with him until the ambulance came—even though the ceremony was going on.
She never sees herself as being important—she completely

forgot herself . . . the handmaid of the Lord, ever ready to
go in haste to serve Jesus in the poor.[34]

I Felt Someone Standing Close to Me

One late night I was suddenly awakened by a severe tooth-
ache. I was on the fourth floor right at the last bed, sitting
pressing my face with my hand. All the others were fast
asleep. I didn't know whom to wake up at midnight, so I sat
in that huge dormitory of sleeping sisters waiting anxiously
for the morning, pressing my tooth to soothe the pain. All of
a sudden I felt someone standing close to me, her hand on my
shoulder. She inquired what had happened to me. I looked
up. It was Mother. I told her what had happened. She said,
"I don't have medicine, but I'll get you a glass of water," and
she disappeared. I remained sitting. I didn't even realize that
Mother would have to go up and down four floors. Anyway, she came with the glass of water and before giving it
to me she said, "Let's say three Hail Marys." So we both
said the prayers. I drank the water. Mother tucked me in
bed, blessed me, and said, "Sleep, now you will be all right."
And sure enough, I went into deep sleep, and the pain disappeared and never appeared again for months.[35]

Mother Rushed to the Gas-Stricken City

Just after the gas leak disaster in the year 1984 that had
taken a heavy toll of lives in Bhopal, Mother rushed to the
stricken city with a planeload of [supplies] along with doctors and the Missionaries of Charity. It was a time when
even the staunch champions of humanity were waiting for

someone to come to the rescue. Immediately after her arrival, Mother Teresa and the sisters got themselves busy with the rescue operations. Her appearance in Bhopal and the initiative taken by her [prompted] others to join her brigade to take up the uphill task of extending help to people affected by the gas leak. Mother along with the sisters knocked on each and every door of the affected localities where even the government officials were scared to reach. The relentless job done by Mother's brigade was a real miracle that inspired people to join the task. During Operation Faith, when the people were sitting behind the closed doors fearing anything awful happening to them, Mother was out in the roads distributing supplies to the affected people and filling them with the courage to fight the aftermath conditions.[36]

With So Much Love and Care

I was on leave on that day when I heard from my house surgeon that Mother was anxiously waiting for me for the treatment of [an MC sister who had met with an accident]. I immediately rushed into the hospital and, coming to the bedside of the sister, found Mother wiping up the blood coming out from the sister's mouth, who was pulseless, bleeding profusely, and almost gasping. Mother very painfully looked at me and said, "Are you Dr. X? I am waiting for you. Please save the life of my child. I will pray for you." I was spellbound to see Mother, who with her motherly appearance was praying for her sister's life. I felt an amazing power and inexpressible sensation, which aroused a strong determination in my mind to save the sister. Already every effort was made by starting intravenous fluid, and several bottles of blood were given, and a group of doctors helped me. Mother was very anxiously and eagerly watching the sister's face. . . . Gradually the pulse was palpable and the respiration became to some extent quiet. We became a bit hopeful, and Mother was also relieved of her anxiety.

The next day, the sister could speak and was more or less stable, and Mother was greatly consoled, and her face became bright and cheerful. She gripped my hands in gratitude and said, "Doctor, please try to hasten Sister's recovery by all means, because she has to take her vows within two months." . . . The sister had two major operations on her jaws (mandibles) and forearm bones. Within a short time, she was out of danger, and Mother asked me to release her from the hospital as she did not feel it desirable and justified to keep that bed occupied in a busy hospital where many poor moribund patients might be refused admission. . . . She took the vows on the scheduled date in St. Mary's Church, and I was present at that ceremony.[37]

Like a Mother Feeding Her Own Child

Mother was very happy to go to Kalighat whenever she got a chance. Mother used to sit and talk to the patients, feed the very sick ones, sometimes with her own hands, like a mother feeding her own child, with so much love and care.[38]

Mother Held My Hand

As an aspirant, my apostolate was in Nirmal Hriday (Ka-lighat). The first few days, I was so afraid to touch the old people. One man had a very big wound on his leg and it was full of maggots. I was so afraid. Then Mother passed that way. She saw me standing with the dressing tray and struggling without knowing what to do, and she knew I was afraid. . . . She held my hand, took the tray from my hand, and she started to clean the wound, and took out all the worms. Then she put the forceps in my hand and she held my hands and made me clean the wound. I did a little, and then Mother continued and finished the dressing by herself. With that my fears disappeared. Then Mother ran and got a cup of hot milk for the patient and made me pour that milk into his mouth little by little, and Mother stood close by watching me and smiled. Then we moved on to another patient, and Mother herself did for each patient whatever was necessary. . . . From that day onward I had no fear. Mother remained at my side that whole morning teaching me.[39]

Her Joy in Doing All the Dirty Work

I was waiting for Mother to do the dressing, but she did not come, so I went to search for her. Then I saw Mother cleaning the [toilet]. I wanted to help, but she told me, "You do the work inside. Mother will do this." Still I wanted to help Mother, so I took a broom and went to help her. By the time I [returned], she had already cleaned the toilet and was rubbing the drain. Then she emptied the dustbins into a trolley.

Mother herself pushed it and took it across the road. She allowed me to hold one side and threw the dirt in the common dustbin outside. Seeing Mother's tender love for the inmates and the dying people, and the joy with which she did all the dirty work (cleaning toilets, washing the bedpans, urinals, the container where the patients used to spit, etc.), which she never allowed anybody else to do, was a big inspiration for me.[40]

Deep Interest in the Person

Mother always manifested love for her fellow human beings by deep interest in a person. If she went to Kalighat, she would go down on her knees, sit beside that patient; she would pat the patient and ask what he or she needed. If that person asked for a rasgulla [a typical Bengali dessert] or something, she would see that the person got it. She would go from bed to bed, touching each one of them, smiling, talking.[41]

Where Is My Friend?

During my postulancy in Prem Dan, I was working in the female ward. Whenever Mother came, she used to visit all the patients first, then the sisters. Whenever Mother came, she used to ask, "Where is my friend?" It was . . . a deaf and dumb lady, found near the jungle, and Mother had picked her up and brought her to Dum Dum first, and from there [she] came to Prem Dan. And [she] was very happy when Mother came. Mother used to go to each patient. Mother was so holy, she cared for each one. Mother's great love touched me. I saw for the first time in my life someone so loving, to each patient, each child, each sister, etc.[42]

I Accept This Gift for the Poor

From the beginning, Mother had the art of begging for the poor. She would pass the word around to those who wished to help her. In this way, she collected books, pencils, clothing, medicines, etc. When she went directly to beg for medicines, she succeeded at times but she also had refusals. I remember an occasion when she took me with her to a doctor in one of the big buildings. She was looking for medicines and help for a little girl, Marcella, who had bone tuberculosis. The doctor was aggressive in his refusal to help. Then Mother got up, joined her hands, smiled, and said graciously, "Thank you." She took the doctor completely by surprise and as she reached the door a message came for her to return to his chamber. The doctor said to Mother, "I gave you nothing and still you said 'thank you.' What if I gave you this?" He handed her what she required. Mother said, "What you did not give the first time was for me, now I accept this gift for the poor." You could see the doctor had never experienced anything like this before.[43]

Carrying the Cross of Christ

When they finally X-rayed my back properly, it became apparent that my spine was badly damaged. . . . I passed the news on to Mother Teresa. . . . I received a letter from her asking me to offer everything for her and the work and to find others to do the same. . . . For me, suffering in itself was nothing. I was a failure and my suffering was . . . destructive. But suffering shared with the Passion of Christ has become a precious gift. The very center of my life is Jesus Christ, and I know that, through his Passion and the Cross, comes a message of supreme hope: our redemption through the resurrection. When I seek an explanation for suffering, I look at my model Jesus Christ, and when I see him tread the way of Calvary, I know that I must simply follow in his footsteps. I try really to live what Mother Teresa tells us to do: to "accept what God gives and what He takes with a big smile." When I'm in pain, when my back is aching, I really feel that I am carrying on my shoulders the Cross of Christ.[44]

Even After Her Death

Mother Teresa—faithful to her mission statement: "If I ever become a Saint, I will surely be one of 'darkness.' I will continually be absent from Heaven, to light the light of those in darkness on earth"—continues her works of mercy even now. Many times patients reported to have seen her at their bedside. Here are two examples:

Thank You, Mother Teresa

Hi, my name is Miguel. I am thirty-four years old. I come from another religion, not Catholic. On June 23, I underwent a surgery on the spine. I entered the surgery room at 1:15 p.m., and I came out at 5:45 p.m. approximately. I woke up out of the general anesthesia about 7:00 p.m. . . . I fell asleep and during my dream I felt that somebody came near my bed and touched my right leg. I opened my eyes and there was nobody. For the second time, hands were placed on the same leg. Again I opened my eyes and there was nothing. The third time, I felt only one hand. I opened my eyes and I saw a hand but only the left hand. I knew whose hand it was because of the border of the sari and her rosary; yes, it was the hand of Mother Teresa of Calcutta, and I opened my eyes more. I could not believe what I was seeing. I could see her wrinkles, her rosary, a little stain bigger than the others, those stains which usually the old people have. I could also see the edge of the nail of the (fat) finger, and I felt how she touched my leg with the palm of her hand. A little bit later my doctor came and said, "I only came to tell you not to be frightened because you won't be able to move your feet, so that you can be calm"; and I, moving my feet, told him, "No! Look, I am moving them," and he was surprised and left. Next Saturday, the doctor came back and told me to try to stand up, and I told him: "I got up already last night to go to the bathroom," and he was surprised again, and he told me, "But someone helped you." I answered him, "No, I did it by myself," and he congratulated me and went. He had planned to discharge me on Tuesday, June 27, and my doctor sent me home on Sunday the 25th. Thank you, Mother Teresa.

Yes, She Is the One!

We are from a very poor ranch [in Mexico]. In spite of our poverty and the fact that we do not have any money, we do not ignore the things about religion. We have a tricycle, and my daughter, Dolores, and I go to sell eggs filled with

confetti and some sweets. We get enough money to eat torti-
llas with salt or chili, rarely for soup. On one occasion when
we were reaching another ranch, a car hit my daughter and
threw her to the ground. She was unconscious. I tried to
help her to come back by striking her face, but nothing.
Without knowing any prayer, I asked Mother Teresa that
nothing may happen to her, that she may not get a blood
clot. I prayed an Our Father, Hail Mary, Glory Be, and
ejaculations to [Mother Teresa]. My daughter regained con-
sciousness eighty minutes after the accident. Later on, my
daughter told me that she had seen a very loving, little old
lady, and she said that she caressed her hair and gave her
the blessing, her dress was white as snow, and smiling she
disappeared. We did not know Mother Teresa [and have not
even seen her in a photo], and we do not have even television. Afterward a young man (the one who helped us to
write our testimony) gave us a picture of Mother Teresa of
Calcutta and my daughter shouted with joy: "Yes, she is the
one!"

REFLECTION

"I was sick and you visited Me." (Mt 25:36)

"Be an angel of comfort to the sick."[45]

"They are sick, [longing] for medical care, and for
that gentle touch and a warm smile."[46]

I will remember the feeling that I had when I was ill and will act with kindness and consideration toward the sick.

How can I alleviate the sufferings of someone who is sick? Can I get him or her the medicine needed? What small act of kindness can I do for someone who is ill: pay a visit, spend some time in conversation, do a small service, like throwing out the trash, reading a newspaper for a blind person, sending get-well wishes, and so forth? Even if I have to overcome my own feelings, how can I move forward to help the sick in their need? Small things done with great love can make a big difference in someone's life.

If I am sick, what can I do to live in a way that my present weakness and limitations do not affect negatively my relationship with others?

How can I help a sick person to see the value that their suffering can have if it is united with Christ's and offered for some good intention? Can I facilitate the sacrament of the anointing of the sick for those I know?

PRAYER

Dear Lord, the Great Healer, I kneel before you, since
every perfect gift must come from You.
I pray, give skill to my hands, clear vision to my mind,
kindness and meekness to my heart.
Give me singleness of purpose, strength to lift up
a part of the burden of my suffering fellow men,
and a true realization of the privilege that is mine.

*Take from my heart all guile and worldliness, that with
the simple faith of a child, I may rely on You.*
Amen.

—*A Physician's Prayer, anonymous,*
prayed daily by Mother Teresa

SIX

VISIT THE IMPRISONED

When we think of those in prison, the first reaction for most of us is that they must be there for a good reason; our inner judgment forms but too fast—we have judged rashly. Our judgment may be true or it may be false. However, this does not change the obligation the Church places on us to practice this corporal work of mercy. What was characteristic for Mother Teresa—in fact, not only when dealing with prisoners, but with anyone—was that she was able to avoid any judgmental attitude. "The act is wrong," she would say, "but why she is doing that you do not know. . . . The intention you do not know. When we judge, we are judging the intention of the sister, of the poor."

Mother Teresa visited prisoners and took great care of them. She did so without prejudice toward anyone, without looking down on anyone, without condescension, but rather with great respect for each person and with great hope. She was always ready to offer someone another chance (and not just a second chance!). She approached each one, independently of the reason for which they were sentenced, precisely with an attitude of mercy, which was partly the fruit of her own conviction that "there, but for the grace of God, go I," and partly the fruit of her compassion for this particular suffering person. If circumstances would have been different, maybe they would not be in their present situation; on the other hand, if I had been in their situation, maybe I would have done the same or worse. Whatever the reason for the suffering, the one who suffers is in need of help, and we cannot remain indifferent.

Mother Teresa started a special apostolate for "jail girls," that is, girls who had been found in the streets (often in poor mental health) and put in jail because of the lack of alternative facilities. With the help of government authorities, she had them released and opened a home for them, where she provided occupational therapy and some small work. In this way, they could work and live with dignity. Further, she would make contact with their families and help them reconcile.

HER WORDS

The Privilege of Being with the Poor

I am grateful to God to have given me this opportunity to be with you and to share with you the gift of God, the privilege of being with the poor, the privilege of being twenty-four hours in touch with Christ. For Jesus has said, and He cannot deceive us, "You did it to Me. I was hungry and you gave Me to eat; and I was thirsty, and you gave Me to drink; and I was sick and in prison and you visited Me, and I was homeless and you gave Me a home. You took Me in." We are trying to do [this], you and I together, to bring that joy of touching Christ in the distressing disguise.[1]

※

Like Saint Paul, once he realized that love of Christ, he did not care [about] anything anymore. He did not care [about being] scourged, [being] put into prison. Only one thing for him was important, Jesus Christ. How [do] we get that conviction? "Nothing and nobody will separate me from the love of Christ."[2]

※

What you have received from Jesus, give generously. He loves me. He took all the trouble to come from heaven to give us such good news, to love one another. We must be able to love, my sisters. Like Saint Maximilian,[3] he was not the one to be chosen. That man said, "Oh my wife, oh my children," . . . and [Saint Maximilian] said, "Take my life." And we know what happened. They put him in jail to die of starvation. We don't know what the pain of hunger is, we don't know; I've seen people die. Real hunger, [for] days. He [Saint Maximilian] did not die, so they gave him an injection. Why did that man do that? Greater love. Would I do that for my sister?[4]

The Jail or the Road

We have thousands of lepers because they are the most unwanted, they are the most shunned people. We have the alcoholics, the distressed ones, the men who have but two places—the jail or the road. We have night shelters and things like that. But . . . for all of us it is not a waste of time to do just the humble work, just to feed the hungry, just to wash his clothes, just to take tender care and love of the unwanted.[5]

✳

We have opened this place in New York for AIDS, as nobody wants these people, as rich as they are. When three men heard they had the disease, they jumped from the thirty-fifth floor of a building. We are taking the sick and dying, and there is a tremendous change in the whole country because the sisters are taking care of them. When I went to the governor, he said, "You are the first and only one who has brought Christ to these people." And he did something unheard of in the United States; he allowed twelve people in the jail with this disease to come out; it was the first time in history, something unheard of in the history of America. They allowed [the prisoners] to come out and die with us. The sisters are doing real miracles there. Father Joseph[6] phoned this morning and what miracles Father is doing with these people. One was baptized, made first Holy Communion and confirmation, and then he died. Sister wrote and said, "What a peace, what a radiating joy there is in the faces of these people when they die." To

me, it has created new hope in the country. Many people
are coming forward now to help. What has happened is
the miracle of God.[7]

※

Yesterday, Sister was telling me there are sisters who are
going to the prison and how, from the time they have
started going, how they have the Blessed Sacrament
in the jail, and the priest who is the chaplain there has
started daily Adoration for half an hour. To see those
prisoners—those young boys and men—adoring. (They
are preparing some of those boys for First Communion.)
[They are] so open to that presence of Christ, that
connecting power. They're hungry for God, they are
very hungry for God.[8]

Appeal for the Life of a Man

Dear Governor,

   I come before you today to appeal for the life of a
man—Joseph Roger O'Dell. I do not know what he
has done to be condemned to death. All I know is that
he is, too, a child of God created for greater things, to
love and to be loved. I pray that Joseph is at peace with
God, that he has said sorry to God and to whoever he
has hurt. Let us not take away his life. Let us bring hope
into his life and into all our lives. Jesus, who loves each
one of us tenderly with mercy and compassion, works
miracles of forgiveness. To you, dear Joseph, I say, trust
in God's tender love for you and accept whatever God

gives you and give whatever He takes, with a big smile.
Let us pray. God bless you.

   —Mother Teresa[9]

When They Leave the Jail

Another thing now we have started in Harlem to do,
the sisters visit the jail, where we have the detention,
what is it called? Anyway, young girls when they are let
out, then anybody grabs them, they can go anywhere.
So when they leave the jail, we have arranged [to] take
them [to] our own place. They need a complete outfit,
and they need to be placed in the proper work. . . . And
in every city you must be having this kind of people; . . .
we will take those girls and bring them to the convent
and then from there [the Co-Workers will] be able to
continue.[10]

HER EXAMPLE: The Testimonies

It Was Rather a Matter of Human Dignity

Our home for the "jail girls" in Tengra, Calcutta, one of
the works dearest to Mother's heart, is a fruit of Mother's
concern to preserve the dignity of the poor, and not just care
for their material needs. These women, most of whom are
to some degree mentally or emotionally handicapped, were
found by the police roaming the streets of Calcutta. For

lack of another facility in which to care for them, they were put in jail, though they had committed no crime. When the government was made aware of this situation, and the large number of noncriminal women affected, the chief minister of West Bengal contacted Mother. He asked her if the sisters could care for these women. It was not, of course, a matter of food and shelter, as these were being provided in the jail. It was rather a matter of human dignity, of providing the kind of environment and care that would help these women to recover, or at least improve, and feel loved and respected. Mother readily agreed to care for the "jail girls," as she called them, if the government would give us land to make a facility for them. This was done, and Mother never tired of drawing the attention of Co-Workers and benefactors to our "jail girls." She even secured the services of voluntary professors and others to help in the education of the women and teach them useful skills such as handicrafts.[11]

A Completely Changed Man

She had a tremendous hope even for murderers. . . . There was a murderer in the USA with whom we became very close friends; he became a Catholic during his life imprisonment. I got in contact with Mother Teresa. She took up the whole case with deep love. He just changed his whole way of life, and through him also other prisoners were changed. Every time I went to Calcutta she would ask, "How is my friend, X? X, the murderer?" He is now a completely changed man. He has become the chaplain's assistant whenever he comes to prison. I had Easter Mass one year. He did a painting for

Mother and another one for myself, which I gave to my father, who had a deep love for her. Oh, [he] can be put to death, but still he can live for Christ. She started correspondence with him in a maximum security prison. Every time I go home I visit him. It is one of the joys of my life. . . . It does not matter if you are in prison, you still can serve Christ there. . . . In a letter to me he remarks, . . . "Ever since I met you and [have] written to Mother Teresa, I often think how different my life could have been if only I had known Jesus Christ before this tragedy happened. . . . I would just like to dedicate the rest of my life to helping others who need my help."[12]

First Home in the USA for People with AIDS

I went with Mother Teresa and two other people at Sing Sing Prison in Ossining, New York. . . . Most people there are serving life terms, and when we went there, these men— many of whom were murderers, rapists, whatever, muscular because of lifting weights—how many got on their knees and started crying when Mother Teresa would pat them on the head and give them Miraculous Medals.[13]

※

For her, they were not criminals. They were made to the image and likeness of God, and so she gave them hope. She always found the right word or the right action to get them in touch with the Lord.[14]

※

Mother decided to open up an AIDS house in New York. It was the first AIDS house, and it began in 1985. In New

York, most of the AIDS patients were homosexuals or drug addicts. And in the Church there was great controversy at that time, because these homosexual groups were very anti-Catholic, and the Church was very vocal against their lifestyle. And some very big priests said, "Mother, don't get involved. Don't touch it. You are going to be criticized, that you are supporting their lifestyle." In her mind these [people] were the lepers of the day. Nobody wanted them. And she went into the prison, and she wanted to open the house, and everybody had an opinion about this. Well, it took about six months. Mother did get the house for the AIDS patients. Mother went into Sing Sing Prison . . . and she gave a Miraculous Medal to these men suffering with AIDS and she said, "I will come for you and get you." And she went to the mayor, she went to Cardinal O'Connor. Mother was tremendously excited. She had had her eye operated on, and she had to wear dark glasses because of the cataract, but she wanted to open the house on Christmas Eve, and she said, "I want to give it to Jesus for His birthday. Let us bring home these men for His birthday."

Christmas Eve in New York—it is impossible to do anything. Everyone said, "Forget it, Mother." [Mother insisted,] "These men have to be released from prison." Mother called the governor and said, "I want you to give me a Christmas gift. I want a Christmas gift for Baby Jesus, and I want you to parole those men in prison so we can bring them home for Jesus's birthday." And the governor said, "Mother, if you want this, there is something you have to do for me. You have to pray for me and my family." She said, "Yes." She put the phone down in the Bronx and she immediately went into the chapel and began praying for him. And the governor was on the phone saying, "Hello! hello!" I picked up the phone and he said, "Where is Mother?" I said, "She has gone into the chapel to pray." He said, "Oh my goodness." He signed a medical pardon for these men on the spot. . . . And these men came in by ambulance. They were dressed like astronauts, so much protective clothing. They came by ambulance with the siren, and Mother was not deterred by the controversy. . . .

Mother had the same rule for this house as she did for the other houses. Again it caused much controversy because they said, "You have to have television; you have to have radio. These men need this. There is nothing else to do." Mother said, "No, nothing doing. We are going to keep the same rule." And what happened was the men began talking to one another, and they became friends. They became like family. Pretty soon they were saying the Rosary. Men from all backgrounds. Some men who had killed, some had been on the streets since they were ten years old. Some had been drug addicts. They were learning the Catechism. And they were like brothers.[15]

Extremely Touched by Her

One guy, an alleged public crime figure, was eleven years in a federal penitentiary, and over that period he had the benefit of confession, of the sacraments, and in line with that we used to send him the rosary beads that the sisters used to make. And I know personally he was touched by that. Two others who, again, were alleged organized crime figures, whom I brought up to personally meet Mother, were extremely touched by her; and Mother embraced them.[16]

She Offered Encouragement, Love, and Hope

In 1991 I was arrested and sent to prison. As I awaited trial, I wrote a letter to Mother Teresa explaining what had happened to me. She wrote back immediately offering encouragement, love, and hope. I was shocked that she would take the time to write under these circumstances. From 1992 until just a few weeks before her death in 1997, Mother Teresa wrote regularly to me and answered every single letter. When I first wrote to Mother, I was depressed and feeling sorry for myself. I shared some of my troubles with her, and from the beginning she encouraged me to forget the problems of the past and focus on the present and the future. She always reminded me of the boundless love of God and always showed me the path to His love. She loved to have me tell her stories about other prisoners and urged me to share her letters to me with them. I did and she always enjoyed hearing stories about them. Here are some excerpts from her letters to me:

> *Thank you for your letter and thank God for all the good He is doing in and through you. . . . Let us thank God for His grace, which is at work in you, and for all the compassion He has kindled in your heart for those behind the bars.*

In His Passion, Jesus taught us to forgive out of love and forget out of humility. I am praying for you that the suffering that has come into your life will be a means for you to come closer to Jesus. Let Him live in you, so you may spread the mercy of His Heart to all in similar situations.

※

I am glad to hear you are free from the past and making use of the present to grow in the love of God through love for the suffering ones around you. Jesus in His agony prayed the longer, the Gospels tell us. Let us also in times of darkness and suffering keep close to Him in the solitude of His suffering and in the intimacy of prayer.

※

A Christian is a tabernacle of the living God. He created you; He chose you; He came to dwell in you, because He wanted you. Now that you have known how much God is in love with you, it is but natural that you spend your life radiating that love.[17]

Never Do Such a Thing Again

A poor woman was talking to Mother and crying. Mother was full of compassion for that lady. Mother saw me passing, called out to me, and said, "Go with this lady; her husband is in jail in Lalbazar. He has stolen a car two days ago and is now arrested. Go to the officer and say, 'Mother [said] to release him.'" I obeyed blindly and promptly. I did not know where Lalbazar was, what it is to be in prison, who [was] the officer. All I knew is Mother said to do it, and I went with this lady who was still crying. Mother saw us off at the gate. . . .

It was eleven a.m. when we reached Lalbazar police station. There we were told that the big officer would come at three p.m. We waited patiently and when he came I said, "There is a man by [this] name. He has stolen a car, and Mother said to release him." He asked, "which mother?" I said, "Mother Teresa." Again he asked, "Who is she?" I said, "Mother" (I only knew Mother as Mother, nothing else). The big officer smiled; he called a police officer and said something to him. We were all called together, put in a police jeep, and taken somewhere else with a police escort. There we entered another office, and I said the same thing to the officer there. He said, "But he is a thief. We can't release him." I said, "But Mother told you to release him." He asked, "What if he steals again?" "I do not know about that; all I know is Mother said to release him." He gave some orders, and I could see from between the curtains that man chained hand and feet together sitting as he could not stand because he was chained. They opened the chain and he was released.

By evening we reached the Mother House. The man was crying, and Mother said to him, "Make a good confession and never do such a thing again. God has given you a beautiful family. Love your children, pray together, say the Rosary each night, and Our Lady will help you." She blessed them and they left. Mother gave them food [to eat and take with them]. Since that day, that man who was a big thief since childhood changed his life, gave up his drinking, his bad company, his evil habits. His friends came to tempt him, but he said, "Mother has told me not to do it again and I promised Mother." Up to this day that [man] is . . . a changed man—poor, struggling to live, but keeping his word to Mother. I am sure Mother prayed for him.[18]

Even After Her Death, Mother Teresa Continues "to Visit" Prison

A sister told my parents [something extraordinary]: Yesterday, she went to the market store to buy candles. There she felt the gaze of a man; she turned to him and said hello; he answered back and asked, "Are you still going to the jail to give food to the prisoners?" She answered, "We are not into that kind of pastoral service (in San Pedro Sula, the sisters only work with HIV [patients], old men, and border kids)." And he said, "I've been watching you because you have the same dress as that nun in 2004, when I was unjustly put in prison, and was two days without eating anything, and she came to give me food." Sister asked, "Only to you?" He said, "No, to all of the prisoners, it was like between eleven p.m. and one a.m. (not visiting hours of course!)." Sister asked, "Was she young?" The man said, "No, she was an old lady." Then the sister showed him a little picture of Mother Teresa and asked him, "Was she the one?" And the man started to cry and said, "Yes, it was definitely her."

REFLECTION

"I was in prison and you visited Me." (Mt 25:36)

"Sick and in prison, [longing] for friendship He wants from you. . . . Will you be that 'one' to Him?"[19]

What is my attitude toward prisoners? That they deserve to be where they are or that it could be me? When I see or hear about a prisoner, do I think: "What could he or she have done to be there?" Or do I see a child of God, my brother, my sister?

Is there a way that I can participate in this work of mercy? For example, could I join a volunteer program or help in some rehabilitation program, and so forth? If I am "imprisoned" in my own prejudices, what concrete steps can I take to learn the truth and correct my mistaken thinking?

Am I imprisoned in my own egoism or pride? Can I get out of myself and offer a helping hand to someone who is in a more difficult situation than I am? Can I have a kind and positive attitude toward someone who is "imprisoned" by addiction? Am I able to approach them and by my understanding love give peace and joy?

PRAYER

O Glorious Saint Joseph,
we most humbly beg of you,
by the love and care
you had for Jesus and Mary,
to take our affairs, spiritual and temporal,
into your hands.
Direct them to the greater glory of God,
and obtain for us the grace
to do His holy Will.
Amen.

—Prayer to Saint Joseph,
prayed by Mother Teresa each Wednesday

SEVEN

BURY THE DEAD

The same delicate care that Mother Teresa showed to the dying was expressed as well in her attention to the dead. She showed great reverence for the innate dignity of every human being, independent of their social status, race, or religion, treating everyone with utmost respect. This was particularly evident in the Home for the Dying (Kalighat), where, while battling for the survival of those on the edge of death, she would make sure that those who died had funeral rites done according to the practices of their respective religions. She could have easily been excused from such effort, as it could have been considered exaggerated, or even extravagant, when there was so much to do for the sick. However, she wanted to show this delicate love even after the person had passed on to eternity. Whatever pertained to the dignity of the human person was important and sacred, deserving of every respect to the very end.

Though today burying the dead has a different connotation than it had in the Middle Ages, when often it meant putting one's own life in danger in plague-devastated cities, this act of mercy nonetheless calls upon us to give due respect to the human body after the person's mortal life has ended. Many a saint has died as a consequence of a disease caught while assisting people during plague epidemics of various kinds, while many others have courageously faced personal dangers to aid their neighbors in danger. In particular, we have the example of Father Damien, who gave his life to help the lepers on the Hawaiian island of Molokai. Indeed, Mother Teresa had great devotion to him. We may not be faced with situations that invite us to such heroic acts, yet we will surely be called to face the reality of death and to carry out those acts of charity that are required of this particular work of mercy.

HER WORDS

Are You Sure He Is Dead?

Once they brought a man dying from the street. The Hindus have the custom where they pray around the body, then they put fire in the mouth and the man starts to burn. They put fire in the mouth of that man and he got up! He said, "Give me water!" They brought him to Kalighat. I was there. I didn't know the story. So I went to see him and he was barely moving. So I said, "This one is already one step up!" So I washed his face. . . . He opened his eyes wide, he gave me a beautiful smile, and he died. I phoned, and they told me the story and asked, "Are you really sure that he is dead?"[1]

That Love of Christ Infected Everyone

When I went last time to Tanzania, all the non-Christian leaders of the tribes came to me just to thank me for the sisters. They said they had never seen God's love in action as [when] they saw what the sisters did for the Burundi refugees. More than twelve thousand people came at the same time, and these little sisters were running in and burying the dead and carrying the sick and all that. It was simply an opening for the whole of that region, for the whole of [the Tanzanian] people. They had never seen anything like that, so living, so real, and yet so full of joy. The sisters told me that during that time even the people in the shops would say, "Come, sisters, take what you need, take what you need." And they would go and take from the shops whatever they needed for the people and without paying anything. It was so beautiful. That shows you that that love of Christ in those sisters infected everybody else. It was, I believe it was something terrible, but again it was the way the sisters did it. The way they touched the people, the way they carried the dead, the way they had to bury them.

They told of a mother, she came with nine children, and by the time she went to the camp she had only one; all the rest had died. And so, whatever the sisters did for that woman and those children . . . it is something that

we must be able to keep . . . up, in our own homes, in
our own area, wherever we are. This is what the people
are hungry for, this is what the young people today want.[2]

Just Hold My Hand

Last Sunday . . . there was a man dying there, and he
didn't want anything. He said, "Just hold my hand and
with my hand in your hand, I am ready to go." There he
sat, was lying there all cold, only his face was still bright,
but that's all that he wanted. He didn't want me to say
anything or to do anything, only to just sit on his bed
and hold his hand, and he felt quite ready to go. Maybe
you will have that experience somewhere someday. This
is very beautiful how much people trust us and how
much they love us that they can trust themselves with us
like that. We have this experience continually all over
the place.[3]

✳

Those who are materially poor can be very wonderful
people. One day we went out and we picked up four
people from the street, and one of them was in a most
terrible condition. I told the sisters, you take care of
the other three, I will take care of the one who looks
worse. So I did for her all that my love can do. I put
her in bed and there was such a beautiful smile on her
face. She took hold of my hand and she said one word
only—"Thank you"—and she died. I could not help but
examine my conscience before her, and I asked myself
what would I say if I were in her place, and my answer

was very simple: I would have tried to draw a little attention to myself. I would have said, "I am hungry, I am dying, I am cold, I am in pain or something," but she gave me much more. She gave me her grateful love and she died with a smile on her face.[4]

I Am Going to Die Like an Angel

I will never forget the man I picked up from an open drain—except for his face . . . worms were crawling on his body. There were holes in his body everywhere, he was eaten up alive. He must have fainted and fallen into an open drain and people must have passed and passed, but the dirt had covered him up, and I saw something moving and I saw it was a human being. I took him out, took him to our house, and he was still. I had not yet begun cleaning him, but the only words he said, "I have lived like an animal in the street, but I am going to die like an angel, loved and cared for." Two hours after, by the time we finished cleaning him, he died. But there was such a radiating joy in his face. I've never seen that kind of joy—real—the joy that Jesus came to give us.[5]

HER EXAMPLE: The Testimonies

Die with Dignity

The first time that Mother had the idea of opening her home for the dying was when she saw a woman on the street, and she took her to the hospital, and she was refused admission. Mother was adamant and refused to budge till that woman was given a bed on the floor. Later she died. Mother could not understand how a human being, made in the image of God, could die in this state. It was then that the idea came to her that she should help people who were refused by the hospitals, especially the poor, to die with dignity.[6]

Hopeless Cases

I have been with Mother when we did not find any hospital accepting the poor who were dying on the street. We went to so many hospitals for care and treatment. They said, "These are hopeless cases." And people died in inhuman conditions on the streets, uncared for. And so Mother's concern was to give them the best, at least to give them a home—to clean them, to feed them, and to make them feel at home. . . . Mother's purpose of founding homes for the dying was not to make a hospital. When I finished my training in medicine, she did not want me to begin a medical institution. Even if I wanted this, she said, "No. When they need such medical care, we will take them to the hospital. We do our part which nobody will do—to wash them, to clean them, to feed them, and then take them to the doctors, to the nearest hospital."[7]

God Created You in His Image

We have to go back to the time when Mother first started the homes in Kalighat, basically to give dignity to the person who was dying on the streets of Calcutta. Here was a person thrown away by society, from life, and did not have the basic dignity of dying in a respectful way. So for her, she was not out to open hospitals and try to cure everybody from everything. She was there to pick up the person from the street, people who were being walked over or walked past, saying, "You are a creation of God. God created you in His image, and therefore I see Jesus in you and want to give you the dignity of dying with respect." She was not out to try to cure every disease and find answers to all the ways people were dying. She was there to look after the person and give that dignity in that last moment of his life. For this she was criticized, for that was the call in her life, and to her credit she gave dignity and respect and love to many, who died in Calcutta and many other places.[8]

They Die as Human Beings

The treatment given in Kalighat [Nirmal Hriday], the Home for the Dying, is far better than the treatment given in the government hospitals. Those who come to Nirmal Hriday are the worst cases that have no hope of survival. Because of lack of treatment, they have reached to such a state that there is no hope of getting well. And yet, due to the loving care and treatment, many of them get well. Also some of them die there, but die like a human being, not like animals [on the street].[9]

What a Beautiful Way to Die

A sister and myself were going with Mother to Tengra for a workshop arranged by the CRS [Catholic Relief Services]. And Mother was going to give a talk. We were in

our small ambulance. As the ambulance reached near Moulali Crossing, all of us saw someone lying on the roadside.
And Mother said, "I think there is a patient lying there." . . .
Our driver said, "That is a mad person," and he crossed the
road to go ahead. But Mother said to him, "Just turn the
car, and let us go back and see." And he turned the vehicle,
came back, and stopped the car next to that person. Mother
and all of us got out and to our surprise we saw it was a
young woman, lying there, burning with fever, and she was
lying in her own excreta, etc. Immediately, we put her in the
stretcher and took her to Tengra. Mother told the sisters to
give her a bath, and change her clothes, and to bring her
to Kalighat immediately. And that patient died next day.
Mother told us, "When I saw her lying there, something
clicked inside me, that is why I turned the car and came back
to see."[10]

Beyond Human Capacity

We both went [to Kalighat]. One of the sisters called Mother
and said, "Mother, there is a person here who is asking for
you." This person on the bed could hardly speak. Mother
said, "What is it?" She bent down and cuddled his head in
her arms, and it was such a wonderful sight to see someone
doing this. It is something beyond the human capacity to
do this to a person full of wounds, pus all over him, and in
such a bad state. We would get sick looking at that sight. He
was smelling. Mother caressed him and asked, "What do
you want? What is the matter with you?" And he smiled at
Mother so beautifully with his broken teeth. Again Mother

asked in Bengali, "Do you want something?" "Yes," he said, "I want to eat a jalebi" (an Indian sweet). So Mother said, "Go get a jalebi for him." So my mother went out, and just outside was a person making them. She quickly bought one. Mother took it and put this jalebi into the man's mouth. He could not swallow it. He was on his last breath. But he took the jalebi, smiled from ear to ear. He tried to eat it and then just died. Mother said, "Look, what a beautiful way to die." Imagine, if death could be so beautiful, I think, this would be a beautiful place that we have, to have had Mother with us. That person who died in Mother's arms, must have surely gone to heaven. These miracles took place every day.[11]

The Same Jesus

Mother used to come very often to Kalighat. On a Sunday she came to Mass. One of the novices offered Mother a stool to sit down. Mother refused to sit on the stool, but she sat at the edge of the bed of a patient who was dying. All through the Mass, Mother's left hand was on the dying person. Mother was partially attending to the man, and fully attending the Mass. She kept on caressing him. The man was dying and even during the consecration time, Mother's one hand was on the man. After Mother received Communion and came back, she put her hand on the man, and that patient died. I could really understand the saying of Mother, "The Jesus who is present in the breaking of the bread is the same Jesus who is present in the broken bodies of the poor."[12]

She Was Seeing Jesus

Our Mother came to visit us in Port-au-Prince in 1980. We went with Mother to the home of the dying. Mother spoke with all of them, each of them was important for her, but Mother then arrived at one bed, where a young man was dying, in terrible pain (he had TB and had developed a terrible disease; he was losing all his skin). Mother stopped near him. I just stood watching, contemplating. I do not remember what Mother said, but I knew that she was seeing Jesus. There was such kindness, such love, such tenderness, such sacredness in Mother's attitude that again I do not find words to express what I saw. I never saw anyone touching a suffering person as Mother did at that moment. It was all divine.[13]

I Am on My Way to Heaven

I was a volunteer in the MCs, the Gift of Love Home for men with AIDS in Greenwich Village, New York, and one night I'm talking to one of the men about ten p.m., one of the residents who was a drug addict. We were talking about different things and he said the best thing that ever happened to him in his life was getting AIDS. And I mean if I wasn't sitting in the chair I probably would have fallen down. Because I'm saying to myself, if this is the best thing that ever happened to this man in his life, what could the worst thing be! And I said, "But why do you feel this way, how could this be the best thing?" And he said, "Because if I didn't get AIDS, I would have died in the street as a drug addict with nobody to love me." That is a miracle.[14]

The Worst Disease, Loneliness

How many people, how many people died in India and other parts of the world with no one at their side? How many people . . . because Mother would always say, "The worst disease in the world is not cancer, it is not AIDS, the worst disease in the world is loneliness," when someone does not have anyone who cares about them. In the Home of the Dying, . . . one Christmas Day when I was volunteering there, I was bringing a dead man into the area to be washed before he was going to be taken away by the hearse, and there was a beautiful sign leading into this area that said, very simply, I AM ON MY WAY TO HEAVEN. How simple! Mother had a rare ability, the gift, the holiness, the miraculous gift to reduce some of the most complex situations in life to very simple situations.[15]

She Went in Ice-Cold Weather

In 1988 Mother went to Armenia, where thousands and thousands of people were buried under debris [after two earthquakes had happened on the same day]. She went in ice-cold weather. . . . Together with the sisters, [Mother] carried out the people who were still alive from among the debris. . . . In Spitak, she has a name that the Armenians will never forget.[16]

While Calcutta Burned with Hatred

In 1963 the Hindu-Muslim riots were happening in Calcutta. People were trapped in pockets all over the city.

Mother called me to her room and told me about the bodies of Muslim patients who were lying in Kalighat and could not be taken to the Muslim place of burial. She needed my father's help. My dad at the time was a colonel in the army. I rang Dad and told him the problem and he came over immediately. . . . Mother and I went to my parents' home at Fort William, where Dad changed into his army uniform and got a contingent of army vehicles to accompany us to Kalighat. We spent the day taking the bodies of the Muslim patients to their burial place and the bodies of the Hindu patients to the burning ghats.

We then went to the Fatima Shrine (which at that time was a large bamboo construction). There Father Henry was saying Mass while the slums around the area were burning, and Christian people who had no home were huddled in the shrine. I remember Mother running up to the altar and whispering to Father Henry to finish Mass, while Dad and I and the rest of the army personnel helped the Christian people into the trucks and we took them to a shelter on Lower Circular Road, which is now the new extension to Shishu Bhavan. I have never been so afraid and so exhilarated at the same time. There was fire all around us. Masses of burning [Molotov cocktails were] being hurled down the streets, and we with these hundreds of men, women, and children were trying to survive. I was just a young novice, but I saw that, while Calcutta burned with hatred, there was Mother Teresa helping the Muslim, the Hindu, and the Christian. Her love for her neighbor knew no bounds. Mother never forgot that day, and whenever she spoke to me about Dad she would recall the horror of that day and the lives we saved.[17]

Today I Have Become a Man

One day when Mother Teresa and Father Gabrić were in Kalighat looking after one of the dying destitutes, Father Fallon and a young Hindu student came in. A few moments later, as they stood there looking, the sick man suddenly died. He happened to be a Muslim. A stretcher was brought to take the dead body away. As the young Hindu watched, Mother Teresa, Father Gabrić, and Father Fallon lifted the body and placed it on the stretcher. Father Gabrić noticed that the young Hindu was hesitating. A struggle was going on in him. He had seen Father Fallon, whom he greatly admired, and Mother Teresa, whose reputation was so great, lift that dead body, and that had obviously made a deep impression on him. Now the three of them were about to carry the dead body away on that stretcher! . . . Something made him feel that he should join in, that he should offer himself to be the fourth man carrying that stretcher, . . . but there was in him that deeply ingrained fear of loss of caste. . . . How could he, a Brahmin, carry the dead body of a Muslim? . . . Father Gabrić understood all that by looking at the young man. And then suddenly the young Hindu made up his mind and asked, "Can I help?" Father Gabrić at once moved to one side, letting [the young man] take the fourth arm of the stretcher. And so the four of them carried the dead man where the dead bodies were kept. When they laid down the stretcher, Father Gabrić heard the young man heave a deep sigh and say: "AJ ami manush hoechi!" [in Bengali]—that is to say, "Today I have become a man!" And he meant, of course, a free man, a man who had overcome those barriers that separate man from man![18]

Mother Would Touch Each One Tenderly

Mother [regularly went] to [Nirmal Hriday, the Home for the Dying] on Sundays. Mother would pray at the entrance with us, put on her apron, take the broom, and start cleaning and doing the humble work. Whenever a dying person was brought in, Mother would be there to attend. Mother would touch each one tenderly and say a few words to them.

Every day, Mother used to wash the mortuary, keep the dead bodies very nicely. One day I saw Mother and one man together carrying a dead body wrapped up with white sheets, taking it to the mortuary. Then I was frightened, but I ran and took it from the man's hand. Then Mother smiled and we put the stretcher down, and with gentle, delicate reverence she put the body on the shelf in the mortuary.[19]

The Mother Fed the Child with Her Blood

To describe God's love for us, Mother Teresa used the example of how an Armenian mother loved her child to the extent of giving her own life for the child's sake. After the earthquake in Armenia in 1988, it happened that this mother and her child were trapped under the debris without being completely crushed. But they could not get out and had no food or water. The mother did what she could to save the child from dying. She had no other way except to cut one of her own fingers and feed the child with her blood, and so that is what she did. When the rescue workers reached them, they found the mother and the child in a terrible state. The mother was worse than the child: her condition was already critical. They tried to save them both, but later the mother died. The child however was saved. This is a story of true motherly love. She preferred to save the child, even if she lost her own life.[20]

REFLECTION

"I had performed many charitable deeds for my kindred, members of my people. I would give my bread to the hungry and clothing to the naked. If I saw one of my people who had died and been thrown behind the wall of Nineveh, I used to bury him." (Tobit 1:16, 17)

"God created you in His image, and therefore I see Jesus in you and want to give you the dignity of dying with respect."[21]

What can I do to help the family of someone who has died? In addition to expressing my condolences, can I offer some concrete service or help?

Respect is to be shown to others even after they have died; at times we can do no more for the dead than to spare them a negative remark. Our being charitable will not change their condition, but it will help us to discipline our thoughts and words, teaching us to preserve the good name not only of the dead but also of the living.

PRAYER

Father,
I abandon myself into Your hands;
do with me as You will.
Whatever You may do, I thank You:
I am ready for all, I accept all.

Let only Your will be done in me
and in all Your creatures—
I wish no more than this, O Lord.

Into Your hands I commend my soul;
I offer it to You with all the love of my heart,
for I love You, Lord,
and so need to give myself,
to surrender myself into Your hands
without reserve, and with boundless confidence,
for You are my Father.
Amen.

—Blessed Charles de Foucauld,
prayed by Mother Teresa on Tuesdays

EIGHT

INSTRUCT THE IGNORANT

Mother Teresa spent about the first twenty years of her religious life as a teaching nun. As a headmistress, teacher of geography and catechism, she was a gifted teacher, fluent in English, Hindi, and Bengali, and had a deep impact on her students. After establishing her own religious congregation dedicated to the service of the poorest of the poor, she became the main teacher of her sisters, and her instructions are still today a treasure-house of spiritual riches. Knowing the opportunity education is and the benefit it can be in one's life and in the lives of others, she sent her first sisters to schools and universities. Moreover, she strove earnestly to offer the possibility of an education to the underprivileged. The first school she opened was a "slum school" under a tree; her blackboard was the ground, and her chalk was a stick with which she traced the letters of the Bengali alphabet. Though the teaching was very basic, she offered the poor children an education that gave them the possibility of being admitted to regular schools; she would then see them through school so they could have the chance to improve their living conditions. Her idea, as she said, was to "go down to lift them up."

Nevertheless, her instruction was not limited to providing basic education. She offered religious and moral instruction whenever she saw it was necessary, especially to people who were deprived of it because of their material need. But what was more interesting in her way of instruction was her ability to direct people to the truth. She knew that "the truth will set you free." Instructing, or informing, someone about the truth can at times be challenging in a relativistic and materialistic world. Yet she never shrank from this duty. Where she could, she brought attention to the sufferings of the poor and oppressed, indicated moral truths to be followed, or spoke about respect for life and in defense of the unborn. She was the most eloquent teacher because she put into practice what she taught.

HER WORDS

The Ground for a Blackboard

When my little ones saw me for the first time, they were asking one another whether I am a goddess or an evil spirit. For them there is no middle. Those that are good to them they admire like one of their deities; and if someone is moody they are afraid of him and they are only continually bowing down to him. Immediately I

rolled up my sleeves, moved the furniture in the room,
took water and the brush in my hands and started to
scrub the floor. They were utterly surprised. They were
only watching me because they have never seen that one
teacher would start doing such work, especially because
it is the job of the lowest caste in India. But seeing me
happy and joyful the girls, one by one, started helping
me and the boys started carrying water. In two hours
the dirty room became a classroom; everything was
clean. It is one long room, which was earlier used as a
chapel, and now there are five classes in it. . . . When
we became a bit familiar, they did not know what to
do for joy. They started to jump and to sing around me
until I [blessed them, placing] my hand upon each child's
dirty head. From that day they called me only one name,
"Ma," which means mother. Ah, how little these souls
need to make them overjoyed! . . . One day a child came
to my school . . . his clothes torn and dirty. I called him
out of the classroom and there with the soap I gave
him a good wash. When I had washed and combed his
hair, I put on him some old clothes that I had got from
the benefactors of the missions. And I sent him again
to the classroom. And watch a marvel! Nobody in the
classroom had recognized him and all started shouting:
"Ma, ma, the new one, the new one!"[1]

✳

Motijhil—The children were already waiting for me
at the foot of the bridge. There were forty-one—much
cleaner. Those who were not clean, I gave them a good

wash at the tank. We had catechism after the first lesson
on hygiene—then reading. I laughed a good many
times—as I had never taught little children before. So
the ko kho [the first two letters of the Bengali alphabet]
did not go so well. We used the ground instead of
a blackboard. Everybody was delighted—after the
needlework class we went to visit the sick.[2]

Make Your Schools Centers of Radiating Christ

Make your schools centers of radiating Christ. Teach
your children, your sick, your lepers, the dying to love
God in their poverty and sickness—teach them to offer
all to God.[3]

✳

I must really say, "Christ lives in me." I must be able to
say that. We have to keep on desiring. The desire will
only be fulfilled when we are face-to-face with God.
Here on earth we must have that desire to live with
Christ in the poor. Jesus said, "I was ignorant and you
taught Me. You took Me to church for Mass." This is
nothing to incite our imaginations; not feelings. Jesus
really said it, "I." So He is the poor we meet everywhere.[4]

✳

I have asked a sister (medical doctor) to conduct a
paramedical course for our sisters so they will be better
able to know, to understand, and to practice the medical
works of the Society. In this way, they will come to give

wholehearted and free service to the sick with greater
dedication, skill, and efficiency.[5]

Know Your Faith Well

Know your faith well, sisters. We must know the faith,
love the faith, and live the faith: Know, love, and live.
It is so important for us to teach catechism. Prepare
your classes well. Don't go with just anything. Take the
trouble to really give. . . . When I was a Loreto nun, I
was in charge of all the school. I was teaching all day
religion, geography, and so on; lots of responsibility,
plus [doing] accounts and so on. All these sisters who
are teaching will also need to prepare.[6]

✳

Teach the people their faith. In the soup kitchen, you
should have at least ten minutes of instruction of the
faith. Teach the Catechism to the children, to the
families. When the sisters first began here, they used to
teach the children in the homes and gather their families
at the same time so that all of them could learn together.[7]

✳

Prepare little prayers, instructions, classes—put them
down on paper, of what you are going to speak to them
[about]. For example, Father B. for years and years, he
takes the trouble to prepare the Mass every day, spends
one hour, in spite of his busy life. It's because for him,
Mass is the most important and sacred and the sisters

too are sacred. Examination of conscience, are you
faithful to teach them to do it with love and to do it with
Jesus?[8]

Teach from Your Own Experience

We are missionary sisters; we are not just religious
sisters. We are bound by that fourth vow [to give
wholehearted and free service to the poorest of the poor].
How do I prepare catechism classes? And now in Mother
House, it is so beautiful, that beautiful preparation
because we are now bound in conscience to teach the
Catholic Catechism because Holy Father has given strict
orders on how to prepare the Catechism. That zeal,
that preparation. The whole lot get together on Friday
afternoon, not just go and then give a little instruction. A
missionary is a person who is a carrier of God's love, and
you cannot carry that love unless you give that love.[9]

✳

We must love souls—to be thirsty. I thirst. We thirst for
love for souls. Whatever work you have to do, the classes
you have to follow, the lessons you have to prepare, put
your whole heart and soul [into it]. It is not how much,
but how much love you put [into it].[10]

✳

Teach the sisters to pray. You cannot teach them from
books only, but from your own experience. When they
come to see you, ask them how did they make their
meditation, how do they make their examination of

conscience. Do you prepare your instructions? Do you
know before you speak to them what you are going
to [say] to them? Connect "I thirst" in all your classes
and instructions. When you tell them about the vows,
connect it with the "I thirst." I was very happy when
Holy Father wrote about "I thirst." He wrote to the
whole Church. I hope slowly they will put [in] every
church also this "I thirst" near the crucifix. Teach them
small prayers that will help them to remain close to
Jesus. Teach them also to appreciate the time they get
for prayer. How many people come here to spend a little
time in prayer; they work extra to be able to come here
and do some [volunteer] work. We are given to do the
same work; how do we do it? The work you have of
taking care of the sisters, do you realize how important
it is?[11]

Do Not Correct, Teach

Holy Father has said, "Do not correct, teach." Whatever
we do for our sisters and our people, the instruction
you give, the food you cook, the same [we] give to God.[12]

✳

When young people come to visit us, I teach them to love
each other. Jesus said, "Love one another as I have loved
you" [Jn 13:34], Very often young men come to us to
work with the lepers. I teach them how to love each other
and how to see God through this kind of love. If you
come to India, I will teach you too. Love in action is the
most dear to me. For this kind of love, we draw strength

from prayer. This is real love and we give our lives for
this kind of action. It is not possible to show God's love
for people without being in loving service to others.[13]

Professor of Love

In London, there are big boys and girls who have not
made First Communion there, in the area where we
are. The sisters have been trying and trying to get the
family together, the young people together to prepare
them for First Communion. Then one day the mother of
one family said, "Sister, why don't you teach me. I have
a better opportunity when they come in the evening
together. My children are there, my husband is there,
I will teach them." And so Sister taught her, and now
even the husband comes I believe early, to be present at
the lessons that the wife is giving to the children. Now
[Sister] has got more than twenty of these mothers from
that simple woman. She has twenty mothers and every
Saturday they come. She gives them their lessons for the
week and they do it.[14]

✳

I will never forget the last time when I was in
Venezuela—we have our sisters working in Venezuela,
we have five houses—and a very rich family gave us land
to build a home for the children. Then I went to thank
them. And there, in the family, I found the first child
very terribly disabled. And I asked the mother, "What is
the name of the child?" And the mother answered me,

"Professor of Love. Because the child is teaching us the whole time how to love in action." There was a beautiful smile on the mother's face. The "Professor of Love"! Because from that terribly disabled child—disfigured— they were learning how to love.[15]

Teach Them to Love One Another

And it is for us, especially for you who have young girls and young boys in your schools, to teach them the dignity, the respect, the love for life. Teach them purity, teach them holiness. Teach them and don't be afraid. Teach them to love one another. A young girl to love a boy and a boy to love a girl—it's very beautiful, very beautiful! Teach them not to touch each other so that on the day of their wedding they can give each other a virgin heart, a virgin body.[16]

❋

I've seen again and again crowds come to Calcutta and nobody wants to work anywhere else except in the Home for the Dying. Why? Because they see the suffering Christ and they receive and then they come many of them come for adoration and most of them, most of them, they say the same thing, "we saw this kind of suffering in our country but we never looked. You have taught us to see to look and find Jesus and do something."

This is the hunger of the young people. Very often we find our young people from all over the place coming to the Hindu ashrams and being caught there and every time when they come out, if they are able to come, I always ask them, "Is Jesus not enough for you?" "But nobody gave me Jesus like that."

That is you, you priests must give Jesus to our young people. There is a tremendous longing for God. I'm sure you know that better than I but with the people that we are dealing, the suffering that we see, we see the young people doing those humble works: cleaning, washing, feeding and there—where they are dying, there is so much tenderness and love. Many of them, after a long time, make their confession and go back to Our Lord. How? That contact with the presence of Christ.

They are longing to learn and you and I have been chosen by Jesus. I have called you by your name Jesus said. You are mine. Water will not drown you, fire will not burn you. I will give nations for you. You are precious to me, I love you. We have that in the Scriptures so clearly, the tenderness and the love of God for us and He wants us to be that tenderness and love to the people.

He wants to use you that's why you have become a priest. You have not become a priest to become a social worker. . . . We . . . cannot give to our people what we don't have. So teach us to pray, teach us to be holy and I think we and our people will be holy because there are places where you cannot go maybe but if you have given us, we can give to them.[17]

The Joy of Spreading the Good News

God has entrusted to you the joy of spreading the Good News that we have all been created for greater things, to love and to be loved. And so, whatever you do, whatever you write, make sure that you remember that you can make people and you can break people. You can give good news and bring joy into the lives of many people; and you can bring much sorrow to many people. So let us always remember that in writing there is always someone being drawn closer to God, or being taken away from Him.

Always write the truth. Because Jesus Christ said, "I am the Truth, I am the Light, I am the Joy, and the Love. I am the Truth to be told, and the Love to be loved. I am the Way to be walked. I am the Light to be lit. And I am the Peace to be given. And I am the Joy to be shared." So let us today, as we have gathered together, let us make one strong resolution that you, through your writing, will always spread love, peace, and joy.[18]

Challenge

I will never forget during the floods, we had terrible floods in Calcutta, and [a group of young men] was busy at the time killing and shooting and burning and doing all kinds of things. And then when this thing started and we were all walking in water up to our necks, these young men came, thirty of them, and said, "We are at your service, use us." We used to stay until ten p.m. working, but they spent the whole night helping, carrying the people on their heads, and the government couldn't understand that it was these university students who were doing all the mischief, and then they were there like little lambs, doing the most humble work. So the young people are hungry for Christ, they are looking for . . . challenge.[19]

It Is Good . . . to Spoil the Poor

Once at a seminar in the name of the whole group, one nun got up and said to me, "Mother Teresa, you are spoiling the poor people by giving them things free. They are losing their human dignity. You should take at least ten *naya paisa* for what you give them; then they will feel more their human dignity." When everyone was quiet, I said calmly, "No one is spoiling as much as God Himself. See the wonderful gifts He has given us freely. All of you here have no glasses, yet you all can see. Say, if God were to take money for your sight, what would happen? We are spending so much money to buy oxygen for saving life, yet continually we are breathing and living on oxygen and we do not pay anything for it. What would happen if God were to say, 'You work four hours and you will get sunshine for two hours'? How many of us would survive?" Then I also told them: "There are many congregations who spoil the rich; then it is good to have one congregation in the name of the poor, to spoil the poor." There was profound silence. Nobody said a word after that.[20]

No Time for the Poor?

Where is that burning zeal that gives without counting the cost? Where is that love for our slum children that takes the trouble to prepare the schoolwork? To find the big children for First Holy Communion? Where is that eagerness [for gathering] the children for Sunday Mass?[21]

✳

Where are we sisters—if we too are the poorest of the poor? Do we know what it means to be hungry and lonely? . . . We meet these people, our poor, every day. Do we know them? [Are we] really one of them? My sisters, it must hurt Jesus as it hurts Mother if we have become so rich as to have no time for the poor.[22]

HER EXAMPLE: The Testimonies

Approachable and Available for Everything

Though [St. Mary's] was a Catholic school, it was the only Bengali high school for girls. Thus both Hindus and Muslims from high society, who were naturally interested in their own culture and language, wanted to enroll their daughters. . . . Mother made no distinction in dealing with them, and they all came for prayer and even catechism classes. Mother was so approachable and available for everything, including spiritual and material needs. Rich or poor, all helped in the cleaning and housework of the school. Regarding food and lodging there was no difference among the boarders. Everyone dressed in the simple uniform of the school.[23]

I was a little nervous since I hadn't been to the city before and didn't know what to expect in this new school [St. Mary's, Loreto]. All my fears melted away on meeting Mother. The day I joined school, Mother Teresa came into the parlor, called me by my name in such perfect Bengali, and greeted me in the Bengali way and language. What a welcome she gave me! Coming to know Mother over the next month, I came to appreciate her as more than a teacher or the headmistress.[24]

Who Will Bring Them Joy?

In 1947 . . . from the bridge, Mother pointed out to me the Belaghata slum. It was such a miserable sight: such poor, naked children, black from the coal dust coming from the pieces of coal they were picking up on the railway line. Mother pointed this out saying, "Look! How poor these children are. They have no joy, but poverty makes them do this work to earn their living. What a miserable life! Who will bring them joy? They do not know Jesus. They have no knowledge of eternal happiness, so in this life they have suffering, poverty, misery, and in the next life too, which is forever. Who will go and give them the Good News that God loves them, that God created them, and that they are His children, so that they will begin to change their life of misery into a life of joy? Will you come with me? But if we go now, they will come to me with their hand stretched out, begging for money because I am dressed like a Mem Shaheb [respectable rich lady]. So we cannot speak to them about God or Jesus. Wouldn't it be nice if we could dress in simple, poor dress and live among them, talk to them, talk about Jesus? He also was poor. He came for them. Will you come? Will you come with me? Wouldn't it be nice? We could succeed in making these people happy in making them know Jesus."[25]

※

Mother had only one aim, to spend her life ceaselessly to proclaim God's love to everyone and everywhere. To do this she did not wait for a diploma or special study except for some months [of a] basic medical course in Patna. When she came back to Calcutta, she immediately went out to the slums. She began Motijhil school for the slum children, cleaning them and teaching them reading and writing. The ground served as slate and blackboard. Of course the little ones soon found in her a real angel of comfort and consolation and began to come in large numbers, waiting early in the morning for her. To find students for the school, Mother would go to everyone's house; we would be with her and call everyone. She would call every child to study.[26]

Give Them Joy

In the year 1948 Mother again came back (to Motijhil). . . . She asked the names of our six sisters and two brothers. When I said that my name is Agnes, then Mother hugged me and took me to her lap. Then Mother said to my mother that she will come here; here are many poor whom I want to help. After that day, Mother would come here every day. . . . She would search for poor children and bring them to school. Mother would walk down from Creek Lane to our place each day. Mother would come at eight a.m. and stay till twelve noon and again come at three p.m. and go back by six p.m. . . . We had nothing. Under the tree shade we would sit writing on the ground. Within a month, Mother brought for us the books, copies, slates, and pencils from somewhere. The sisters started to teach us. In our place one person fell sick; she had a big boil; she was suffering from unbearable pain. Mother took her on her lap and brought her to a room next to ours. Like this, from different places, Mother brought five patients and kept them there in that room. Mother would look after these sick people, and the sisters would teach us. . . . Mother would not take leave even on Sunday. She would take us all to Baithakhana Church at eight o'clock in the morning. . . . Sunday was the happiest day for us. . . . My First Communion was held when I was eleven years old, and before this I didn't know anything, neither to learn nor to read nor to pray; all were taught by Mother. . . . I had completed my studies at Moti-jhil. At Moulali I studied till class eight.[27]

※

One Sunday evening we went out, the four of us: Mother, Sister Agnes, Sister Trinita, and myself. Mother gave each one of us something to carry; we went to Beleghata, one of the very, very poor areas. We had some games up to four o'clock. All the men were given to me; Sister Trinita took the boys. Sister Agnes took the girls and women, and we stood against the wall, and they had races. Whoever came first among the men got the soap as the first prize, the women got the blankets, the children got the sweets, and the boys got the chalk and slates. The next week also we did the same, and you could see the joy on their faces. Coming back home, Mother said, "You see what you brought to the children? Joy. These people do not know Jesus. We have Jesus. We go to Mass. So the only way to give them Jesus was to give them joy."[28]

The Joy on Mother's Face

Sunday schools: Our time to rise on Sundays was 4:30 a.m., and sisters prepared children and adults to receive the sacraments: Holy Communion, confession, confirmation. Mother wanted every sister to go for Sunday school and teach the Catechism, as far as possible. Most of our poor children could not afford the normal outfit for first communicants, so this was provided. It was so beautiful to see these little "angels" running all the way with their sisters to Baitakhana Church, for Holy Mass at 6:30 a.m. on the feast of the Holy Guardian Angels, October 2, each year. . . . And the joy on Mother's face to see these over a thousand children, many of them above the normal age—the fruit of Mother's zeal.[29]

✴

Before Mother left from Shkodra for the first time . . . she went up to the Children's Home on the first floor. The children gathered around her, those who were able to walk and

who were mentally all right. She immediately began to teach
them the Our Father in Albanian, but she taught it in such a
nice way, she made it into a kind of tune with a rhythm, and
they repeated line by line after Mother. Mother repeated it
again and again. All the children were smiling happily as
they were learning.[30]

Pain and Compassion on Her Face

Mother would go and beg from other nuns to take our children as day scholars. She sent some of the boys to the Jesu-
its, some to the Salesians. She took the trouble to have them
admitted. It was something more than what we could give.[31]

✳

When I was in Loreto Entally in charge of the junior school
in the 1960s, I had some of her orphans from Shishu Bhavan.
One was a disturbed child and caused much trouble for the
matrons and the teacher. The staff, after helping and accepting her as much as they could, felt she was disturbing
the whole section, so they convinced the superior to send
her back to the MCs. When I met Mother Teresa sometime
later, she remembered the case and showed much regret that
the child had been sent back. There was much pain and
compassion on her face when speaking about the child.[32]

Sacrifice Money

The sisters would pick up the children and take them to
school. As most of our children were too poor and hungry, bread was ordered for them at the Mother House and

sisters would collect their share for each class in each school. Children in England saved their pennies to enable our poor children to get a daily slice of bread; and a glass of milk was made possible by the sacrifice of thousands of Danish children, while the children of Germany with their "sacrifice money" provided a daily vitamin pill for the children of India. Children were helped to clean themselves, comb their hair. Slates and chalk were provided, and for the older ones, exercise books and stationery. Their clothes were also taken care of. After the Assembly and marking of registers, there were classes in the rudiments of learning: reading, writing, arithmetic, singing, games. In the meantime, arrangements were being made to get them into regular existing schools.[33]

Allowing Others to Share in the Joy of Giving

Shishu Bhavan, a home for unwanted, abandoned children, opened in 1955. As the children grew, Mother initiated a child welfare scheme by allowing a generous Hindu lady . . . to sponsor the first ten children for ten years. Many followed her example in India and abroad and it included a sponsorship scheme, which provided fees for education, outfits, etc., for schoolgoing children. When the work grew too big for us, Mother passed it on to the diocese through the parishes.[34] When I was in Amravati in Maharashtra, a college student gave me some scrapbooks for the children studying. When Mother came to see me, I told her about it. Mother said, "I am so happy to see that. I would like to go and see the students." When I informed the college, the professor arranged for the students to gather and meet Mother. There were about three hundred college students there. Mother went and spoke to them, and Mother said the same thing: "In the ignorant children Jesus will say, 'I was the one you taught.' So you keep helping the sisters. I am so happy."[35]

No One to Help Them

I told Mother that when I was at home I was working, and the money I got, I used to spend for my younger sister's education, and now my sisters had no one to help them. . . . Seeing my difficulty, Mother took two of my sisters under her care and arranged for their studies, but later they told Mother that they also wanted to be religious, so both of them joined us. Through this kindness and concern for my own sisters, my sisters and I were greatly inspired to give our lives completely to God.[36]

Mother Arranged for Their Studies

My sister had four girls. They were studying in the boarding school and had problems with their fees, as they could not pay. They were being sent away from the school and when I told this story, Mother helped them so they could continue their studies.[37]

Under the Mango Trees

In Tabora, Mother saw us taking catechism class under the mango trees. Whenever she came to visit us, she asked us, "Are you still teaching children under the mango trees?"

Mother was so happy to see the children being gathered and taught the faith. She also told us, "Before starting the dispensary, pray with the people. It's not enough to give medicines. Give them God."[38]

Not Only the Material Needs of the Poor

Mother not only took care of the material needs of the poor, but she also organized Sunday schools for the poor Catholic children: Catechism to be taught to Catholics studying in government schools, after-school programs to help the children with their studies, summer day camps for children in poor neighborhoods, days of prayer and recollection in retreat centers for married couples, homeless men and women residing in our homes, and shut-ins, and other activities that have brought people together, improved relationships, broken down barriers to love, opened up people to friendship, and eased their pain and loneliness.

She consecrated homes, especially in the month of June, to the Sacred Heart of Jesus. She insisted that families should pray the Rosary, that parish priests must have weekly hours of Adoration with the people in their parishes, with the opportunity for receiving the sacrament of reconciliation. . . . She repeatedly said that the work of the Missionaries of Charity was not social work, but God's work, and that whatever we do, we do to Jesus.[39]

She Took Immense Pride in Each Child

I was in close association with her while I was working with the children of Shishu Bhavan, especially during Christmas and Easter. It was during this time that Mother's wonderful ways revealed themselves to me. She gathered children around her just as a shepherd gathers his flock. She took immense pride in each one of them and their accomplishments. Once after the children performed the Hoop Drill for her with all the colors of the flag, she was so overwhelmed that she did not wait for them to come to her to be blessed. Instead, she went to them and blessed them. When she blessed them, the five fingers of her palm symbolized the saying "I did it [to] you." She made each gesture meaningful and made the children understand that everything they did was for a purpose and that purpose was Jesus.[40]

If a Mother Can Kill Her Own Child, What Is There to Stop You and Me from Killing Each Other?

In September 1994 Mother sent a message to the UN Conference in Cairo saying openly, "I speak today to you from my heart, to each person in all the nations of the world, to people with power to make big decisions as well as to all the mothers, fathers, and children in the cities, towns, and villages. . . . If a mother can kill her own child, what is there to stop you and me from killing each other? The only one who has the right to take life is the One who has created it. Nobody else has that right; not the mother, not the father, not the doctor, no agency, no conference, no government." This took a lot of courage to say, which is proved by the criticism Mother's words elicited.[41]

REFLECTION

"In that same hour He rejoiced in the Holy Spirit
and said, 'I thank you, Father, Lord of heaven and
earth, that Thou hast hidden these things from
the wise and understanding and revealed them
to babes; yea, Father, for such was Thy gracious
will. All things have been delivered to Me by My
Father; and no one knows who the Son is except
the Father, or who the Father is except the Son and
any one to whom the Son chooses to reveal Him.' "
(Lk 10:21–22)

"Help a child who has difficulty in the school
with his homework. Share with others what you
know."[42]

Are there areas of my life, especially my spiritual life,
where I need to realize and recognize my ignorance and
take steps to learn, especially the wisdom of "little souls"?
Am I obstinate in my attitude of superiority and unwilling-
ness to learn and improve? Do I have the courage to stand
for what I know is right and true, in spite of contrary opinions around me? Is my stubbornness and unapproachabil-
ity an impediment to spreading Gospel truths and values?
Do I teach not only with my words, but with my example,
with the spirit of doing good to others.

PRAYER

*Grant, O Merciful Father, that Your divine Spirit
may enlighten, inflame, and cleanse our hearts,
that He may penetrate us with His heavenly dew
and make us fruitful in good works, through Jesus
Christ, Our Lord.
Amen.*

*—The closing prayer of the Litany of the Holy Spirit,
prayed by Mother Teresa on Mondays*

NINE

COUNSEL THE DOUBTFUL

Mother Teresa received crucial assistance concerning her spiritual life through various counselors whom God provided along the way, most especially when she faced the excruciating interior darkness that lasted for decades. She was immersed in a deep interior trial, as one of her guides attests:

> In our meetings, Mother Teresa began to speak about the trials of her inner life and her inability to disclose them to anyone. . . . I was deeply impressed by the honesty and simplicity of her account, and the deep anxiety she was going through in utter darkness: Was she on the right path or had she become the victim of a network of illusions? Why had God abandoned her totally? Why this darkness, whereas in her earlier life she had been so close to God? She had to lead her sisters, initiate them into the love of God and into a life of prayer, which had been wiped

out in her own life as she lived in total emptiness:
Had she become a shameful hypocrite who spoke to
others about the divine mysteries which had totally
vanished from her own heart?[1]

As she agonized through such a long and painful interior trial, she was deeply grateful for the counsel and support she received from the few spiritual directors with whom she was able to share this suffering. Having experienced firsthand the relief that good counsel can bring to a weary soul, she was eager to offer counsel to whomever was in need of it.

Mother Teresa had a notable gift to be able to set at peace a "restless and troubled mind." Her method was simple: first she would listen. She would listen attentively to the account being related to her, but even more she would listen to the pain and confusion that accompanied it. At times it was said that she could "read hearts." She could certainly demonstrate a remarkable understanding and compassion that indicated that her heart was open to share in another's suffering. Constantly aware of her own weakness, especially her interior darkness, she assumed a humble and unpretentious attitude toward all. This attitude helped many to be completely open with her and to experience her compassion. In this heart-to-heart exchange, she was able to listen without prejudice and without a judgmental attitude, giving advice in a way that was often unexpected. With her "vision of faith," she was able to look at the issue at hand from "God's perspective" and then point people in the right direction.

In listening to or advising others, Mother Teresa promoted neither a personal agenda nor a preconceived solution. She was open to learn from the situation, looking for a way to resolve the issues as circumstances unfolded. Even when the solution to their difficulty or situation was not immediate, people found solace in her advice and guidance. While she didn't claim to have an instant solution, it often was, in a certain sense, "instant" because she was able to orient the issue to God in prayer, trusting that He would take care of it.

HER WORDS

I Give What I Have

Deep down in every human heart there is a knowledge of God. And deep down in every human heart there is the desire to communicate with Him. And therefore, the word that I speak . . . is true, because I am a Catholic, and a sister totally [consecrated] in vows to God. Naturally I can only give what I have. But I think everybody . . . knows deep down in their hearts that there is God, and that we have been created to love and to be loved; that we have not been created to be just a number in the world. But we have been created for some purpose, and that purpose is to be love, to be compassion, to be goodness, to be joy, to serve.

You see that in animal life [even], there is love between animals, there is the love of the mother animal to the little child, to the little animal to which she has given birth; it is engraved in us, that love. So I don't think it is difficult for you; you can express that in your own words; but you know very well that every single . . . person . . . knows that God IS love, and that God loves them, otherwise they would not be, they would not exist; and that God wants us to love one another as He loves us. We all know! Everybody knows—how God loves you. Each one of us knows. Because otherwise we cannot exist. The proof of our existence is that God—somebody who is higher, somebody who is greater—is holding us, protecting us.

Life is life, and the most beautiful gift of God to a human family, to the nation, and to the whole world [is] the child. And therefore if the child is born a disabled child, we cannot destroy it. We cannot destroy the unborn child; we cannot destroy the born child. If your parents did not want you, you would not be here today. If my mother didn't want me, there would be no Mother Teresa. So I think it is good that our parents wanted us. And it is for us to help our people. If a mother is not able to take care of that deserted child, it is for you and for me to help them to take care of that child. That is the gift of God to that family.[2]

Our Heavenly Father Will Provide

Malcolm Muggeridge, a British journalist and author, made a documentary on Mother Teresa and her work. He had many questions about the faith, but was eventually received

into the Catholic Church at seventy-nine years of age. The
following is a letter from Mother Teresa to him.

God, our Heavenly Father who takes care of the lilies
of the field and the birds of the air—we are much more
important to Him than the birds and the flowers of
the field—has provided abundantly all these years, is
providing and will provide. You remember our TV talk,
how neither you nor I never spoke or asked for money
and see what God did.[3]

Unless You Become a Little Child

I think I understand you better now. I am afraid I could
not [provide an] answer to your deep suffering. . . .
I don't know why, but you to me are like Nicodemus
[Jn 3:1], and I am sure the answer is the same—"Unless
you become a little child" [Mt 18:3]. I am sure you will
understand beautifully everything—if you would only
"become" a little child in God's hands.

　　Your longing for God is so deep and yet He keeps
Himself away from you. He must be forcing Himself to
do so, because He loves you so much, as to give Jesus
to die for you and for me—Christ is longing to be
your food. Surrounded with the fullness of living food,
you allow yourself to starve. The personal love Christ
has for you is infinite. The small difficulty you have
regarding His Church is finite. Overcome the finite with
the infinite. Christ has created you, because He wanted
you. I know what you feel—terrible longing—with dark
emptiness—and yet He is the one in Love with you.[4]

Let It All Be for Him

I think now more than ever you should use the beautiful gift God has given you for His greater glory. All that you have and all that you are—and all that you can be and do—let it all be for Him and Him alone. Today what is happening on the surface of the Church will pass. For Christ, the Church is the same—today, yesterday, and tomorrow. The apostles went through the same feelings of fear and distrust, failure and disloyalty, and yet Christ did not scold them—just "little children—little faith—why did you fear?" I wish we could love as He did—*now!*[5]

Your Home Must Come First

You had once asked me to leave the Co-Workers [because] it takes you from [your wife] and the children. They come first. I will miss you, but your home must come first. You could remain a Co-Worker without having the burden of a chairman, as you already have so much to do with the Order of Charity. I still keep praying for this, but your home is first. You and [your wife] must decide. Your happiness and love for each other is the only thing I want for you—whether you are in or out of the Co-Workers. [You and your wife] will always be the same to me.[6]

Only Cling to the Living Christ

Your nephew, like so many in this hard and sad time of fight for the faith, is going through his purification. If he only clings to the living Christ—the Eucharist—he will come from his darkness radiant with new light—Christ.[7]

Respect Each One as a Child of God

Respecting each person as a child of God—my brother, my sister. I know how trying this must be at times. If you find it hard to see Jesus in the distressing disguise of someone, see that person in the Heart of Jesus. He loves her with the same love with which He loves you. This will help you to greater love, especially to the one most in need of it. You are in my daily prayer as you have done so much for Jesus in the Co-Workers. May Mary, the Mother of Jesus, be Mother to you.[8]

Do Not Play with Fire

Counsels of Mother Teresa to a priest having difficulties.

It is perfectly true that you are fully free to decide, but remember: in the parish you were very happy and you really did very well, all for Jesus. And you had the great love of your parents and the cardinal and your people—yet after much prayer you gave it up to be an MC deliberately. Knowingly [you] chose to be the Poorest of the Poor—chose to be an MC and so belong to a community. I have your [earlier] letters—they are full of the spirit and the joy of MC.

I am very sure the devil is trying his utmost to break through and destroy the little community. Don't allow

him to use you as his weapon. This is your chance for
Total Surrender. Give Jesus a free hand to do with you
as He wants, a true MC. You know Mother's love for
you. All these years you have been longing for this—and
now when it is yours, do not lose it. This trial is a gift
of Jesus to you to draw you closer to Himself so that
you can share His Passion with Him. Remember, He
has espoused you in tenderness and love, and to make
this union more living [He] made you His priest—His
Eucharist. You have as much vocation to be an MC as
I—to be an MC Priest of the Poorest of the Poor. Do not
play with fire—fire burns and destroys.

Pray often during the day: Jesus, in my heart I believe
in Your tender love for me, I love You, and I want to be
only all for You through Mary as an MC. Let us pray.[9]

Smile

Mother's advice to a schoolgirl.

Smile. Whenever you meet anyone, greet him with a smile.
The utility of smiling is that it will keep you always
acceptable to everyone. At the same time it will make
you, your face, look beautiful. If you are ever angry,
try to smile rather forcefully and soon you will see, you
have forgotten your anger, smiling with everybody.[10]

Jesus, Be in This Person

When you speak, look at the person in front of you. Say
this prayer in your mind: Jesus, be now in this person

when I speak to him and help me to see You in him.
Bless me, so that I may speak to him with all sincerity,
as I would speak to You. Look at me through his eyes
and help me to succeed. If I fail to please You in this
person, give me courage that I can bear the pain meekly
and cheerfully.[11]

HER EXAMPLE: The Testimonies

Coming with Frowns and Scowls, Going Away with Radiant Faces

Although Mother had to deal with crowds whenever she
attended a meeting, she always gave much time, attention,
and interest to individuals. I often marveled at her untiring
energy, her calmness, and her charming smiles that seemed
to have an effect stronger than analgesic drugs. I have seen
people coming to her with personal problems, with frowns
and scowls, who a little later went away with radiant faces.
She had the gift of touching hearts with peace, of anointing
them with the oil of gladness and joy. She wrote to us, "God
did such great things for all of us, especially for you. . . . If
we only let Him do it, He does it so beautifully. With some
help I am sure you will make it into a real Nazareth, where
Jesus can come and rest awhile with you. I am really happy
for you. . . . The sunshine breaks all darkness, even spiritual darkness. I saw your faces full of smiles already, thank
God."[12]

What Can I Do For You?

When [someone] came to her, she did not question whether
he was a sinner or a good person. . . . She was always ready
with a smile or a word or a medal, a message or something.
"What can I do for you?"

She had a tremendous capacity to listen to people, and to
hear what they were really saying, even behind their words.
She was wise and always was welcoming.[13]

What Would Jesus Do?

As I came up the steps, she pulled me across. "Father, I have
to speak to you immediately." . . . [She] said, "Father, I got a
phone call this morning from the governor. . . ." "What did
he want, Mother?" "He wanted to know if he should pass the
order of execution on this man . . . who had murdered two
people in cold blood, and the people were demanding that
he be put to death, and the governor wanted to know what
he should do—should he give him life imprisonment or the
death sentence. I don't know why he should ask me, Father,
I just don't understand the situation. So I told the governor
I would pray about it. 'You call back later.' So he insisted
he was going to call back at eight-thirty." "Oh Mother, I
understand he is a politician. If he passes the death sentence,
he favors one group: if life imprisonment, he favors another
group. He wants you to get him out of the trouble." "Oh
now I understand, Father." After some days, I got a note,
I have the Xerox copy here. It says, "When the governor
called I told him that 'you must do what Jesus would do if
you were in His place.'"[14]

Mother Never Embarrassed Her

In 1997 a well-to-do lady came to Mother for help. She had a serious drinking problem and had failed in her many efforts to break the habit. . . . The lady fell on her knees beside Mother's wheelchair, sobbing. Mother never embarrassed her but with great kindness and gentleness told her to spend some time before Jesus in the tabernacle and to pour out her troubled soul to Him as a friend would do. In that short time, you could actually perceive grace at work. This lady spent the next hour deep in prayer before the Blessed Sacrament. Mother returned to her room after prayer and she was quiet and pensive, but she never mentioned anything about that lady's struggle. The beautiful thing was I saw that lady return the next day and make her confession. I will never forget the radiant peace of her face. She promised to hand over her salary for the sisters to hold in case it would lead her into temptation again. She had made a firm resolution to turn away from alcohol.[15]

My Answer Is "Silence"

Fourteen women had gathered before [Mother]. A young lady came forward to ask what she should do when her husband argues with her, making faces and often using harsh words. "Shall we quarrel and retaliate? What shall we do, Mother?" the ladies asked again. [Mother] remained silent. Silence was then freezing on the other side too: an uncomfortable situation. But then Mother smiled and she said, "My answer is, 'Silence.' You would remain silent. Silent not in fear or oppression, not in weak heart or in thought that you may be thrown out of your own place. But silence to show your deep hatred, your disliking toward all harshness and ugliness. Remember, there is God in you and God in the person you face at home; he too is Jesus! God wants us to show our strength of mind, our obedience toward truth and beauty, our calm and fortitude of mind, because we believe in Him. We cannot do what may make God sad. To have faith in Him is to have faith in yourself, your mind, and your inner God, who lives in our heart. When I say, 'Love one another as He loves you!' let us not forget that God has given us His best love. He has also put His essence of love into our heart, so that we can give the same love to others. Give your love even to those who appear brute to you, so that you do not [make] the same mistake as he did [with] you. Silently, with your action, make him understand that he is really missing something in his life—he is missing [loving] you. He is cultivating ugly wrath and hatred, selfishness, and ill behavior in himself. God made him beautiful too, but he is destroying his own beauty. He will realize it someday. But don't put yourself to cultivating the same as him. Let us remember, fire cannot be put [out] with another fire. We need water. Water to destroy fire. Similarly, let us give beauty against all ugliness. Kindness against all rudeness. Good words against brute words. Even if you ask for separation, do it with love and friendship, not hostility."

Several questions in between were asked to Mother regarding divorce, separation, atrocities to women, etc. In reply to another question, Mother said, "Let us unite in a family and not separate. Let us not forget that, if we ask for a divorce, we also choose to pain our children with our cruel decision. Let us pray from the first day of our conjugal life, so that we may live together. The family that prays together, stays together. Let us make prayer a daily habit. Prayer not to murmur a few words and spend some time, but prayer with the heart and fervent wish, prayer that should come from within. We do not unite (a husband and wife) to separate, but to face the challenges of life united."[16]

As Bombay Burned

During the riots of 1992–93, as Bombay burned, many citizens rushed to the city's aid. Two of them came up with a unique idea. There was no one who could bring the message of peace more effectively to this troubled city than Mother Teresa. Unfortunately, Mother Teresa's health was failing. It would be impossible for her to make the journey to the city. [They] then found a solution. A team of filmmakers would fly down to Calcutta together and film a message from Mother. This message would be telecast on all the major channels, as well as on cable television. [They] contacted Mother Teresa, who immediately agreed. When the team reached the Mother House in Calcutta, they found the nuns not very welcoming. Mother Teresa had been unwell the night before, yet she had insisted on going out early that morning to visit the riot victims in Calcutta. The team decided to wait for Mother Teresa. Early that evening she returned. She looked exhausted. However, when she saw Dr. P, she broke into a smile. She said she was ready to start filming immediately. But first she felt the team should eat something. "They must be hungry," she said to one of the nuns, "they have come a long way." The team was given a simple meal of bread and butter, bananas and tea. They all agreed that it was one of the nicest meals they had ever eaten.

For the next few hours Mother Teresa worked with the film crew. It was demanding work, but she never faltered. Even when she was asked to do yet another take because of some technical fault or flaw, she never complained. Her message to Bombay's citizens was, as always, simple yet effective. She asked them to love each other as brothers, to be good to each other, to care for each other.

The next morning, the team had to leave Calcutta at five a.m. Mother Teresa was there at the gate to wish them good-bye. Barefooted, with a rosary in her hand, she said a short prayer for all of them. As they left she pressed a few medals of Our Lady into their hands. Even today, six years later, all of them have those medals. In times of stress and trouble, those medals blessed by Mother Teresa bring them solace and peace. Mother Teresa's message was broadcast the following week over all the major channels. No one who saw it was unaffected. It was a message of love and peace from God's chosen messenger.[17]

The Best Teacher Is Our Lady

I took the superior's promise just with Mother. After the promise, Mother gave me a small instruction. Mother told me to put my hand in Mary's hand and take each step with Mary. I also asked Mother how to pray better. Mother told me, "The best teacher is Our Lady," and to ask [Our Lady] to teach me to pray as she taught Jesus. She also told me to do every action with a prayer and do it for God and not for anyone else to see. Look at Our Lady; she pondered His words in her heart. If I want to be a true MC, I must learn that silence which enables me to ponder His words in my heart and so grow in love. "Be open to Our Lady," Mother said, "like a child is open to her mother. Tell her everything that you have in mind. She is there to help you in your everyday need. Pray the Rosary daily and with devotion, and place yourself with Mary in each of the mysteries." During those precious moments, I felt Mother was there just for me. Her whole concern for me was to be a true MC, as Mother always wants us to be. . . . She was a real mother to me.[18]

How Proud I Was

I was appointed superior. I felt I was so small, an inexperienced person, etc. Therefore, I wrote to Mother on this matter, how will I be able to take up such a big responsibility? I was so young, thirty-one years old. I'm [such an] insignificant person; I was afraid: a big community, with a formation center, an apostolate such as Shishu Bhavan, Nirmal Hriday, dispensaries, leprosy work, shipments, the Co-Workers of Mother Teresa, etc. I thought I had written a very humble letter. In answer to this, I got a nice letter in return telling me how proud I was, that I wanted to do all the work myself, instead of allowing Jesus to do the work through me. I never expected such a letter, but it opened my eyes, taught me to surrender, and thanks be to God my mission . . . was a success. Praise the Lord.[19]

The Devil Just Wants to Disturb You

In London, I was on night duty in our home for homeless women. A big fire broke out, and before I even knew there was a fire, ten women had lost their lives because of that fire. During tertianship, the devil began to taunt me, telling me the fire and deaths were my fault. It became a mantra, which I could hear in my head and in my heart. I tried to push it away with reason, because of all the years of peace I had experienced, but it would not go away. Mother came to Rome to receive our vows, and although I had a long talk with Mother, I did not mention this taunting. I had a gnawing sense that I should speak with Mother, but I kept arguing that Mother was too busy and it really wasn't necessary.

Finally, the day of profession arrived and it was nearly time to leave for the Church. I made the decision to mention this to Mother. I walked into Mother's room and Mother was alone. I began to speak: "Mother, please may I speak with you just for a minute about the fire in London?" Mother stopped me by raising her hand high in the air and saying, "You had nothing to do with that fire. You are not to blame for it. God allowed it to humble us." I then told Mother I never took the blame before that; I was always in peace until this year. Mother said, "The devil just wants to disturb you because you are taking final vows. He doesn't want you to take your vows and he hasn't been able to get you in another way, so he's trying with this. Go now and be at peace." With those words Mother blessed me. From that moment, the devil's taunting stopped and never returned.[20]

This Sister Should Not Remain an MC

I spoke with Mother about a finally professed sister in the community who, in my observation, had a very serious problem. I believed that because of this, the sister should not remain an MC. I did not tell Mother the name of the sister. When I finished speaking, Mother smiled so lovingly. Understanding was written all over Mother's countenance. Mother gently looked away and said, "She did not have a mother's love." This was absolutely true. The sister's mother died when she was [very small]. Mother knew I could not help this sister, so Mother told me she would change her. The change took place only six months later. Mother was not in any way as concerned about this as I was, and Mother in no way considered that the sister should be dispensed from her vows.[21]

Speak Also Beautiful Things

In the community there was some problem among the sisters. And I found very often that my superior was crying. I used to notice very often that many senior sisters were going to Mother House. One fine morning Mother arrived in the community. She gathered all of us and gave us an instruction. Mother said, "I am so happy that some of you come to see me and inform me about what is happening in your community, but remember, sisters, Mother is not a dustbin. Don't speak only ugly things to Mother. Mother also likes to hear about the beautiful things about the sisters. Come and tell Mother all the good things that are happening. Your superior is a beautiful person. Speak also beautiful things about her." Mother encouraged all of us to find all that is beautiful in our superior and speak to Mother when next time Mother comes.[22]

Reaching Out in Love

A rich woman came to Mother and asked her to bring peace between her and her daughter. Mother advised her to do little acts of love for her daughter, without letting her know that it was she who was doing it (e.g., put on her table a flower that she likes, prepare the food that she likes, etc.). And it did work. The daughter was touched by the effort the mother was making to reach out to her in love.[23]

Make Sure to Smile

One time I was visiting Mother and she sensed that I was just not myself. I told her that I had had a difference of opinion or a misunderstanding with my own superior. I was feeling quite down about it. She took me by the hand and gave me some practical motherly advice. She said I should find some excuse to meet with my superior as soon as possible and make sure to smile all the while [that I was] with [that superior]. She said she always did that whenever she might have had a difficult moment with one of her sisters.[24]

I Do It for You

"I shall not do it. He is not good. I don't work for bad people." I was quite in wrath. The person standing before me was Mother Teresa, listening to all my angry words. "If you are in trouble," said Mother, "and quite compelled to do something for a person you dislike, do it like this." Then spreading her right palm in front of my face, she touched her right little finger with her left thumb and said, "I do it for You," starting with "I" on the little finger, she ended with "You" on the thumb. The five fingers she touched for five words. "Commit your work to God and say to yourself, 'God, this work I am not doing for the wretched person. I do it for You.' And do it for God. Let your mind be an instrument of His will and your hands do His work. If you practice this, you will find so many of the works that we dislike have smoothly been done without paining you." I found this a simple but effective method to do many works that at times are so essential and yet so much disliked.[25]

Carry On, Sister!

Another time we went to Otis Street [on the occasion of] a final profession at the basilica. On this one day, Sister M. was taking out the garbage, and she used the back shortcut so she wouldn't have to see the visitors. She was carrying a big black plastic bag of garbage. Mother came charging out of one of the back rooms almost on a run; she dodged me but ran smack into the bag of garbage held by a shocked Sister M., who froze and didn't know what to do. Mother simply laughed and instead of being annoyed because the garbage bag was beginning to drip, took the bag out of Sister's hands and waited for her to become composed, and put it back in her hands again. "Carry on, Sister!"[26]

REFLECTION

"Come to Me, all who labor and are heavy laden, and I will give you rest. Take My yoke upon you, and learn from Me; for I am gentle and lowly in heart, and you will find rest for your souls. For My yoke is easy, and My burden is light." (Mt 11:28–30)

"Christ, who being rich became poor and emptied Himself to work out our Redemption, calls us to bear witness to the true face of Jesus, poor, humble, and friend of sinners, the weak and the despised."[27]

Am I open enough to seek and accept the counsel of others when I am in doubt, in confusion, in darkness? Do I act impulsively in a situation where I lack clarity, or do I seek the advice of others? Am I humble enough to consider others' advice and to take it into account?

Am I willing to listen to others? Do I take time to listen? Am I patient with others who are in doubt and darkness? Is the advice that I offer the fruit of my prayer, my reflection, and my intention to do the best for the person in need? Is my advice mixed with my own agenda or does it reflect a lack of real concern?

PRAYER

Breathe in me, O Holy Spirit,
that my thoughts may all be holy.
Act in me, O Holy Spirit,
that my work, too, may be holy.
Draw my heart, O Holy Spirit,
that I love but what is holy.
Strengthen me, O Holy Spirit,
to defend all that is holy.
Guard me, then, O Holy Spirit,
that I always may be holy.

—Saint Augustine's prayer to the Holy Spirit,
prayed daily by Mother Teresa

TEN

ADMONISH SINNERS

Admonishing sinners was one of the works of mercy that Mother Teresa practiced with utmost tact. She knew herself to be a sinner (and thus not better than others); for this reason she could show understanding and sympathy even when correcting others. The sacrament of reconciliation (confession) was one of her favorite manners of making things right with God and others, and she had a great appreciation of it. She would not miss her own weekly confession and would recommend this encounter with God's mercy to others as a source of forgiveness, healing, inner peace, and reconciliation.

"Hate the sin, love the sinner" was a principle much ingrained in Mother Teresa's manner of dealing with people. She knew very well how to separate the sin from the sinner, the wrong from the person who did it, always respecting the person's dignity in spite of the fault committed. This uncommon ability was at times misunderstood and taken as leniency or a lack of courage. Yet she would not miss an opportunity to correct the wrong. This she would do, though, without condemning the wrongdoer; rather, she would encourage the person, calling them to repentance and a change of life. She was not correcting others because their wrongdoing was annoying or affecting her, but out of love for God and for the sinner himself, since by that sin he was damaging his relationship with God, with others, and with himself. She would do everything possible to help the person reconcile with God and find their own inner peace. She corrected people not to put them down, not to crush them, but to build them up, ultimately, because, as she would say, "I want you to be holy."

With her sisters, Mother Teresa could be strong and exacting. Yet they never kept away from her but went to her when they did something wrong. "With you my sisters, I will not be satisfied by [your] being just good religious. I want to be able to offer God a perfect sacrifice. Only holiness perfects the gift." That was her standard, yet the sisters knew that they did not need to hide their errors from her and could go to her with all their mistakes and uncertainties, as her words brought relief, comfort, and healing. She was a true mother and consoler.

HER WORDS

I Am a Sinner

During the Stations, when you are facing the Passion of Christ, look at the Cross. I can find my sins on the Cross. . . . We can be sinners with sin and we can be sinners without sin. Are you really in love with Christ? Can you face the world? Are you so convinced that "nothing can separate me from Him"? [Rom 8:39] Cut me to pieces and every piece will be yours.[1]

✻

See, that Prodigal Son could go back to his father only when he said, "I will rise, I will go, I will tell. I will tell my father that I am a sinner, that I am sorry" [cf. Lk 15:18–19]. He couldn't tell his father, "I'm sorry," until he took that step, "I will go." He knew that in his home there was love, there was kindness—that his father loved him. Our Lady will help us to do that. Let us do it today: rise and go to the Father, and tell Him that we are not worthy to be here, to be His own.[2]

✻

How unlike [Jesus] we are. How little love, how little compassion, how little forgiveness, how little kindness we have, that we are not worthy to be so close to Him—to enter His Heart. For His Heart is still open to embrace us. His head is still crowned with thorns, His hands nailed to the Cross today. Let us find out, "Are the nails mine? That sputum on His face, mine? What part of His body, of His mind, has suffered because of me?" Not with anxiety or fear, but with a meek and humble heart, let us find out what part of His body has [suffered], [what are] the wounds inflicted by my sin. Let us not go alone but put my hand in His. He is there to forgive seventy times seven, as long as I know my Father loves me, He has called me in a special way, given

me a name, I belong to Him with all my misery, my sin,
my weakness, my goodness . . . I am His.[3]

The Sacrament of Mercy

How great and tender is the love of the Father to have
given the sacrament of mercy where we go as sinners
with sin and we return as sinners without sin. Oh, the
tenderness of God's love! If we would only allow Him to
love us. "Be not afraid—I have called you by your name,
you are Mine. Water (sin) will not drown you, fire
(passions) will not burn you. You are precious to Me. I
love you. I have carved you in the palm of My hand. You
are Mine" [cf. Is 43:2, 49:16].[4]

❊

The beginning of holiness is a good confession. We are
all sinners. There is holiness without sin, for we must
become sinners without sin. Our Lady did not have to
say, "Pray for us sinners." I am a sinner with sin. When I
make a good confession, I become a sinner without sin.
How do I become a sinner with sin? When I deliberately
say that word something tells me, "don't say." That is
why we have confession. I hope you make good use of
confession every week.[5]

❊

Confession is as important to Jesus as it is to us. It's a
joint action: Jesus and I. Just as in Holy Communion:
Jesus and I. I cannot be forgiven without Jesus. Jesus
cannot forgive if I don't tell [my sins]. More important

than Mother's instruction or Sister's instruction is *one good confession*. "I will rise and go to my Father."[6]

Do I Make a Good Confession?

Do I make a good confession? Examine your confessions. Do you make them with a real desire, with real sincerity to say the things as they are, or do you say "half-half," hiding something or taking away something? The devil is very clever. Jesus has said, "Do not be afraid." If there is something that is worrying you, say it in confession and once you have said it, do not be busy with that anymore because sometimes, after many months, the devil is after us until he breaks our love for confession. It is not meant to be a torture.[7]

✳

Confession is Jesus and I, and nobody else. Confession is a beautiful act of great love. . . . We don't measure our love by mortal sin or venial sin, but when we fall, confession is there to cleanse us. Even if there is a big gap, don't be ashamed, still go as a child.[8]

✳

Confession is just that, acknowledging sin. Never postpone confession whenever you have done a deliberate act. . . . What a wonderful gift. That is why confession must not be used for gossip but to acknowledge my sin: deliberately I have answered back, deliberately I have given things without permission. Like a little child, like that Prodigal Son, go and say

it in confession; never hide, otherwise for life it will eat
you up.[9]

＊

Each time when you fall, go to confession and say, "I am
sorry." God is a merciful Father and He will forgive you.
The devil cannot move me or touch me even a small bit
unless I say "Yes." So you must not be afraid of him.[10]

＊

Do not be ashamed and think, "Oh, what will Father
think of it?" Father is there to take away your sins from
you. We tell our sins to God and obtain forgiveness from
God. God takes away our sins. We must be simple like
a child: "I shall arise and go to my Father." And what
does God do? "Bring the robe, the ring, the shoes, the
fatted calf" . . . and see the great joy. Why? Because "My
son was dead and has come back to life" [Lk 15:22–24].
Same for us; but we must have that simplicity of a child
and go to confession.[11]

＊

Don't create scruples in your mind. . . . If by mistake you
accept this pleasure, go to confession, and remember
God's mercy is very, very great. . . . See the greatness of
God's love—Mary Magdalene, Margaret of Cortona,
Saint Peter, Saint Augustine. To Saint Peter, Jesus said,
"Do you love Me?" [Jn 21:15ff] That is the condition.
Never say, "Tomorrow"; don't play with chastity.
The devil will say to you, "Oh don't worry [about] it.
Mother has told you all those things. Mother doesn't

know. I know better. You're a human being, you feel that pleasure." In spite of the temptation, willfully say, "I don't want it." See Maria Goretti, "Die yes, sin no." Saint Agnes, "Die yes, sin no."[12]

✳

Even if we have fallen and have committed a sin of impurity, have the courage to go to confession. Saint Margaret of Cortona was like a prostitute, a big sinner, but to prove that God had really forgiven her, every year on her feast day her body becomes full and complete. Make one good confession and finish. Never, never, never think about it! Except to say, "For these and all the sins of my life, especially sins of impurity, I am sorry," as an act of humility.[13]

Our Lady Will Help You

Our Lady will help you to remain pure. If I read that thing, I may be caught. You must have the courage to protect yourself. Why do we have dogs? To warn that somebody is coming—just by the dog barking we know that someone is there. The devil is a barking dog. You are inclined to that person, there is someone who will divide your love for Christ, or you want to give things without permission. You cannot be only all for Jesus unless you go to confession.[14]

✳

Our Lady had a clean heart so she could see God. She had a humble heart. We too can see God if we are really pure of heart. That is why we need confession, not to go and talk, but to go in a sinner with sin and come out a sinner without sin. If we have that love among us, we can give it. If we are disturbed inside, we cannot give love—we can go on pretending, but there will be just none.[15]

✳

As pure as the Immaculate Heart, as pure as the sunshine—nothing will come between Jesus and me. Make use of confession. "I know I should not have done that"—anything that is a deliberate refusal. Something is telling me inside the heart, "Don't," and I do it. Go to confession. . . . You've been impatient with dispensary people, make up for it.[16]

Jesus Washes Our Sins

Why do you make a general confession? Not because I am doubting, but to make that connection, to realize how good the Lord God has been to me—the goodness of God. . . . We make our sincere and humble confession not to the priest, but to Jesus.[17]

✳

How pure the priest must be to pour the Precious Blood on me, to wash my sins away. How great that priest is to say, "This is my Body." You must never doubt that word, "I absolve you, I free you." Even if that priest is a bad priest, he has the power to forgive you, to make you free.[18]

✳

The moment Father says, "I absolve you," Jesus comes
and washes our sins. The Precious Blood of Jesus [is]
poured on our souls to purify us and cleanse our souls.[19]

Standing Before Jesus Like That Sinful Woman

Before you go to bed . . . do you really look at the Cross?
Not in imagination. Take the Cross in your hands and
meditate. . . . . We see our own sisters struggling with a
bucket of water. Am I like that little bird, trying to take
away that little thorn? Do I have compassion? Jesus had
compassion on the sinners. That sinful woman standing
before Jesus, Jesus did not condemn her [Jn 8:11]. That
is confession. I too need to be forgiven. Confession
is nothing but standing before Jesus like that sinful
woman, because I have caught myself in sin.[20]

Confessions Must Be a Real Joy

Saint Ignatius has in mind as a rule, confession—an
expression of our need for forgiveness, not discouragement.
Confession was not instituted on Good Friday but on
Resurrection Sunday, so it is a means of joy. It was not
established as a torture, but as a means of joy.[21]

✳

A priest who is a writer of books makes confession every
day. I asked him, "But what do you say?" He said that

after writing, he reads through and corrects [what he has written], but sometimes he reads it for the sake of pleasure or pride. So he goes for confession. Cardinal Sin of Manila—such a holy man—said to me, "I make confession nearly every day. In the archbishop's house there are a lot of priests, so I catch any of them." See, sisters, confession must be a real joy. I must not neglect confession. Negligence is one thing we have to confess. I must go to confession with love because I have an opportunity to make my soul clean, to become pure. Confession is coming face-to-face with God. When I die, I have to come face-to-face with God, but now I have the chance to go to Him with sin and come away without sin.[22]

We Must Acknowledge Our Sinfulness

That man Zacchaeus [Lk 19:1–10], he wanted to see Jesus and tried in many ways. He could not see Him until he accepted that he was small—that acceptance led him to the next step—the acceptance of the humiliation to climb the tree and let all the people know that he was very small. The people were surprised that such an important man should climb a tree to see Jesus. Zacchaeus was small in body, but for us our sinfulness is our smallness. We must acknowledge it by going to confession—as a sinner with sin—and we come out as a sinner without sin.[23]

When Temptation Comes

Let your purity be really pure. Whatever has happened,
I want you to go to confession. I want your purity to
be pure, your chastity to be chaste, your virginity to be
virgin. Don't busy your mind with yourself. Temptation
comes to us all; it is meant to be a wonderful way of
growing. Temptations against our vocation will come,
but be like the Little Flower [Saint Thérèse of the Child
Jesus]: "I belong to Jesus and nobody and nothing will
separate us." The temptation came to Saint Paul, and
we must be able to say what Saint Paul said, "I belong to
Christ." Then the people will come and see only Jesus,
because we will truly be carriers of God's love.[24]

✳

When temptation comes, remember the three things:

1. I don't want it. Then the devil cannot touch you.
   You are safe.
2. Be busy—as long as you know and say, "I don't
   want it," you are all right.
3. Turn to Mary. This is something very precious
   for her to give to Jesus.[25]

Seeking Out Sinners

With the coming of Jesus, He shows in His own person
that tender love, that compassion . . . except when He
saw the hard-heartedness and unbelief of the Pharisees.
Otherwise He was gentle and meek, and anyone who

acknowledged Him had a place in the Heart of Jesus. It was that tender love and compassion that caused Him to feel pity for the crowds, to cure the sick, and to seek out sinners.[26]

✳

We are all so small, sinners, miserable, and so on, but God stoops down to each one of us and asks us, "Will you come?" He does not force us. This is the wonderful, tender freedom that God gives us. You can grow in the love of your vows so fully that you become a living saint.[27]

✳

I think of Our Lady most when we face ourselves as sinners. When we say the Hail Mary, that part, "pray for us sinners," let us say it with our whole heart and soul. She is the one who will obtain for us a pure heart. She is the one who saw there was no wine [Jn 2:3]. Let us ask her to see in us that we have that sinfulness—no holiness—and to tell Jesus. And she will tell us, "Do whatever He tells you" [Jn 2:5]—to obey.[28]

Do Not Kill the Little Child

It is true; some of you have done the wrong thing in killing the unborn child in your womb through abortion. But turn to God and say, "My God, I am very sorry for killing my unborn child. Please forgive me. I will never do it again." And God, being our loving

Father, will forgive you. Never do it again—and believe me, God has forgiven you. Also remember your action does not harm the child. Your little one is with God for all eternity. There is no such thing [as] the child [punishing] you or your family. The child is with God. Your child loves you, has forgiven you, and is praying for you. He is with God, so he cannot do any harm but only love you.[29]

❋

The presence of nuclear weapons in the world has created fear and distrust among nations, as [they are] one more weapon to destroy human life, God's beautiful presence in the world. Just as abortion is used to kill the unborn child, this new weapon will become a means to eliminate the poor of the world—our brothers and sisters whom Jesus Christ has taught us to love as He has loved each one of us.[30]

❋

Mistakes are being made all over the world. That mistake about not keeping a pure heart, a pure body, which we can give to God, we can give to each other. And it is not wrong that a young woman and a young man love each other. But today that part of beautiful purity has been more or less neglected, and mistakes are made. But I beg of you, *help* the parents, *help* your children to *accept* that little one, *not to kill* the little child. To accept. Mistakes we all make, and mistakes can be forgiven. But to murder an innocent child is a very big sin.[31]

No *Time for the Children to Be Loved*

We didn't have these difficulties before because the
family was always together. The children knew their
parents, and the parents knew their children. But now
the parents know their children less and less, because
they have no time. Or they sit for hours before television
and never exchange words between the children and
themselves. And I think television is a good thing if it is
used properly. But television has also been a means of
separating the parents from their children. They have
no time to exchange love, for the children to be kissed,
to be loved; they need that. Because that hunger for love
is there in every child's heart, the child goes out to look
for it. That has brought much loneliness into the lives of
the children. To kill that loneliness, they do all kinds of
things.[32]

Correct Yourself

A mother went to a holy man with her boy, who had a
bad habit of eating [between meals], and this man said
to her, "Bring him to me after a week," for he realized
that he too had the same bad habit and he could not talk
to the boy with a clean, sincere heart unless he corrected
it himself.[33]

✳

We must realize our faults and correct ourselves. Why
did I become like this? Because I am proud.[34]

✳

You have to know yourself; if you are not sincere with
yourself, you will not correct the mistakes. Now is
the time to correct your mistakes. If you really love
Jesus, you will be happy to know and correct yourself;
otherwise it will go on and on with you.[35]

＊

There is no meaning in showing temper when you are
corrected. Then there is no sense in joining a religious
society if you don't want to be holy. We must watch
our moods very closely and check them in the very
beginning. When we find out that we are inclined to be
moody and hysterical, watch, watch, watch. Women are
inclined to that—we live on our feelings, but as religious
we can't do that. Because I am very fervent today, don't
think I [will be fervent tomorrow]; I am not what my
feelings make me, but I am what I am before God. I beg
of you, sisters, watch yourselves well in the beginning.
Be harsh with yourselves now, rather than later on when
it will be so much more difficult. That I am inclined to
be dragged down—that is all right, but I must not give
in to that inclination.[36]

Never Correct in Public

Do not be harsh in your voice when you have to correct.
Never correct in public. Always [speak about] the
correction you want to give to a sister first with Jesus,
and ask yourself, "How would Mother correct me if I
was guilty of the same fault?"[37]

Correction does not mean shouting and saying just anything that comes to your lips. Correction is a token of love. You give it because you love the sister.[38]

Do not allow any uncharitable, harsh remarks to come from your lips when you correct your sisters. So much hurt has come into so many hearts due to hurtful, harsh words. . . . I do not know why you have to do it, when I have never done it to you. Not one in the Society, from the beginning to this day, can say that I have hurt any of you with my words; maybe sometime when you found obedience difficult, you thought Mother was hard on you. It was not I; it was you who were hard on yourself for not accepting to obey.[39]

Silence Cannot Be Corrected

If we keep silence, silence cannot be corrected; if we speak, if we answer back, we make mistakes.[40]

Very often I have the answer and I don't give it. I wait and I am always grateful to God for giving me this opportunity, because silence cannot be corrected. Mary could have told Joseph that the child she was expecting was the Son of God. That little unborn boy (John the Baptist) knew that Jesus had come. Joseph, standing here, did not know [Lk 1:39–41]. Mary knew that Joseph was going to run away. Let us make that marvelous resolution. Let us control our tongues from getting dirty. I will love Jesus with undivided love by loving my sisters and the poor as He did. My tongue must be clean; tomorrow Jesus comes on my tongue.[41]

✳

I remember my mother. They say she was very holy. One day three of us were [saying] not nice things about the teacher. It was night. [My mother] got up and [turned] off the main switch. She said, "I am a widow. . . . I have no money to spend on electricity for you to talk evil." And we had to do everything in darkness—go up and down, wash, go to bed.

My sister was a dressmaker. We had a board on the wall: "In this house no one will speak against another." One day a very rich woman came to give orders to my sister. She started talking against somebody. My mother said to that lady, "See what is written there." [The lady] got up and went. My mother said, "I'd rather beg in the street than to bear uncharitableness in my house." Do you have that courage, sisters?[42]

Remain Faithful

There has been much disturbance in the religious life of sisters, all due to misguided advice and zeal. Something of that oneness with Jesus and oneness with His Church has been lost. There is more love for freedom in action and the way of life. Like in many laywomen, so also in our religious, the ambition to be equal to men in all things, even in the priesthood, has taken away that peace and joy of being one with Jesus and His Church. I would be grateful if you would help us to love, obey, and remain faithful to the Church and the Vicar of Christ and so come back to our full consecration by living the true life of the spouse of Jesus Crucified.[43]

HER EXAMPLE: The Testimonies

Jesus Wants You to Be a Saint

If she spoke to a person in deep sin she would never say, "You are a sinner." She would say, "Jesus wants you to be a saint," and such and such is wrong. She tried to make that person understand what God was calling them to be. She didn't judge. She would remind everyone of how special they were to God. And that was what used to move people. It wasn't "change yourself so God will accept you and love you," but rather that "God accepts and loves you as you are even in your sins, but He loves you too much to leave you as you are." She knew from Jesus that making people feel loved would [challenge] them to respond in love.[44]

She Made Us Aware That She Was Disappointed

Once it happened that we failed to show respect for Mother Cenacle. She complained to Mother about us. Mother made us aware that she was disappointed and hurt by our behavior.

She did not scold us, but at mealtime she went around the refectory outside saying her Rosary instead of coming into the room with us. We all felt so miserable. We went to ask pardon from Mother Cenacle. This made us realize the love and respect [that Mother] had for authority. She had such concern, compassionate love, availability, and approachability. The word *Mother* was not only on our lips, but also in our hearts. She could manage us, "rebels" as we were.[45]

I Did Not Expect This from You, My Own Child

Mother had learned each one's temperament and need, and so treated us accordingly. If we tried to say something that was not nice, she would put her hand on our mouth to stop [us from] speaking. There were times when we would behave badly and say things to Mother that were not nice. Mother would accept it by saying, "I did not expect this from you, my own child. This is good for me. Thank you." She would pray and wait for us to cool down and come back to her to say sorry. If we did not come back by evening, she would call for us so that we could make up [with] her. After this, she would never mention it again. There were times when Mother was very strict with me and did not spare me when I used to be stubborn. But it was done with love and for my good. After correcting me, she would make it a point to call me or to give [me] something so that I would not keep feeling hurt.[46]

Like Eve After Eating the Forbidden Fruit

It was rainy season and we had to carry our umbrella. I was feeling uneasy to carry the big umbrella in the crowded trams because I had the biggest men's umbrella. . . . Before we could escape the gates, behold, Mother was standing there. She asked me why am I going out without an umbrella. I answered her, that mine was broken. . . . Mother told me to go upstairs and see in Mother's room there was an umbrella, to take that and go. I went up and saw it was a brand-new one . . . and the same size as mine. I could not refuse it. I took it to the Sunday School. . . . I do not know what made me think to travel back by the double-decker bus. . . . For me it was something wonderful to travel in it. . . . I climbed the second story of the bus and sat near the window and enjoyed the sight.

Just as we crossed the Howrah Bridge, a thought suddenly came to my mind: if we get down in front of the Mother House, Mother or any other sister would see us. Now fear entered in my heart. So we planned to get down near Sealdah. From there we walked toward Mother House. . . . As Adam and Eve after eating the forbidden fruit experienced the fear of God, so too we both of us. . . . When the time came to get down, there was no rain and I forgot to take the umbrella in the bus. My whole body was cold. Fortunately, we were late for community lunch. . . . My conscience was haunting me to go and to tell Mother. . . . No courage . . . Mother called me. . . . She knew my fear because by the time I went to her, the umbrella had reached her. I do not know when and by whom it was brought. . . . Anyway, Mother made me kneel down and asked me the details. At first, I went on telling lies after lies. . . . I told her that I lost the umbrella in the tram. Mother asked me the tram number because she knew that we did not travel by tram. She made me speak the truth. . . . I did it after much pressure from her side. Once she got the whole truth, she made me speak my faults one by one for each item. . . . She did not say much. Only I remember Mother saying, "Never to do it again." See Mother's compassion and love for me. Patient and kind.[47]

✳

Mother would not scold me for wrong done, but she would call me and tell me sweetly, "You have been so good, what has happened to you now?" Then she would give a blessing with both hands. That was the way Mother used to correct in her later years.[48]

We Can Only Change Them by Our Love

Some of our orphan children were naughty, and one day I punished them by not serving the lunch for them, and I said at the table that I did not give them lunch. Mother made me leave my lunch and go and serve their lunch. She said, "We can only change them by our love, not by our punishment."[49]

With Great Patience She Corrected

In Shkodra, Albania, Mother would feed the children; as they were spastic and gravely handicapped, they made their whole face dirty after each spoon they were fed. Mother never left the children dirty and she wiped their mouths after each spoon she fed them. With great patience, she corrected the aspirants and showed them how to wipe the mouths of the children. The love with which she herself did it spoke more than her corrections. I remember specially one child who was so disfigured in his body. He was also full of fear and screamed a lot, and screamed even more when someone approached him. Mother gave special attention to him, began to be able to hold his hand, etc., and after a few days he smiled whenever he saw Mother. Then Mother would call us to his bed and so "introduce" us to him as her friends, so that he would accept us too.[50]

This Is Not the Way We Deal with Christ

As a young religious, I was placed in a leprosy hospital. Once an elderly crippled couple had a little difficulty in the hospital and they came to Mother House. They wanted to meet Mother. Somehow Mother could not meet them; so every day they came to the Mother House, disturbing the sisters. One day the sisters rang up to me and said, "A couple of your patients are sitting here and are disturbing the whole house. Why don't you do something?" As I heard this, I was angry, and in my anger, I came running. As I reached in front of the Mother House, I could see this couple: the man with an artificial limb and so deformed, a very frail person. In all my anger, I lifted him and put him in the ambulance. After a while I could see Mother coming down. She said, "Brother, you have a fourth vow. What is our fourth vow? Wholehearted free service to the poorest of the poor. Did you make this vow?" "Yes, Mother, I did make the vow."

"What did you do here now?" She said it very politely and without many words. I could feel the motherly way of correction, and Mother said, "This is not the way we deal with Christ. The poor man is Christ. He is the distressing Christ. All that this poor man is showing to us is Christ on the Cross that we have come across. We should not run away." The way Mother gave me that correction soundly influenced my life. To this day I remember . . . and cherish it.[51]

A Shock Treatment

When I first went for leprosy work as a postulant, I was afraid of getting the disease. After a week, I went to Mother to tell her that I could see a patch on my forearm. Mother believed me and asked Dr. S. to examine me, and he said there was nothing, not even a spot. Then Mother called me and said, "I am going to change your place of work. I think you are not worthy to serve the lepers." It came as a shock treatment for me. From that day, I prayed to get over my fear of the disease, and whenever there was an opportunity I would go to them.[52]

The Truth in Charity

When a prime ministry of India introduced sterilization of adults to decrease births, [Mother] wrote to that [person] and clearly said, "Aren't you afraid of dying and having to answer for this terrible sin?" She allowed the letter to be given to the press and quoted in the newspapers because she believed the issue to be that serious. She didn't back down. She spoke the truth in charity.[53]

Speak the Truth

In 1979 Mother Teresa received the Nobel Peace Prize. . . .
Passing through Rome on her return to India, she came to
our seminary and gave us a talk. . . . It seems that the day
following the event of the Peace Prize, a priest came for Mass
in the convent where Mother was staying, as MCs were not
yet in Norway. After Mass the priest told Mother that he
had listened to the broadcast of her speech the night before
and had become quite upset. Mother had spoken out against
abortion for the first time, and she had spoken strongly
that abortion was nothing less than murder, and how can
a young woman commit murder like that? The priest said
that she would just alienate young women by speaking in
that fashion. Mother said to us, "I just looked at Father and
said, 'Father, Jesus said, "I am the Truth" [Jn 14:6], and it
is for you and me to speak the truth. Then it's for those who
listen to accept or reject it.' " Mother believed in the radical-
ism of the Gospel message, and she loved souls too much to
be influenced by human respect.[54]

You Need to Come Back to Your First Love

One cardinal . . . brought a group of theologians. He said to
Mother, "I would like you to tell them what is really in your
heart for them." She turned to them and said, "When we
read the Gospels and read the passage where Jesus rebuked
religious leaders of that day, can you truthfully say that you
would not stand in that position to be rebuked today?" And
then she went on to say, "You need to come back to your
first love."[55]

I Prefer to See the Good

One day [Miss X] began to complain about the corruption of government services. Everything required a bribe. In fact, she wanted Mother to intercede on behalf of someone [who] could not get a permit from the city without putting down a great deal of money. [She] said, "Mother, can you help because [this city] is so corrupt. You cannot get anything unless you pay people off." Mother immediately said, "You know our people are so beautiful." And she started telling us of how many gifts they bring at Christmastime. And the woman said, "Yes, Mother, that is very nice, but let's face it. The vast majority are just out for money." The second time Mother interjected a ray of hope: "You know [they] have a beautiful custom. They take a handful of rice and put it aside for the poor." And she started a story about the family sharing rice. This woman became frustrated and shouted, "Mother, will you wake up? [This city] is a hell of corruption!" A great silence settled over us. It was embarrassing to hear the woman speak like that. And again Mother became very quiet. She looked at the person, straight in the eye, and she said, "I know very well there is corruption, . . . but I know also there is good! I prefer to see the good."[56]

There Is So Much Good

Once I said to Mother, "Mother, there is so much evil in the world." Mother paused a moment, looked intently at me, and said, "Sister, there is so much *good* in the world."[57]

With Folded Hands She Begged Them

In 1992, when the Hindu-Muslim riots broke out in Calcutta, Mother and some sisters, with children who were
going to be adopted, were going by ambulance to the airport. On the way they encountered open fighting and violence between the Muslims and Hindus. Mother got out of
the ambulance, and in the middle of the danger put up her
hands for them to stop. With folded hands she begged them
to put an end to the fighting and reminded them that they
were all brothers.[58]

She Admonished Him Gently

One day when I was a novice, a [poor] boy aged about fourteen years entered Mother House, climbing the wall, and
broke the lock of the [warehouse] and took out some boxes
of soap, plates, etc. It had happened in the morning while we
were at prayers. He was waiting to carry his booty when the
portress would open the door. The sister [portress] shouted,
"Thief, Thief." We all rushed to the site. The boy out of
fear hid in one of our bathing rooms. We told Mother and
were gleefully waiting to see the punishment of the culprit.
To our utter amazement, Mother took the boy by the hand
and brought him with great compassion near the gate. She
herself opened the door, admonished him gently, "Don't do
that again," and let him go as if nothing had happened.[59]

It Could Happen to Me and You

Two of the men in the shelter were seen by people in the
neighborhood masturbating in the window. So these people

were understandably upset. . . . Lo and behold, at that point, Mother comes to town. [A Co-Worker] says to Mother, "What should we do?" And Mother said, "You know this is very, very, very bad, these men must go to confession." I have to be honest, at this point I was waiting for her to say and then throw them out, right? She said, "It's very, very bad, these men they must go to confession, but it could happen to me and you tomorrow." I don't know but for me in my life that statement was like a wrecking ball hitting me in the back of my head, and it's something that I'll never forget to the day I die. . . . I mean I was haunted by that statement, and only after Mother died not only did it mean so much in terms of her holiness, but the real kicker, which I not too long ago realized, [was that] she really meant it.[60]

Never Doubt the Mercy of God

Once I came to Calcutta for a retreat. I was much worried about a sin I had committed. So I went to see Mother. I wrote all my faults and especially my sin, which was disturbing me, and gave it to Mother to read. She read the whole thing. Then she tore it to pieces and she said to me, "I am putting all this into the Heart of Jesus, and never, never doubt the mercy of God. Once you have confessed your sin, remember God has forgiven you and He has forgotten everything." And Mother explained to me about God's great love, forgiveness, and mercy. Then she took a picture of the Immaculate Heart of Mary, wrote on it "Be a Mother to me" and "God bless you, Mother," and at the back of the picture she wrote "I forbid you to be busy with the past, put your trust in our Lady," and gave it to me. And that sin of mine, instead of taking me away from God, was an instrument in making me humble, drew me closer to Him, increased my devotion to the Merciful Heart of Jesus. Thanks to Mother.[61]

REFLECTION

"Let the word of Christ dwell in you richly, as you teach and admonish one another in all wisdom, and as you sing psalms and hymns and spiritual songs with thankfulness in your hearts to God." (Col 3:16)

"We are all poor, for we are all sinners."[62]

"We are not sinless, but we must be sinners without sin."[63]

Do I recognize that I am a sinner with many sins? Am I willing to recognize my own mistakes and sins and accept correction from others? Do I become aggravated if someone points out my mistakes to me? How can I respond more graciously to those who point out my errors to me?

Do I allow myself to take the path of least resistance and avoid taking a stance for what is true and good? Do I lack courage to do or say what is right because I am afraid of the opinion of others?

Do I make good use of the sacrament of mercy, of reconciliation?

What are the ways that I can help someone realize that

what they are doing is not right, or in what way can I encourage them to do better? Is there a way that I can show with my example the way of truth and the good?

PRAYER

ACT OF CONTRITION

O God, I love You with my whole
heart and above all things. I am heartily
sorry for having offended You, because
You are so good. I firmly resolve, with
the help of Your grace, not to offend You
anymore. And I shall do whatever You
will ask of me.
Amen.

ELEVEN

BEAR WRONGS PATIENTLY

Patience, serenity, and evenness of character were qualities that those around Mother Teresa noticed in her. Her characteristic calm was a sign of a well-balanced and mortified person who could place things in proper perspective and accept trials as a part of life. She demonstrated this admirable equanimity especially when she was treated unjustly by others. Even when she was being wronged, slighted, or misunderstood, she was patient; she knew that these deeds were done by poor, weak, and sinful human beings like herself, and thus she could be tolerant and even gracious.

In a vision that she had at the very birth of the Missionaries of Charity, Mother Teresa had seen Christ crucified bearing all possible wrongs patiently out of love for her and for all. She was thus eager to do likewise in imitation of Him and to show her love for Him. "If I am the spouse of Jesus Crucified, then I must have some resemblance to Him—some sharing of identity with Him to show that I belong to Him." Practicing forbearance was thus an opportunity for her to quench His thirst for love. At the same time, she would be united to the poorest of the poor, who daily suffer many wrongs and injustices. It is only natural to struggle to accept and persevere in bearing the wrong done to us. Our first reaction might be to avoid certain situations, and that may be the right thing to do. However, there will always be situations impossible to evade, so it will be necessary to face the wrong done to us either intentionally or unintentionally. Mother Teresa never expected special treatment nor demanded special privileges, but even when she was treated worse than others, she was able to respond generously. At times it was a question of willing to be a victim of others' limitations, selfishness, or lack of thoughtfulness, but she accepted people's behavior without letting others notice that she had been wronged.

Ultimately, she saw these trials or wrongs as being permitted by God for reasons that she might not always be able to understand, but she knew He could draw good from them, as Saint Paul affirms in Romans 8:28 ("God makes all things work for the good of those who love Him"). She thus willingly accepted these trials and sufferings, and, uniting them to the Cross of Christ, she offered them for her own purification and for the salvation and sanctification of souls.

When the situation was reversed and she had wronged someone, she made it a point to be the first one to apologize. But going even further, she would be the first one to seek reconciliation even when she was not the one who had done wrong.

HER WORDS

Back at Home

I remember my mother and father; they could have a
difference of opinion, but afterward my mother used to
look at the clock, as she knew the time when my father
was coming home, and [she would] run upstairs to make
herself up every day. We used to play tricks on her. It
was so beautiful. They could disagree, but they used
to come back together as if nothing had happened, day
after day. You see this is something we have to learn
from our parents, their care for each other.[1]

Share the Passion

It is very natural because we are human beings and our
Lord must have felt like that sometimes, even crying,
and He felt very lonely, and . . . when He was dying,
He said, "Why have you forsaken Me?" [Mk 15:34]
The greatest suffering of Jesus was His loneliness, His
rejection in Gethsemane. I feel that the Passion of Christ
in Gethsemane was much, much, much harder for Him
to accept than the Passion of the Crucifixion because the
very heart of Christ was crucified by being rejected, by
being left alone, by being unwanted, unloved, uncared
[for]—just left alone like that. And I think we, if we
really belong to Jesus, then we must experience that
loneliness; we must have that experience, that feeling of
being unwanted even by Him sometimes. He must have

a free hand. If He chooses like that, all right, . . . so we have to tell Jesus, "Okay." If He wants us to share that Passion of Gethsemane, it's only being relived, and if we really belong to Jesus, we must experience that Passion of Christ. We must experience it. And [it is] sometimes a long time, sometimes a short time, maybe—it depends; He's the Master, He can choose. He can come to us in His Passion, He can come to us in His resurrection, He can come to us as a child, as a preacher, in whatever form He wants to come.[2]

✳

People are very hard to deal with, but Jesus said when they slap one side, show the other side [Mt 5:39]. Sometimes they hurt us. Be happy, share in the Passion of Christ. Stress that point, look up and see Him. If we are humble like Mary and holy like Jesus, they will see Jesus in us and we will see Jesus in them.[3]

✳

Why was Jesus humiliated and crucified? For our sake. It was a terrible humiliation, difficult to accept the Crucifixion—He perspired blood. Also in our life we may have to face many situations—very painful. For Jesus there was no "Oh, but, . . ." no condition. It was a terrible humiliation for Jesus, and we claim to be the spouses of Jesus Crucified. Examine yourself: How did you accept [humiliation]? Have you grown in that tender love?[4]

✳

Then we see Him on the Cross. He could have come
down when they were asking Him to do so. Very
easily He could have done it. They would have been all
frightened and walked away. He could have done that in
Gethsemane, but for love of you and me, He remained
on the Cross. Let us not try to escape the Cross or
humiliation but grab the chance to be like Him, to live
His Passion in us. A carrier of love means a carrier of
the Cross. If I want to be a true MC, I must be a real
carrier of the Cross. Maybe, carrying the Cross on the
way we fall. It is very beautiful to make the Stations of
the Cross, in seeing Our Lady meet Jesus on the way,
or asking Simon to help you carry [the Cross] when
you fall on the way. So many people were on the way to
Calvary—Our Lady, Simon, Veronica, the women. Are
we Veronica to our sisters in the community? Are we a
Simon to our superiors? Are we a mother to our poor as
Mary was to Jesus at the Fourth Station [of the Cross]?
Ask Jesus to deepen your love.[5]

Remember What We Have Done to Hurt Our Lord

We are surprised how the people hurt Jesus: they
slapped Him, spat on Him. What we throw in the drain,
we throw on Jesus. And Jesus—not a word. Each time,
when we say ugly things, uncharitable words, we are
doing the same thing to Jesus—"You did it to Me."
Terrible . . . throwing, spitting—that's where Veronica
came in and wiped His face. Spitting on Our Lord—
"You did it to Me." When? Now. We think that what
they did, we are not responsible [for]; it is exactly what

they did to Him [that] we are doing now. Today I want
you to go before the Blessed Sacrament; [go back and
examine] in my own family, as an aspirant, postulant—
take a direct look at Jesus. Whatever you did to that
sister, to that poor person: "I am spitting on Him."
Make this your own and you will see how your whole
attitude will change. Just this morning I was with Jesus.
Instead of words of love, I give dirt; sin is dirt, that
evil. Jesus gives us a word of love. If you want to know
if your heart is all right, [examine] your words; my
hands are acting, my feet are acting, my tongue is acting
through speaking.[6]

✳

Today see if you can look up at the Cross and say: "For
my sins"; "I will get up and go to my Father." . . . Let
us remember the things that we have done to hurt Our
Lord. Why are we—and not [the other sisters]—here
today? Maybe others have done [something wrong]
only once and they are not here. This is the mystery
of God. That is why now we are saying the Rosary in
reparation for the sins committed by each one of us, here
within our own Society. Let us ask Our Lady to be the
Cause of Our Joy by opening our eyes to see sin in our
lives.[7]

✳

Maybe [someone] said a word that hurt me before and
that hurt is preventing me from having a clean heart,
it is preventing me from seeing Jesus. I will not be able

even to pray because only in the silence of the heart, God speaks. If I am not at ease in speaking to God, I [must] examine if my heart is pure. I don't mean impurity, but something that prevents me [from seeing, from listening]. From the fullness of my heart I speak to God and God listens. We need a clean heart if we really want to pray, to serve the poor.[8]

You Will Be Able to Face Any Wrongs

I want you to spend your time being alone with Jesus. What does it mean to be alone with Jesus? It doesn't mean to sit alone with your own thoughts. No, but even in the midst of the work and of people, you know *His presence*. It means that you know that He is close to you, that He loves you, that you are precious to Him, that He is in love with you. He has called you and you belong to Him. If you know that, you will be all right anywhere, under any superior; you will be able to face any failure, any humiliation, any suffering, if you realize Jesus's personal love for you and yours for Him. Nothing and nobody! [Rom 8:39] Otherwise you will be so preoccupied with unimportant things that slowly you will be[come] a broken sister.[9]

Be Ready to Pay the Price He Paid for Souls

Jesus says, "Amen, I say to you, unless the grain of wheat falling into the ground die, itself remaineth alone. But if it die, it bringeth forth much fruit" [Jn 12:24].

The missionary must die daily if she wants to bring souls to God. She must be ready to pay the price He paid for souls, to walk in the way He walked in search [of] souls.[10]

※

How very often very small misunderstandings— repeated—become a cause of so much suffering. In the name of Jesus and for the love of Jesus, accept these little gifts from Him. Look up at that little hurt and see the gift of Jesus only. He . . . accepted so much suffering and humiliations because He loved you. Will you not accept the little correction or hurt because you love Him?[11]

※

You write "my vocation"; yes, yours and your husband's is to let God do with you what He wants. Give Him your eyes, that He may see; your tongue, that He may speak; your Heart, that He may love; your whole being, that people may look up and see only Jesus. You, as you are all only for Jesus, are helping me much more now than all the talks put together. All the sacrifices you had to offer when Bishop broke your Co-Workers—and the result of it all, the great gift the Holy See has given to your Missionaries of Charity, the "Decree of Praise."* You had to pay for it.[12]

※

* Pontifical recognition whereby the MC Congregation was placed directly under the authority of the pope, February 1, 1965.

You are the spouses of Jesus Crucified. Be that joy, that peace wherever you go. Whatever work is given to you, do it with joy. Be heart and soul and mind only all for Jesus. If you are only all for Him, you have nothing to fear. The greatest suffering, the greatest humiliation will be the greatest gift for you.[13]

✳

A clean heart can see God. "I was hungry, you gave Me to eat; I was naked, you clothed Me." What does it mean, "You did it to Me"? Are your hearts so pure [that you can] see Jesus in your sisters, even the one that hurt you? Never, never say an uncharitable word.[14]

Grab the Chance

When the superior corrects you, when she blames you, when you are not at fault, go [in]to yourself for a minute [and examine]. If you are guilty, say sorry. If you are not guilty, grab the chance, offer it for your community, for Mother, for your intentions. . . . Grab the chance because this humiliation will make you a beautiful sister. I can talk to you all day about humility and you will not improve. But by accepting humiliations, you will become a humble sister. And we all have them— humiliations we will have all our life.[15]

✳

What is your reaction when [you are] reproved or corrected? Examine it. If your reaction is to grumble,

then you are not using the eyes of faith. Watch your
thoughts, your words, your actions when corrected.[16]

✳

If I'm really humble, I will answer, "Yes, thank
you." Pride speaks boldly, and it destroys on its way
everything that is lovely and beautiful. That word
you speak in anger because of that correction—say,
"Oh, she is partial"—goes around, and by the time it
comes back to you it is something different. Just like
that sin of Adam and Eve. They ate maybe only one
bite of that apple and yet that act has affected mankind
through all time till the end of the world. If we are really
humble, we will be truly Christlike, we will do things
pleasing to Him. Then we will be on the way to true
sanctity. Nothing will make us holy except if we have
started on that road. Unless we have learned to accept
humiliations, nothing else, not even lots of work for the
poor, will be of any value.[17]

✳

Is it better to be blamed for something that you have
done or for something you have not done? If you
learn to do this, if you learn to accept whatever He
gives and give whatever He takes with a big smile,
you will have learned to be humble. That prayer that
I have taught you will help: "In union with all the
Masses being offered throughout the world, I offer
You my heart. Make it meek and humble like Your
heart."[18]

❋

Even if your superior sometimes may not understand
you or say things that may hurt you, that little
hurt should not come between you and Jesus. That
humiliation will bring you close to Jesus. Never answer
back in that humiliation. Suffering has to come,
humiliation and loneliness [have to come], because you
are going to be the spouse of Jesus Crucified. A garland
is not given to you, a crown is not given to you, but
the Cross is given to you. "You are my Spouse, share
with Me."[19]

❋

If you are determined to become holy, grab [each
humiliation] as your chance; do not let it go down into
your heart—[let it go] straight, from one ear in and
from the other out. These little humiliations are the gifts
of God.[20]

❋

In everybody's life there are continually throughout the
day many of these beautiful gifts—chances to show
our love for Jesus in those little things, these little
humiliations. And if we are humble, if we are pure
in heart, then we will see the face of God in prayer
and so be able to see God in one another. It is a full
circle, sisters. Everything is connected. The fruit of our
prayer is that love for Jesus—proved by accepting little
humiliations with joy.[21]

❋

It's very easy to grumble. Never do. You came here
because you love Jesus. Today you will have to show
your love by accepting. Today you get a bad correction
and it hurts you. Never answer back. Unless you are
asked, if she [the superior] asks you, "Have you done
this?" you may say yes or no. If she doesn't ask you, if
she blames you, if she even shouts at you, [ask yourself,]
"Is it true?" Only that one question you ask. If your
heart is clean, say: "I'm sorry, I will not do [that]
anymore." If not, accept[ing] this will teach you to
become a humble sister. Accept. Never, never—after
correction—never become moody. Moodiness is [the]
fruit of pride. Revenge: "You have hurt me. I have no
means to hurt you back. So I get moody." Grab it. That's
humiliation that will teach you to become a humble
sister. [A] clean heart will give you joy.[22]

❋

Never allow bitterness to touch you if you want to be
happy. If you really give yourself to God, humiliation,
failure, success, sorrow, pain is in that "yes." When we
forget that "yes," . . . bitterness comes into our heart.[23]

❋

Don't waste time. Don't worry about what she said or
if she hurt you, be busy for souls. Feel that you have so
much to do and to pray [for].[24]

❋

When the people praise you, let it be for the glory of
God. When the people despise [you], don't let it hurt
you. [When they praise you,] don't let it make you
proud. Let it go in through one ear and out through the
other. Never let it go into your heart. . . . People will
always say many different things.[25]

※

Always be the first one to say sorry. Never let it go out
of your mouth what you have heard from others. Never
repeat. If you are hurt, don't give back [don't try to take
revenge]. The joy of our life is just this [to forgive]. That
sister who hurt you, who was not so nice with you, is the
poorest of the poor. If you don't care to smile or forgive,
you are refusing Jesus.[26]

※

In difficult times—[those are] the times of surrender,
never be insincere, never exaggerate, or think one thing
and write another. Never write more than necessary;
never write when you are hurt or when a sister has upset
you. When you feel free, then write. The mistakes you
make, do not disown or hide [them], but be the first one
to write it before others say it of you. You are getting
what Jesus wants you to get. If you are sincere, holy,
humble, you will get exactly what you must get, nothing
more, nothing less.[27]

※

Remember Nazareth, His own place, they wanted to stone
Him when He explained the Scriptures [Lk 4:28–29].

You have to suffer for the truth. You will have to say, but do not say without praying: "Let me say for the glory of Your Son." Be only all for Jesus through Mary. Live that. They called Him a liar, Beelzebub, He never answered; only when they slapped Him, "Why do you slap Me?" [Jn 18:29] It's a great humiliation for [a] man to be slapped in public. Accept humiliations. Without humility you cannot be like Jesus and Mary; accept.[28]

Jesus, for Love of You

In the Carmelite monastery, where the Little Flower was, they had an old nun whom no one could please or satisfy. She was always grumbling and so no one wanted to take care of her, but the Little Flower, because she loved Jesus, volunteered to take care [of the old nun]. So every day the litany began, "O, you are too slow or too fast, you will kill me, or what are you doing, can't you walk"—all the ways one grumbles. The Little Flower obeyed that nun each time and did what she wanted because she wanted to be all for Jesus, her crucified Spouse. Stupid things maybe, but for God nothing is stupid the moment we say, "Jesus, for love of you."[29]

✳

How I wish I was with you these days—just to be there—I know and I can imagine the wound caused by Bishop's action. But what about the terrible wound to the Heart of Jesus, who loved him first? We all feel so bad and this [is] only in our feelings, but Our Lord's wound is deep and painful because the wound was caused by the one He so loves. We must pray that he returns to Jesus, and I am sure He will not despise a broken reed. Don't allow pain and sorrow—[it] does not matter how deep—[to] preoccupy you, for Christ wants your love now. You can love Him for all those who do not love Him. He must receive all the love He longs for from you both. Jesus must love your home so much.[30]

✳

Poor Jesus—so much suffering for Him and yet the Cross, Nazareth, Bethlehem was His first love. He being rich, became poor for love of us. Don't let anything separate you from the love of Christ, even friends like Bishop ——, [but] draw your mind to think differently. Cling to Christ. He is the same Love that loved you first. Let us not judge. No one . . . Don't allow all kinds of thoughts and rumors to upset you. Fix your eyes on Christ. He is the same yesterday, today, tomorrow: a love that [will] always burn, a strength that never falters, a joy that always fills. . . . Keep close to Jesus with a smiling face.[31]

[For] so long I had no news from you and then the sad news of the university. This is our chance to show our love for the Church. She needs us now more than ever. Let us all be generous and stand by Christ in His Passion. I feel as if I hear Jesus say in this confusion, "Will you also go away?" He is the Love worth loving, the Life worth living, the Light worth burning, the Way worth following. Remember Pilate and Caiaphas, and yet Jesus obeyed them because they had "power from above." The good bishop has "power from above"; therefore, all of us must obey—Christ will speak to us only through him—Jesus did not stop loving us because Caiaphas the high priest was so cruel and made terrible mistakes. Let us be very, very close to our Mother the Church through our bishop, in total surrender, loving trust, and cheerfulness.[32]

✳

My sister may not have worms [like the homeless man on the street] but see that harshness. She is really hurting me. So I give back. . . . If that sister has said that to you, it is bad, but why [has she] done it? You don't know. Don't judge. You will have peace in the community if you don't judge.[33]

Sharing in the Sufferings of Our Poor

See, our poor people have to suffer so much; we are the only ones who can help them. Offer your pain to Jesus for them. Share in His pain, humiliation, Passion. Nobody ever has gone through more pain and humiliations than Jesus [did], all for you. Now we have our chance to accept all this for love of Him.[34]

Just think how much Mary loves Jesus. She always kept close to Him: in His humiliations when they wanted to stone Him and when they called Him Beelzebub, on the way to Calvary, when [He was] on the Cross, when they beat Him, nailed Him, spat on Him, made Him die as

a criminal—and Mary was not ashamed to own Him
at all times as her only love, as everything she had and
owned. She stood by Him. Do we stand by our poor in
their sufferings and humiliations?[35]

Why They and Not Me or You?

Abbe Pierre[36] came once to Nirmal Hriday. I think it
hurt him very much, he kept on saying, "Why they and
not me?" over and over again. When he went back to
France, he wrote a beautiful article entitled, "Why they
and not me or you?" When I visit the poor, it hurts me,
it must hurt you, if you are really the spouse of Jesus
Crucified. It is Christ Crucified, Calvary again, that is
why we [need] the penances, because we want to share
in the Passion of Jesus.[37]

HER EXAMPLE: The Testimonies

When someone was difficult or troublesome to Mother,
Mother went out of her way to be more loving to that
person.

All for Jesus

In Nirmal Hriday, many dying patients were sent by Calcutta Municipal Ambulance, and also MC sisters brought
them from the streets of Calcutta. Most of the days the

patients were dying. A group of people were writing in the newspaper that Mother is taking out the blood from the patients and because of this . . . many patients were dying. I asked Mother to protest about this, but she was quiet and calm. She told me, "This is all that God wants. One day these people will understand their mistake and they will be sorry for this." Mother's word came true. One of those people was suffering. That time nobody wanted to look after him, but universal Mother was always [there] for him. She gave him love and those people understood their Mother.[38]

❈

"Let the people criticize us, saying that Mother has a lot of money, but she has not built hospitals and nursing homes and things like that." Mother was above all that. She did not pay much attention to all this, nor did she allow us to dwell on such things. She would always make the sign of the Cross on her mouth and say, "All for Jesus." That was the word in her mouth: All for Jesus.[39]

Mother Forgave This Patient, Rehabilitated Him, and Helped His Family

One of our leprosy patients in Calcutta was violent with Mother at the Mother House gate. . . . One of our young neighbor boys saw this scene from his window. He came down, caught hold of [the man], and threatened him, and [the man] ran away at once. Mother forgave this patient, rehabilitated him, and helped his family.[40]

A Good Instruction on How to Be Kind

There was [an orphan boy] who also gave endless trouble at the Mother House pretty often. He too wanted only money, and when Mother refused, he went down to the parlor to break all the chairs. Mother went down to him and just looked at him. He stopped and asked pardon. But on another occasion, he came while the whole house was resting in the afternoon. He started giving trouble and ran and hid himself in the toilet in the novitiate quarters. A sister decided to call the police, and they came fast, but they did not leave fast enough. The bell rang to wake us up, and, like all of us, Mother was on her way to chapel. She looked down and saw the police and asked what it was all about. When she was told it was [the orphan boy], Mother was very upset. "Why did you not wake me up, instead of calling the police?" She went down to the police, took them aside, and spoke to them. "He is our boy, my child. He will not do it again, let him go free." Then turning to [him], Mother asked, "Is it not true?" and [he] shook his head to say, "Yes." The police took him outside the gate and set him free. But we professed sisters got a good instruction after our tea on how to be kind and forgiving even when our children and people are difficult.

A Very Ugly Letter Against Mother in the Newspapers

In a city of India, when the sisters opened a dispensary to serve the needs of the poor, a certain doctor began to lose some of his patients and became very angry with the sisters. In his anger, he wrote a very ugly letter against Mother in the newspapers. Mother went to this place, and, finding out from the sisters what had occasioned the article, Mother went to the doctor's residence and knocked on the door. What a shock for the doctor to find Mother at the door! Sweetly she said, "Doctor, I am Mother Teresa. I have come to tell you many things which you don't know about me." He invited her in, completely shaken. She did not tell us what else she said to him, but he became a Co-Worker and began to help the sisters in our dispensary.[41]

Don't Worry About Me

When Christopher Hitchens published his horrible documentary on Mother, called *Hell's Angel,* I was rather furious. . . . I called her up, and I said, "Mother, we are so sorry that something like this has happened," and I was burning with hatred, bitterness, revenge. How could somebody allow his own selfish motive to arrive at such a point where he could malign a person who is doing so much in the name of the Lord, and yet, being human he did it; and my concern for Mother Teresa: "Oh! How she must be feeling!" Her concern was, "But what's wrong with you? You should be praying for him; don't worry about me. We have to love him; we have to pray for him." I don't know, but this was one thing that was very public and her whole attitude was that we have to love him. We have to pray for him. So her life was a life of loving not only those who were close to her, but even those who were her enemies. . . . [Later] when I met Mother in Calcutta, she asked me if they were still speaking bad things about Mother. I said, "Oh no, Mother, that's all over," and Mother said to me, "If they did all kinds of things to Jesus and called Him Beelzebub, then who are we? All for Jesus through Mary," and she clasped my hands tightly. I will never forget that.[42]

❋

Whenever I told her, "Mother, they are saying this about you," she would say, "Everything is in the hands of Jesus. There is nothing to worry [about]."[43]

Don't Judge
Mother did not despise anybody, never accused anyone, and never blamed anyone. Rather, she always excused. She used to say, "We do not know the intention or situation that makes people fall. We cannot judge." She wrote, "One of the sins I have never had to confess: doubting the actions of any people, including you. Often I see wrong is being done and I can't say it is right, but why that person acts or speaks like that I don't know. This keeps me free from judging, what Jesus said" [Mt 7:1].

Let Us Pray for Them
Uncharitable talk was something she detested. If a sister began to complain about someone, Mother would immediately sign her own lips [with the sign of the Cross] to remind the sister to keep silent. When someone told her that she was being criticized or slandered, she would say, "Let us pray for them," and she sometimes even looked on it with humble

humor, laughing at herself. She would tell us sometimes, "Let us learn from it and correct ourselves where we have gone wrong."[44]

One time, two sisters had a terrible clash. Mother tried to make them see each other in a better light, but the one at greater fault poured out her anger on Mother using ugly words. She turned to run out the main door. Mother moved fast and held her most lovingly while trying to make her understand. I am convinced that the sister is still with us, a good, hardworking, loyal MC because of Mother.[45]

I Was Very Upset

I remember one time I was very upset and Mother noticed. She called me to her room and asked me, "What has happened? The sun has gone down before [its] time? It is only three o'clock." When I explained to her, she gave me a precious lesson to practice. She said, "You see, Jesus is burning in your heart in love. You love Him and He loves you. That burning love is there, but there is something missing. He needs some incense to complete the glory of God. This morning you prayed, 'Help me to spread Your fragrance,' so He provided the incense. It is up to you to pick it up and offer it to Him in gratitude. Give it to Him with all your love, and you will see the fragrance from Him within your heart. It cost Jesus to love you. You also must share in paying some price if you want to save souls in loving Jesus."[46]

Mother, One of the Babies Is Dying

I started looking at my watch and I said to her, "You know, Mother, if you want to take that plane, we've got to go." And she said, "Yes, you're right, I'm coming." So she stood up and made motions to leave, but then all the sisters had to be blessed again! I could feel my irritation rising; it was like, please, please let's get going! I kept trying to maneuver Mother toward the car, but then someone else would say something and distract her. Eventually we got there and I held the door open for her and really felt like just shoving her in, when suddenly the superior said, "Mother, one of the babies is dying." Mother stopped in her tracks and said, "Bring the child to me."

By now, I'm over-the-top, so to speak, and I exude this attitude of "we don't have time for dying babies. You have a plane to catch." I mean really! . . . Anyway, I'm not saying anything, but my body language, my tutting and sighing, says it all. Mother did not say to me, "You're being very rude and impatient. Stop it. Look what you're doing. I'm talking about a dying child. What is the matter with you?" Neither did she dismiss me with, "Move to the side if you're so annoyed. I'll catch the plane in my time." She didn't tell me off at all or point out my dreadful behavior. She just very lovingly put her hand on my arm and said, "I will come, but I need to see this child." With all my faults, in that moment, she took care of me too.

Mother must have seen Jesus in the distressing disguise of the badly mannered, because having bad manners is a form of poverty too. You know she didn't point out how rude I was being; she embraced me and held me in my rudeness, and the result was, I melted, I just melted. The tiny dying child was brought to her. Mother must have seen thousands of children in that state and yet she took time to pray and to tuck a little Miraculous Medal into the infant's clothing before getting into the car. It was an exquisite incident that I was privileged to witness and be a part of. It was not an act put on for my benefit—that was the way Mother was; so how many other exquisite simple acts of love must she have performed in her life? It's amazing to think about.[47]

A Difficult Sister

We had a sister who was difficult. . . . One day at lunch that particular sister said at the table that she didn't want to eat the food; she said that just by looking at the food she lost her appetite. We all felt embarrassed, but not Mother; she acted [like] a real mother. She made her eyes big and told one sister to get something else for her. Then Mother took up the conversation. When the sister came with the food, Mother smiled and then she remained at the table with the sister while we had to get up, as it was time already. Mother did not tell that sister to make [a] sacrifice and eat or to do what all of the rest of us did, etc. I saw that many times, that Mother loved the sisters unconditionally, . . . Mother trusted the sisters, and that she had great hope for each one of us, even the "poorest of the poor."[48]

Only Busy with Helping Her

On one occasion a sister was in trouble. Mother managed to get her to see the priest. While the sister was with Father,

Mother was pacing up and down the veranda, rosary in hand, obviously praying for that sister, not busy with the wrong or the suffering the sister had caused Mother, but only busy with helping her.[49]

Can't You Give Jesus Your Good Name?

Once feeling hurt and upset because a sister was speaking against me, I told Mother I could not manage anymore. I thought she would give [me] some sympathy or ask: how? who? what? etc. Mother's answer was a surprise. She looked intensely at me for a moment and said, "But can't you give Jesus your good name?" I then understood, a little, the level on which Mother functioned. She did not focus on difficulties, incidents, people as such—everything was Jesus. What is He telling me, asking from me, giving me? That is, Mother sought the deeper truth in the situation—the Truth of Love—and she responded in that Truth. That is why when one asked Mother how to be really holy, the answer was invariably the same: "Take what He gives and give what He takes with a big smile." That's how, it seems, she could be twenty-four hours with Jesus—in love—and make her life something beautiful for God. To live like this consistently would require *heroic faith*.[50]

Only Your Kindness Will Help

One priest was giving us a hard time in the mission. When Mother came to visit us, we told Mother about him. Mother told us, "God put him here that you may love him and be kind to him. Be careful not to speak uncharitably about him, but help him and be kind to him. He is the poorest of the poor now." I have never heard Mother speaking about or against anyone even when it is true. I spoke to Mother about a person, and she immediately made me stop. She would say, "Be kind to her. Only your kindness will help her."[51]

The Boy Managed to Pull Out the Money from My Bag

At Christmas[time], while in the market, I found a very miserable and malnourished boy there. I was so happy [that he would] be our Christmas gift, and I must take him home. As I walked, the boy followed me. While I was trying to pick up the fish, the same boy managed to pull out the envelope with 960 rupees from my bag. I saw the boy running, and I could hardly believe it was done by the same boy. Seeing my anxiety, people made a search in the whole bazaar but could not trace the boy. In all my sorrow, I canceled the [shopping] and went home and asked pardon from my community. . . . I presumed [that as] restitution I would carry that many buckets of water from the main tank to the toilet tank. . . . Meanwhile, I wrote to Mother explaining everything. In February, there was a retreat in Mother House. With trembling and fear, I went to Mother; once more I narrated the whole story. Mother listened to me so beautifully and said a sentence beyond my expectation. "Never mind, Sister, that boy might have been in need of that money." Never a word of judgment, or condemnation of that boy, or finding fault [with] my careless ways.[52]

The Power of Mother's Love

There was a lot of trouble in Calcutta because of the unrest among Hindus and Muslims. At noon Mother and I were going out to Park Street. Before we reached Park Circus, we saw a big gang of people, with stones, and sticks, knives, swords. . . . They were trying to destroy many houses. From far [away], Mother lifted up both her hands and asked the driver to [blow the] horn. People noticed that Mother was inside the vehicle. They all threw away the stones, etc., and came running to the car. As they came close to the car, Mother joined both her hands. She never uttered a word to them. She showed them a sign with both her hands for them to go back. They all touched Mother's feet, took her blessing, and returned like lambs. Mother waited till all the people had gone back. That day I realized the power of Mother's love, which brings peace to troubled hearts. I was wondering why Mother did not speak a word to them. Then I realized Mother's own sentence, "If I speak I have to stand by one, not by all, and then I get stuck with politics and stop loving." Mother was very wise; she knew when to speak, and when not to speak, and her action in this moment was accepted as a sign of her love and a cause of peace.[53]

Meet Our People in the Home

The government of Assam was giving Mother a large plot of land for AIDS patients. The chief minister insisted Mother should come to accept the land. In the afternoon, when Mother [arrived], a huge crowd had come to meet Mother and take her blessing, etc. A well-dressed lady came in, started to talk all kinds of things against the work, against the poor, as if all that we were doing was useless. Mother gently patted her and said, "I have nothing to say to you, but I want you definitely to go around and meet our people in the Home, and then I will meet you." After some time, the lady returned. She was weeping profusely and she told Mother, "I came empty hearted, and I go back with a heart full of satisfaction. Mother, my hands are empty; I have nothing to contribute toward your work." She then broke the thick gold chain from her neck, removed the locket that was the symbol of her marriage, kept it aside, and the chain she placed in Mother's hands, saying, "Mother, please don't refuse me; you must accept this." Mother took it graciously. And Mother led her to the parlor and spent some time with her. She was a changed person altogether. Her life was changed by the invitation of Mother that she visit the Home before she [said] anything.[54]

My Son

There was a leprosy patient who was giving a lot of trouble to the sisters. For three days he would lie down near the gate, not allowing our vehicle nor the sisters to go out. He was throwing stones and broke the window of the vehicle, etc. . . . He was very dissatisfied, and we could not give in to his unreasonable demands. When we were in this desperate situation, Mother arrived there, with some visitors from Calcutta. As soon as Mother arrived, all our other patients went and told Mother everything. Mother got down from the ambulance and spoke to [the leprosy patient] kindly. She said, "My son, I am going to take you with me to Calcutta, and I will [settle you in] Titagarh with the brothers." The man immediately got up; he touched Mother's feet, took her blessings, and got ready to go with Mother without a word. Mother took the visitors around, spent some time with the sisters, and went back to Calcutta, and our patient also got into the car with Mother and went with her like a little lamb. All of us were awestruck at the way Mother handled the situation.[55]

Leave the VIP Enclosure

The Holy Father came to [India]. For the Mass of the Holy Father, Mother was in the VIP area in the front row. Then the bishop's secretary came and told Mother to [leave] the VIP enclosure. All the sisters who were sitting with her felt very bad. But Mother immediately got up from there and went back. It was the pro-nuncio and the cardinals who had taken her to the VIP enclosure, even though the bishop [had not given] her a VIP pass. When the Holy Father came on the stage, he noticed Mother was not in the front row, and he asked Mother to come right up front to the first row. And Mother came back to the first place. All the sisters were very angry with the bishop because we felt that the bishop wanted to humiliate Mother, who was not in the least affected by all this. When the bishop's birthday came, Mother went with all the sisters to wish the bishop a Happy Birthday. She gave us all a chance to make up with the bishop.[56]

Mother Apologized

Once Sister A. and I went to pick up Mother from [the airport]. There Sister brought a new book. In the car I was reading that book. Mother told me gently, "Do not read that book without permission." Sister A. said, "Mother, she asked permission." In the house, I was standing alone and Mother took that chance and apologized for correcting me without asking first. I was really impressed.[57]

REFLECTION

"Put on then, as God's chosen ones, holy and
beloved, compassion, kindness, lowliness,
meekness, and patience, forbearing one another
and, if one has a complaint against another,
forgiving each other; as the Lord has forgiven you,
so you also must forgive." (Col 3:12–13)

"Accept what He gives—give what He takes—with
a big smile."[58]

Do I make connections with the wrongs I bear and the wrongs Jesus bore for me on the Cross?

Do I consider the immense wrongs done to the poor, the humiliations and privations? What are the wrongs done to me in comparison to the wrongs they suffer?

Am I aware that I might be doing something that can be an annoyance or a bother to others? Do I realize that I might lack thoughtfulness toward others, that I might be trying to them (for example, having a loud conversation when someone is trying to work or study, being too noisy when someone is trying to rest)? Am I so busy with myself that I cannot think about others' needs?

How do I react when others show a lack of thoughtfulness toward me?

What wrongs can I bear patiently, including those small offenses, which Saint Thérèse of Lisieux called "pinpricks," that do no more than produce personal discomfort or inconvenience for me?

Can I accept that I am being overlooked? That I am not given due consideration?

PRAYER

Lord, make me a channel of Your peace,
that where there is hatred, I may bring love;
where there is wrong,
I may bring the spirit of forgiveness;
where there is discord, I may bring harmony;
where there is error, I may bring truth;
where there is doubt, I may bring faith;
where there is despair, I may bring hope;
where there are shadows, I may bring light;
where there is sadness, I may bring joy.

Lord, grant that I may seek rather
to comfort than to be comforted;
to understand than to be understood;

to love than to be loved;
for it is by forgetting self that one finds,
it is by forgiving that one is forgiven,
it is by dying that one awakens to
eternal life.
Amen.

—Saint Francis's prayer,
prayed by Mother Teresa daily after Holy Communion

TWELVE

FORGIVE OFFENSES WILLINGLY

Mother Teresa's capacity to forgive was one of her qualities that impressed even those who did not share her religious convictions. Coming from an Albanian culture in which "blood feuds" were traditional, she knew well how terribly difficult it can be to forgive and the devastating effects of failing to forgive. It was said of her that she had a "biblical faith"; this faith gave her the motivation and strength to forgive those who offended her in some way, big or small.

One of the principal reasons that she was so forgiving was that she was aware of her own sinfulness and need for God's mercy and forgiveness. She also knew that she could be hurting others unintentionally, and that she would be happy to receive forgiveness.

Whether the offense was small or great, Mother Teresa was willing to overlook it rather than seek revenge or distance herself from the offender; she likewise refused to harbor resentment or keep a grudge. She went even further: she was concerned for the one who hurt her, for their emotional and spiritual well-being, which had been compromised because of the wrong they had done.

"Be the first one to say sorry," she would advise her sisters, being herself usually the one to take the first steps toward reconciliation, even when she was the one who had been wronged. And if the other party persisted in their ill will (as was the case, for example, with some of her more adamantly unjust critics), she would forgive and pray for that person.

"Have the love to forgive and the humility to forget" was her advice when anyone was faced with any offense. There are hurts that one might not be able to literally forget, but the desire to "forget" was the expression of her desire to "wipe it out" from her mind, leaving the rest to God. She would then act as if nothing had happened with that person and show even greater kindness.

Clearly, there are offenses that demand justice and reparation, but what we often deal with are "pinpricks," the little injuries that we inflict on each other due to our selfishness, pride, or thoughtlessness. Mother Teresa wanted to avoid exaggerating these little hurts that are part of daily life, because these wrongs can very easily be blown up into larger issues, leading us to become resentful or hold a grudge. Even because of little things, relationships can be ruined.

HER WORDS

God's Mercy Is Much Greater
Even on the Cross He has nothing to say but words of
forgiveness, "Father, forgive them, they know not what
they do."[1] The Passion of Christ is the surest proof of the
humility of God.[2]

※

If something happens, if we should fall, let us remember
that the Father is a merciful Father. He will always
forgive.[3]

※

We must pray that the mistake is not made. But when
the mistake has been made, God's mercy is much greater
than the mistake. God will forgive.[4]

※

I think [about] what it means that God will not destroy
[sinners]—every sinner is a bruised reed—and God will
not destroy them [Is 42:3], because God's mercy
is much greater than all that the bruised reed can be.
And I think, I always take that as we [are] sinners before
God and yet He will never destroy us; He will always
have that tremendous, tender mercy for each one of us.[5]

※

We have to implore God to forgive sins: our own
and the sins of others. We may offer everything for

the conversion of sinners. The value of the Precious Blood is infinite. Let us be united with Him in our work. Every drop of the Precious Blood may cover everything in our daily life; so we offer [everything] to Christ, Our Lord.[6]

To Be Able to Pray We Need to Forgive

To be able to pray we need to forgive. Then our hearts will be free to pray. And we must really pray and make many sacrifices to create peace in our own house first. We cannot work for peace, nor give peace, if we do not have that peace in our own hearts. That is why many things are made to destroy life; it is because peace is destroyed in [our] own hearts. Just as we have love in action, so we also have destruction in action.[7]

※

Suffering makes it important, first of all, that we pray, because we need courage to forgive. And to be able to forgive we need lots of love in our hearts. Forgive! And also we must know that we need to be forgiven. And for that we need a humble heart. So humility and love will help us to forgive each other; and instead of hurting each other we will begin to love each other and to see what is beautiful in each other. Every one of us has something beautiful. If we only take the trouble to see it, we will be able to love that person—even that person who hurts us most. If we have a free heart, we will be able to forgive that person.[8]

When somebody fights with you, you should always
forgive; and if you are the one who is fighting, there is
a time to say that you are sorry. And if someone fights
with you, you must forgive that person, and you must
not keep any grudge against that person. That's what
Jesus told us, to love one another.[9]

Make your family something beautiful for God in love,
peace, unity, and joy. Even if you pray ten minutes
together, it is worthwhile. It is worthwhile. Get together,
always together, always together, even when you have
misunderstandings, get together. Forgive and forget and
you will be really filled with God's love, really have the
peace of God in your heart. This is very, very important,
especially nowadays when there is much turmoil
in the world, all over the world, all over the world,
everywhere—so much pain, so much suffering.[10]

Say Sorry to Each Other

First of all, I think we have to say sorry to each other, to
forgive each other, to ask for forgiveness and to forgive.
Unless we are free from anything that is holding us back,
we cannot be free to love. Love is freedom, and we must
love until it hurts. And we can do that only if we pray,
for prayer will give us a clean heart, and a clean heart
can see the face of God. When we see God's face in each

other, we will be able to live in peace and happiness, for what we have been created, to love and to be loved.[11]

✳

In the Gospel, we often see one word, *"Come,* come to me *all"* [Mt 11:28]. "He that cometh to me I will not cast out" [Jn 6:37]. "Suffer little children to come to me" [Lk 18:16]. Always ready to receive, to forgive, to love. And to make sure that we understand what He means—[Jesus] says, "Amen, Amen, I say to you, as long as you did it to one of these My least brethren, you did it to Me." . . . One thing that will always secure Heaven for us [are the] acts of charity and kindness with which we have filled our lives. We will never know how much good just a simple smile can do. We tell people how kind, forgiving, and understanding God is—are we the living proof? Can they really see this kindness, this forgiveness, this understanding alive in us? . . . Be kind and merciful. Let no one ever come to you without coming away better, happier. Be the living expression of God's kindness. Everybody should see kindness in your face, in your eyes, in your smile, in your warm greeting. In the slums, we are the light of God's kindness to [the people].[12]

Forgive and Love

Our Holy Father has proclaimed the holy year as a Year of Reconciliation. The word sounds long but it really means: *forgive and love.* Reconciliation begins not first with others, but with ourselves: by allowing Jesus to

clean us—to forgive us, to love us. It starts by having a
clean heart within. A clean heart always forgives and is
able to see God in others and so love them. . . . Forgive
and ask to be forgiven: Excuse rather than accuse. Do
not go to bed when you remember "that your sister has
something against you," as Jesus said. Even if we are not
guilty, still let us take the first step of reconciliation.[13]

✳

Today I want to speak to you about forgiveness. I beg
of you, sisters, forgive one another and ask pardon
from one another. There is so much suffering and
unhappiness because of unforgiveness. . . . Remember,
sisters, in the Our Father we say, "Forgive us our sin as
we forgive." If you do not forgive, you are not forgiven.
Look deep down in your heart. Is there any bitterness
against any person? Then try to find that person or
write to that person—maybe a sister or a poor person
or someone at home. Forgive. Otherwise you are not
free to love Jesus with an undivided love. Do not keep
any bitterness in your heart. There are so many who
can't forgive. Some say, "I forgive, but I can't forget."
Confession is forgiveness—the kind of forgiveness that
God gives—and we must learn that kind of forgiveness.
So many years ago someone said this or did that, and so
I say, "She said this, she . . . and she . . . and she . . ."[14]

✳

In one place there was a priest who was against the
bishop and priests for some reason. There was so much
bitterness in his speech each time I visited him, and he

said to me, "I will not forgive. I won't." This time when I went, I told him, "This is your chance; say sorry to your bishop. That is the only word the bishop wants from you." And I was praying and the sisters were all praying inside. When I finished the prayer, he said, "Mother Teresa, give me paper." So I gave him the paper and I was so happy. I took him to the bishop and gave him the paper; otherwise he might change his mind, and I told him, "This is not enough; say 'I forgive' "—and he did.[15]

✳

We need much love to forgive, but we need much more humility to ask for forgiveness. And this forgiving and asking to [be] forgiven is [what] Jesus taught us when he taught us to say the Our Father. "Forgive us our trespasses as we forgive those who trespass against us," and this is for us life. This is the joy of loving.[16]

✳

When you come to that part in the Our Father, stop and ask yourself, "Is it true what I am saying?" I think Jesus suffered much more just hanging from that Cross. He said, "Learn from Me for I am meek and humble of heart" [Mt 11:29]. You cannot be meek, you cannot be humble, if you don't forgive. It is not necessary to have a big thing to destroy us. Examine [yourself]: if I'm not able to see God—why?[17]

✳

Don't say, "I'll forgive, but I can't forget." When
Jesus forgives in confession, He forgets. Don't say a
lie—when you ask pardon and when you don't give
forgiveness. Unforgiveness is the greatest sin of pride.
Ask forgiveness and give forgiveness.[18]

✳

If I forgive, then I can be holy and I can pray. . . . All
this comes from a humble heart, and if we have this we
will know how to love God, to love self, and [to love
our] neighbor. You see in this is simple love for Jesus.
There are no complications and yet we complicate our
lives so much, by so many additions. Just one thing
counts: to be humble, to pray. The more you pray,
the better you pray. How do you pray? You should go
to God like a little child. A child has no difficulty in
expressing his little mind in simple words, but they
express so much. Jesus said to Nicodemus, "Become
as a little child." If we pray the Gospel, we will allow
Christ to grow in us. So one thing is necessary for us—
confession. Confession is nothing but humility in action.
We call it penance, but really it is a sacrament of love, a
sacrament of forgiveness. That is why it should not be
a place of talking for long hours about our difficulties.
It is a place where I allow Jesus to take away from me
everything that divides, that destroys. When there is a
gap between me and Christ and my love is divided, then
anything can come to fill up the gap. If you really want
to understand the love of Christ for us, go to confession.
Be very simple and childlike in confession: "Here I am

as a child—going to her Father." If a child is not yet
spoiled and has not learned to tell lies, he will [confess]
everything. This is what I mean by "childlike" and this
is what we must imitate in confession.[19]

✷

During the day, share very often in the Passion of Christ.
I'm sure you will get all the graces to be holy if you are
faithful to that total surrender. Even if you have made
a mistake and have been uncharitable, say sorry. The
moment you say sorry you can be forgiven.[20]

✷

Jesus has called you by name—"You are Mine"—"You
are precious to Me"—"I love you." If He is like that
with Me, He must be like that with my sister also. She
too has been called, and [she too] is the spouse of Jesus
Christ. I'm repeating myself again and again, because
for me, the way I understand it, those words "I belong
to Him" mean that even if I sin—He accepts me as I
am. Then why do I keep that grudge against my sister
in my heart? If I have not forgiven my sister, then I have
not understood His love for me. Look at the Cross and
see where are you. Jesus need not have died like that,
need not have been born to go through that agony in
Gethsemane.[21]

Is There Unforgiveness in My Heart?

How can you carry any ugliness against your sisters
when you have to carry Jesus? Open your heart to that
sister—ask her to forgive you. This is the best confession
you can make. You will only be able to forgive and
forget if you have given back to her the burden of your
hurt in love. Unforgiveness will prevent you from giving
love. Only if you are able to forgive will you be able to
fulfill that Gospel of "Love one another as I have loved
you." Only then will you be able to love God with your
whole heart.[22]

※

Whatever I do, I do it for Jesus. When we pray, when we
begin to pray, we do it for Jesus. What is your love and
respect for the poor? That harshness becomes a slap for
Jesus. Sometimes we can't forgive, even once: "She has
called me bad names." Jesus could destroy everything
with one word. He forgave. Not forgiving can destroy
you for life. We keep on thinking of that word that
sister said, but we need to acknowledge our sin, to be
able to forgive. We must forgive—don't wait. Is there
unforgiveness in my heart? It's an obstacle for life. When
it's too late, nothing can be done.[23]

※

My brother had a little pimple here, and within a
short time the cancer had become a big root—after
just three months. The same thing happens for us
with unforgiveness. Don't believe the devil. Get it out.

Maybe you have a grudge against your superior, maybe against your sisters, maybe against your parents. As a novice, as a junior, the devil will come to you with very beautiful ideas. Don't allow the devil to cheat you. What a wonderful gift you will give to Jesus on your wedding day—a pure heart.[24]

✳

If there is still something in your heart [against a sister] and that sister is far away, go to the tabernacle, ask Him to touch the heart of that sister. Let her feel that you have forgiven her. We are sent to be God's love—God loves the world today, we are sent to be God's love.[25]

✳

You all had superiors. Sometimes they tell you things that are not nice, maybe the way they say it is not nice. Did you accept it? Maybe a change of place, a change of work, a change of partner, a change of food, and so on. If only you can accept, there will be no difficulty. But you do not accept, and then there is so much difficulty and so much bitterness in the heart. There isn't that total forgiveness. Show me a bitter sister and I will show you a proud sister. A bitter sister is always a proud sister also. Bitterness and pride are twin sisters—moodiness goes with it. A humble sister will not be bitter nor moody.[26]

Wonderful Experience of Forgiveness

That lady who came and taught hymns—her grown-up
children sent her to India to have a holiday, just to forget
her troubles. What happened? After thirty-five years of
oneness with her husband, that love and fidelity, where
has it all gone? She told me that her husband has such a
big position; he is the best surgeon. . . . Now he told her
that he doesn't want her anymore, because somebody,
another woman, is after him. She came to ask my
advice, and I told her that "only you can save him; your
prayers and sacrifices can bring him back to you. He still
loves you, so you forgive him and pray for him."27

※

I had a wonderful experience and example of forgiveness.
A family—a husband and wife—were not happy for
many years. They were fed up with each other, so they
planned to go each their own way. The sisters visited
them and prayed. And when I went there, the sisters told
me about them. So I called for both. They came. The
wife cried and cried, but her crying did not do the action
[of asking for forgiveness], only when she said, "I ask
your pardon," and he said the same thing, "I ask your
forgiveness." She was looking at him smiling and he was
looking at her smiling. For the last few years, they were
just hurting each other, but that day they were so happy
and went [home]. Next day evening—they came again
to see me and I was so happy. Both looked at each other
and were smiling again.28

※

There is another story of a man who had so many sins
and did not make confession for many years. One day he
decided to make his confession. So he wrote four pages
full, all the sins of his past life, and he went to make
his confession. Page after page he read. After reading
the fourth page, he thought, "Maybe I have left out
something." So he looked back onto the first page. He
found it was clean and empty. Nothing was there. Then
he looked onto all the pages. Something had happened.
He was so happy and he told his story of confession
to others. We receive this kind of forgiveness from
God, and we need to forgive others with this kind of
forgiveness.[29]

Forgive Me, Forgive Me

We have opened a house in New York for AIDS, and
these are the people of today who are the unwanted.
But what a tremendous change has come in their lives
just because those few sisters are taking care of them,
because they have made a home for them, a home of
love, a gift of love; that they are wanted, that they are
somebody to somebody, changed their life in such a
way that they die the most beautiful death. Not one has
died distressed. The other day Sister told me that one
of the young men (all are young people), and one of the
young ones, was dying and couldn't die, so she asked
him, "What is it? You are struggling with death, what
is happening to you?" And he said, "Sister, I cannot
die until I ask pardon from my father." And so Sister

found out where the father was and she brought him. And something most extraordinary [happened]: living gospel, the father embracing his son, "My son, my loved one," the son begging his father, "Forgive me, forgive me," and the two of them clinging to each other in tender love. After two hours, the boy died. See what love can do. Father's love, child's love. So this is [a reason] for us to open our hearts to God, because we have all been—every one of us—that man in the street, that person there, this one, that one—everybody has been created for greater things, to love and to be loved. And if in the world today we are [seeing] so much suffering, so much killing, so much pain, it's [because people] have lost that joy of loving God in their hearts. And because that has gone, they cannot share that love with others.[30]

My Own Son Did This to Me

I remember once finding an old woman in a dustbin, burning with fever. She was much bigger than I, so I had trouble getting her out of the bin. But with Jesus helping, I managed to do it. As I was taking her to our home, she did not say a single word about her terrible fever or great pain, or the fact that she was dying. No, the only thing she kept saying was "My son did this to me! It was my own son who did this to me!" She was so bitterly hurt by the fact that her own son had thrown her away that I had to work very hard, and it took me a long time to help her finally to say that she forgave him. She said it just before she died. . . . And if you could love

and console even one person suffering like this, it would
be a wonderful thing, because that person again is Jesus
in his painful disguise.[31]

I Forgive Him Because of God's Love

A man in Poona wrote in the paper many ugly things.
He called me a hypocrite, a religious politician, [he
accused me of] making others Catholic, and about the
Nobel Peace Prize and many other bigger adjectives.
I wrote back to him that I felt sorry for him. I really
feel sorry for him because he hurt himself much more
than he hurt me, and I believe that many people wrote
to him ugly letters because of what he had said. It
was written in the newspapers: Mr. R. calls Mother
Teresa "Hypocrite." I wrote back to him that I forgive
him because of God's love, and I invited him to come
and see Shishu Bhavan. When he got that letter, he
got more angry and began to write many more things.
He called me "Mister," so I was thinking of calling
him . . . "Miss." It was again written in the newspaper:
"It is not that she is not sincere, she is very sincere, but
she is leading the people the wrong way. She is still a
hypocrite." You see, sisters, we must accept. That man
got very angry because I said, "God bless you, I forgive
you." So, sisters, when you are scolded, forgive and you
will be all right anywhere. If I had used other words, I
would have lost the chance of giving God's love, God's
joy. . . . We must become holy at any cost. Mother
receives many humiliations—more than you do—but I
think they are beautiful chances.[32]

I Begged His Forgiveness

A few days ago a Hindu man came to the Mother
House. Every month, he makes many little sacrifices—
two dollars, two and a half dollars—and he brings it to
the Mother House—not much, because he is poor. His
father had died and he was very sad. He had gathered up
all the leftover medicines and came. I was in my room
because I was not feeling well. The sister told him just to
put the medicine down there on the floor. He was very
shocked. Another sister came to me and begged me to
see him because he was so depressed. When I came, he
told me, "Mother, in the whole of my life I have never
received this kind of rudeness; she was so harsh, she
hurt me so much." I joined my hands and begged his
forgiveness, [said that I regretted] that it had happened
in our house, and I took his medicines in my hands.
He kept his eyes looking wherever that sister went and
repeated, "I'm sorry, Mother, but I had to tell you." I
was ashamed that it had happened in our house. The
man left with a sad face. I called that sister and told
her, "If you had been a little more gentle and kind, you
would not have blocked the way of Jesus to that man."
She said, "Mother, I am sorry, I will not do it again."
But that man had gone away, he never heard those
words; the words she had spoken to him before could
not be taken back. For life that harshness will remain
with him. I beg of you, sisters, if you have a hot temper,
control it.[33]

HER EXAMPLE: The Testimonies

Always Ready to Forgive

Each and every individual whether good or bad is acceptable to Mother. Her attitude of openness, understanding, accepting, forgiving, and encouraging [a person] to do better—there is always one more chance to do better with Mother just like [with] the Heart of Jesus. We always try to draw a line: seven times like Saint Peter; but with Mother it is always seventy times seven. Mother had been criticized for this, much.[34]

Don't Hurt Jesus

Mother Teresa was very patient, and even if she met with ill treatment from the sisters as she sometimes did, she would always say, "I forgive. Don't hurt Jesus." She didn't think so much of getting hurt, but of hurting Jesus.

❋

There were so many misunderstanding complaints [about me], but Mother was always ready to forgive just like Jesus, always with a smile. Not once [did] she discourage me. Mother was always there, no one understood but Mother. When the heart is full of sorrow, you go to Mother, [she] just looks into your eyes and automatically everything vanishes. No matter what crime you committed. Only be open to her and she was there to help and solve the problem with her forgiving love and compassion.[35]

✳

If we had done something wrong, we could go to Mother and say sorry. She would forgive and forget at once, and never bring it up again, even if we committed the same fault again and again. In Mother there was always the forgiving and forgetting. Mother, at the beginning, never neglected to correct us. And sometimes her corrections were quite strong. She wanted us to grow spiritually. As the years went on, we found Mother more gentle in her corrections and more quick to forget and forgive. Mother always used to tell us, "Don't hurt Jesus. He loves you." This helped us a lot. When there were difficult moments, we could see Mother praying all the more. She never left or ran away from the difficulty to pray in the chapel. No, Mother, in a second, would become so closely united to God and overcome the difficulties. We knew she received the answer from God. We could feel that Mother was united to God all the while, always attuned to the will of God with joy. We, who lived with Mother, saw how she never gave up loving Jesus with that deep personal love.[36]

Whenever We Made a Mistake

Sister X was very sick. Sister Z and I were sitting on a wooden bed and were talking to Sister X. And one more sister came and sat on the bed, and the bed broke. Now we were very afraid to go and tell Mother that we had broken the bed. Those days Mother had no money; we just had enough money to live on. One by one we went to Mother and spoke our fault. Mother did not scold us; she was very kind. She only said, "Next time do not sit on the bed and break it." Mother used to correct us when we did something wrong. But whenever we made a mistake and owned up to it and said sorry, she was very forgiving and understanding.[37]

What Happened, My Child?

In the novitiate I had a fear of Mother. One day my mistress punished me. She sent me to Mother. When I went near Mother, she asked, "What happened, my child?" Then I said, "Mother, my mistress told me to see you because I did not do my homework." Then Mother did not scold me at all. She gave me her blessing and told me, "Next time do the homework," and she sent me back. From that day my fear went away completely. I knew Mother has a really loving heart.[38]

I Could Trust Mother

I was having a hard time dealing with the guilt and shame [of] a sin I had committed. I knew without a doubt I could trust Mother to keep my secret and to continue to love, accept, and respect me even though I had disappointed Mother, but I knew I could trust Mother to not condemn, reject, or humiliate me. After I told Mother the whole story, Mother first asked if anybody knew about it, and I told her only the priests who heard my confessions. Mother looked at me with such love and tenderness in her eyes. She said: "Jesus forgives you and Mother forgives you. Jesus loves you and Mother loves you. Jesus just wanted to show you your poverty. Now, when a sister comes to you with the same thing, you will have compassion for her." I asked Mother not to tell anyone, and she promised she would not in such a tender way. Mother never asked me: "Why did you do that? How could you do that?" Mother never said: "Aren't you ashamed? You caused such a scandal." Mother never even said: "Do not do that again." As I thought of and prayed over my meeting with Mother, I cried all the more and was filled with peace and gratitude. I went back to Mother the next day and thanked her for the great lesson she taught me. I told Mother all the things she never asked me. Mother beamed with joy and said: "See, I never thought of that; I just said what came to me." Mother blessed me again with great affection and I went my way with a happy heart.[39]

The Prodigal Mother

Once when a group of us (novice mistresses) were having instruction from Mother, a sister knocked at the door to say that Sister so-and-so had come. We knew she had been in a lot of trouble, and I was wondering how Mother would act. As soon as the sister came in, she knelt down crying, and Mother blessed her and welcomed her with such love that she could not say a word, and then turning to us she told us to go and get her a cup of tea: *The Prodigal Mother.*[40]

I Forgive Him

[In India, there was a TV program because of] Christopher Hitchens's first TV program, which I saw. I told [Mother] about it. I have to say her first reaction was that of anguish. And she said to me, "I have done so much work in this country. Is there nobody who will speak up for me?" And it was then that the seed was born in my mind that I had to do something. She had through her prayerfulness overcome this. The next time I mentioned this to her when I met her, she said, "I forgive him." It was an incident that [she had put out of] her mind. She had forgiven him completely. It was as if she didn't know, like a child, what he had said. So she had risen above it.[41]

We Make Mistakes

When we were in Ethiopia, a lady came and videotaped our children's home, when we were not there. And then she put all our work on the television as though it was her work. People started to call us and ask: "What happened? Are you going away?" So we said, "No, we are not going." We came to understand this particular lady had made this program on TV as her own. We had a meeting with the president. Mother came and Mother said, "Sisters, forgive her. She did not know what she was doing. We have to learn to forgive. We make mistakes, people make mistakes." So she had forgiveness for everything.[42]

God Has Forgiven Me

We once discovered a man from the slums who was dying, but he was very bitter. He was a Catholic, but he was unwilling to see anyone, not even his family. We tried to talk to him a little; he smiled and asked us who had sent us to him. Then, in the course of our conversation, we told him that he needed to have a clean heart in order to go to heaven.

For this he needed to forgive everyone, even his own wife and children, because God also forgives us without keeping any account of our misdeeds. He agreed by nodding his head that he approved of what we had said, but he was reluctant to see a priest so as to make his confession. We felt sorry for him and we prayed our Rosary on the way home. We told Mother, "This man is going to die, but he refuses confession." Mother asked us, "How old is he?" We said: "About forty-five." Then Mother said, "Let us offer forty-five rosaries to Our Lady . . . for this man so that he may accept making his peace with God." We divided the number of forty-five between three of us and Mother.

The next day when the Rosaries we had promised to Our Lady had been completed, Mother asked us to visit him again. He told us that he would like to make his peace with God, and that he had not been to confession in a long time. On our way back to the convent, we stopped in St. Teresa's Church to give to Father a little note with the man's name and the name of the hospital. In two days we visited [the man] again and he was so happy. He asked us to bring his family to visit him. He said, "God has forgiven me and I want to forgive my people completely." We came home with such joy to tell Mother. We thanked Our Lady together for this great gift of peace to this dying man.[43]

If We Would Have Been in Their Situation

As Mother wanted to see most of Albania for the sake of foundations, we went a lot by car. Many times along the road there were crowds of people who had come to greet Mother, whom they all considered to be "their Mother."

Whole villages came out to meet her. Mother stopped and prayed with them, gave out medals. Mother remained so small, so calm, so silent, as they were crying out: "Long live our Mother," etc. Even when single persons recognized her (as she was sitting in the front of the car) and waved to her, she asked to stop so as to greet the person, always with the same love and calmness. She never refused anyone. When we told Mother about the stealing and cheating that was going on in Albania, Mother said: "If we would have been in their situation, we would have been worse."[44]

REFLECTION

"So if you are offering your gift at the altar, and there remember that your brother has something against you, leave your gift there before the altar and go; first be reconciled to your brother, and then come and offer your gift." (Mt 5:23–24)

"Sisters, receive forgiveness to give forgiveness."[45]

"If someone fights with you, you must forgive that person, and you must not keep any grudge against that person. That's what Jesus told us, to love one another."[46]

Am I aware that I stand in front of God as a sinner in need of forgiveness and mercy? Do I realize that God forgives me and calls me to forgive others?

Is there a person in my life whom I hold a grudge against and do not want to forgive?

Did I allow a small offense to grow out of proportion, and because of a trivial matter have I refused communication with a family member or friend? At times I might have even forgotten what the real issue was (or maybe I now realize that it was not as serious as I considered it at the time), but now my relationship with that person is broken or injured and the gap between us seems unsurmountable. Is there not a way to bring about reconciliation? What steps can I take to bridge the gap (e.g., send a message, extend an invitation for a meal and talk over what took place years ago) and reestablish the relationship? Can I show kindness to the person who offended me?

If someone has committed a serious offense against me and I am still holding a grudge and feel unable to forgive, can I do something concrete to move toward forgiveness? Can I at least pray for the grace to forgive and/or pray for the person who injured me?

PRAYER

O Jesus! grant that you may be
the object of my thoughts and affections,
the subject of my conversations, the end of my actions,
the model of my life, my support in death,
and my reward eternally in your heavenly Kingdom.
Amen.

—MC *prayer book, prayed daily by Mother Teresa*

THIRTEEN

COMFORT THE AFFLICTED

"I looked for one who would comfort Me, but there was no one" (Ps 69:20), was a reference to Jesus's Passion that Mother Teresa often quoted. She used to exhort her sisters: "Tell Jesus, 'I will be the one.' I will comfort, encourage, and love Him. . . . Be with Jesus. He prayed and prayed, and then He went to look for consolation, but there was none. . . . Try to be the one to share with Him, to comfort Him, to console Him." As she was eager to console Jesus, so she was eager to comfort those who were in need of comfort; in each of the afflicted, she saw Jesus in His distressing disguise pleading for consolation.

Mother Teresa was a person with a strong character and great determination, but at the same time, she was tender-hearted and moved by others' pain and sufferings. Frequently, when faced with much suffering, either our own or that of those around us, we tend to close—"harden"—our hearts in order to "protect ourselves" and not get too personally involved. As useful and legitimate as this may be, when we close our hearts, we are not reflecting how God's Heart works, how it goes out to those who are in pain. Mother Teresa wanted her heart to reflect God's Heart.

Mother Teresa was deeply moved by each person's suffering, and for this reason she was able to offer comfort at a very profound level, "getting at the people's heart." Whenever people with diverse forms of suffering came to her for comfort, she was ready to offer a word of consolation, a smile, and at times nothing else but a promise of prayers. And people would leave her consoled and with renewed hope, and with the ability to see a brighter future. This was not due to her words, which were in fact very simple and unassuming. Rather, it was the compassion that she had in her heart for the afflicted that made the difference, her heart-to-heart communication. By entering into their suffering, she was able to "love until it hurts," as she used to say.

"Comforter of the Afflicted" is one of the titles of Our Lady given in the Litany of Loreto. Mother Teresa's daily prayer to Mary was "give us your heart, so beautiful, so pure, so immaculate," and it was at the school of Mary that she learned to have a compassionate heart and to reach out with love and comfort to those who were afflicted in body or in spirit.

HER WORDS

Face yourself: Do you really love Jesus? Am I the one to comfort Him? You have all seen the picture of Christ in His Passion where it says, "I looked for one who would comfort

Me, but there was no one," and Mother wrote on it, "Be the one." Are you really the one? Can He really turn to you for comfort? Are you the one He can rely on especially today in this turmoil of sin? Are we that comfort, that consolation?[1]

Bringing Jesus to Suffering People

The Jesus who becomes bread to satisfy our hunger also becomes that naked person, that homeless and lonely and unwanted person, that leper or drunkard or drug addict or prostitute, so that we can satisfy His hunger to be loved by us through the love we show them. Bringing the presence of Jesus to people suffering like this makes us contemplatives living right in the heart of the world.

※

The people are asking for spiritual help, for consolation; they are so afraid, discouraged, in despair; so many commit suicide. That's why we must concentrate on being God's love, God's presence, not by words, but by service, concrete love, listening.[2]

First and Last Contact with Love

Nirmal Hriday—the living tabernacle of the suffering Christ—how clean your hands must be to touch the broken bodies; how clean your tongue must be to speak the words of comfort, faith, and love; for, for many of them, it is the first contact with love, and it may be their last. How much you must be alive to His Presence, if you really believe what Jesus said: "You did it to Me."[3]

My Brother, My Sister

And Christ has said so often, "Love one another as I have loved you." And we know how He loved us. He gave all for love of us that we may be able, like Him, to love others, especially the people who have nothing, who have nobody. . . . There are many people who suffer from different poverty, spiritual poverty. Being . . . left alone, unwanted, unloved, uncared for. And I think you and I, who have been created to love and to be loved, we have been . . . created for greater things. We are not just a number in the world. A child of God. And that person is my brother, my sister. And therefore, that's why Jesus insisted so much on that love for one another.[4]

Be Kind

Sisters, you and I have been sent. A missionary is a person who has been sent, and we have been sent to do what? Charity. A Missionary of Charity is what? A carrier of God's love. What a beautiful name the Muslim men have given to the sisters. Indian men, they don't call them Missionaries of Charity, they call them "Carriers of God's love." What a beautiful name.[5]

*

Our poor people are becoming poorer day by day. I beg you, my sisters, be kind to them—be a comfort to the poor and take every trouble to help them. Open your eyes to the needs of the poor. Put into living reality your vow to give wholehearted, free service to the poor—to Christ in His distressing disguise.[6]

*

Be a true co-worker of Christ. Radiate and live His life.
Be an angel of comfort to the sick, a friend to the little
ones, and love each other as God loves each of you with
a special, most intense love. Be kind to each other—I
prefer you make mistakes in kindness than that you
work miracles in unkindness.[7]

Smile at Each Other

For today, besides the material poverty that makes
people die of hunger, die of cold, die in the streets,
there is that great poverty of being unwanted, unloved,
uncared for, having no one to call your own, having no
one to smile at. And sometimes it happens to our old
people whom we call shut-ins . . . they are nobody, they
are just there, they're unknown, they are known by the
number of their room, but they are not known to be
loved and to be served. For knowledge always leads
to love and love to service. Do we really know that?[8]

Heal the Suffering

You people who are dealing with medical work, you
are dealing with suffering, you are dealing with people
who come to you bearing great pain, great suffering,
and with great hope that you will do something, that
you will give them something, the joy of being relieved
of the pain. How terrible it is if they come to you with
fear, with fear that you will destroy something in them.

There is a group of doctors and nurses being formed
who came to me and said, "Please help us to make
our life, our work, . . . consecrated, something holy,
something beautiful for God." So [those doctors] have in
themselves the determination that through their work,
doing this beautiful medical work, they will heal the
wounds, they will heal the suffering, to give joy.[9]

✳

And the suffering and the pain, it's only a sign given
to that person, that individual person, that she—that
person—has come close to God, that God can share
His own Passion with that person. It is not always
easy to accept it, but this is where we must come in,
in the people's life, and help them to accept [what is
happening]. And I often say, I wonder what the world
would be if it didn't have people to share their suffering
and to offer their suffering.[10]

✳

I'll never forget I met a lady who was in the most terrible
pain. I have never seen a person in such great pain. She
was dying of cancer with terrible pain, and I said to her,
"See, it is the kiss of Jesus, a sign that you have come so
close to Him on the Cross that He can kiss you." And
then she joined her hands and said, "Mother, please tell
Jesus to stop kissing me."[11]

They Let Them Talk and Talk and Talk

In England, Mother has started a small group, a
listening group, and they go to these old people,
ordinary old people's houses, and they just sit and listen
to them. And they let them talk and talk and talk. If
only [they have] just that one person to listen, they go
there. Very old people love to have somebody to listen,
even if they have to tell the story of thirty years ago,
but it is good to listen, and I think it is a very beautiful
thing. . . . Once you start visiting those places, these
people, you will very soon find that maybe a little thing
will please that person, and that little thing you can [do
for them]. . . . You can find out what they need, go once
and see, then you find out—a book, a card, only that
simple contact with them.[12]

My Mother Doesn't Want Me

I [will] never forget that young man in England; I saw
him in the streets of London. He had long hair and I
told him, "You shouldn't be here, you should be at home
with your parents." He was only twenty-two, twenty-
three years old. Then he said, "My mother doesn't want
me. Every time I went home, she locked me out because
I have long hair. She doesn't want me and I can't cut
my hair." So he chose the street [because] his mother
didn't want him. Quite possibly that good mother was
concerned about the hunger in India and worked for
the people all around her, except her own child. When
we returned, that young boy was lying on the ground.
He had overdosed himself with drugs. We had to take

him to the hospital. I don't know whether he survived, because I don't know how many things he had taken. What will be the reaction of that mother facing that child when they meet again? "You didn't want me." So let us begin to want each other.[13]

They Have Absolutely Nobody

Now in the New York area where our sisters are working there are a number of places, but in one place especially there are people, something like [the] people we pick up from the streets of Calcutta, a little more neglected than our people. . . . Sisters go there once a week. . . . We . . . go there and do this humble work, such as cutting nails and washing and feeding and changing the clothes and making the bed a little bit comfortable. . . . I have been there some time ago and I thought it was terrible, and since [then] things seem to be much worse than they were before. We are trying to find out who is the person to contact who will give us complete permission to go [there] daily. . . . You could find out people like that, especially the shut-ins. In every place we have these people, in every place; in hospitals there are people whom nobody visits, they have absolutely nobody. So like this man in this place, he waited for the sisters to come to wash his mouth, because for a whole week nobody gave him anything to wash his mouth. The next week, when the sisters went, he had died already.[14]

Comfort the Many Lonely

A wealthy man said to me, "I have a big house in
Holland. Do you want me to give it up?" I said, "No.
But what I want you to do is to go back and see: Do you
want to live in that house?" "Yes," he said. "And I also
have a big car; do you want me to give that up instead?"
I said, "No. But what I want you to do is to go back and
see some of the many lonely people who live in Holland.
Then every now and then I want you to bring a few of
them at a time and entertain them. Bring them in that
big car of yours and let them enjoy a few hours in your
beautiful house. Then your big house will become a
center of love, full of light, full of joy, full of life." He
smiled and said that he would be so happy to bring
the people to his home, but that he wanted to give up
something in his life. So I suggested, "When you go to
the shop to buy a new suit or clothes, or when someone
goes to buy for you, instead of buying the best that would
cost $55, buy one for $50 and use that extra money to buy
something for someone else or, better still, for the poor."
When I finished saying this, he really looked amazed.
"Oh, is that the way, Mother? I never thought of it."
When he finally left, he looked so happy and full of joy
at the thought of helping our sisters, and he was already
planning to send things to the sisters in Tanzania.

Words of Comfort

As soon as I heard about the terrible earthquake in Kobe,
Japan, I sent a message to the archbishop offering the
service of our sisters. Six of them went to the city to

bring God's love and compassion to the people, especially the elderly. They walked through the streets of the city where more than five thousand people died, offering words of comfort, hope, and encouragement as well as supplies to those in need. Let us pray for the people of Kobe and for all people suffering from natural disasters, war, and violence that by uniting their pain and suffering to that of Jesus, they may find strength and healing.[15]

Joy of Sharing His Suffering

You have done much and you are still doing much for the glory of God and the good of the poor. So do not be afraid—the very Cross is the sign of His great love—as He gives you the joy of sharing His suffering and humiliation with Him. . . . These are but means to greater love.[16]

Let Jesus Be the Victim in You

You have said "Yes" to Jesus and He has taken you at your word. . . . God cannot fill what is full. He can fill only emptiness, deep poverty. And your "Yes" is the beginning of being or becoming empty. It is not how much we really "have" to give, but how empty we are, so that we can receive [Him] fully in our life and let Him live His life in us.

In you today He wants to relive His complete submission to His Father. Allow Him to do so. [It] does not matter what you feel, as long as He feels all right in you. Take away your eyes from yourself and rejoice that you have nothing, that you are nothing, that you can do nothing. Give Jesus a big smile each time your nothingness frightens you.

This is the poverty of Jesus. You and I must let Him live in us and through us in the world. Cling to Our Lady, for she too, before she could become full of grace, full of Jesus, had to go through that darkness. "How can this be done?" But the moment she said "Yes" she had need to go in haste and give Jesus to John and his family.

Keep giving Jesus to your people not by words, but by your example, by your being in love with Jesus, by radiating His holiness and spreading His fragrance of love everywhere you go.

Just keep the joy of Jesus as your strength. Be happy and at peace. Accept whatever He gives, and give whatever He takes, with a big smile. You belong to Him. Tell Him, "I am Yours and if You cut me to pieces, every single piece will be only all Yours." Let Jesus be the Victim and the Priest in you.[17]

✳

I pray for you that Our Blessed Mother may keep close to you as she kept close to Jesus at the foot of the Cross. Share everything with her, and ask her to be a Mother to you.[18]

If We Have Jesus, We Have All
Your welcome letter has brought me joy and sorrow: joy that you are all well, that you have taken your great loss so beautifully, with real Christlike fortitude. I am really proud of you. And sorrow for the things [that are]

gone, but I could not help thinking, maybe Our Lord has allowed this to free you, to make you share in the Tenth Station of the Cross—"and they took away His garments from Him." These people have done exactly this to you. Forgive and forget and smile. Thank God you were not in the house when they came. God knows what would have happened to any of you. I know what both of you feel, but both of you are young and strong. The house can be furnished, but do it in the spirit of the Vatican Council, beautifully, worthy of the temple of God dwelling within. Here we are also sharing the Passion of Christ. Famine, floods, disease, unrest—so much suffering, so much misunderstanding. The pain of seeing my people suffer so much is very great. The Church within the nations at war—more suffering— I often very often say just, "Thank God, there is God in whose hand we are." Our homes are full, full with children unwanted, with sick and dying people, with old people whom no one wants, and yet we must keep up smiling in total surrender to God and loving trust in our neighbors—whoever they may be. He is the Light that will never be extinguished. He is the Way that will never go wrong. He is the Truth that will conquer. He is the Life that will never die. If we have Jesus, we have all. So let us keep close to Jesus with a smiling face.[19]

The Suffering, the Greatest Wealth

I am praying much for you that you may make use of the ability and suffering that have come into your life as means to real holiness. Let us thank God for His

love for you, for His presence in you, and for the grace
with which you have accepted your affliction as a gift of
God. It must be hard—but the wood of the Cross was
hard too. Do not ever think your life is useless because
you cannot do what others do. The Cross of Jesus and
the suffering of our Blessed Mother and of so many
Christians are the greatest wealth of the whole world.
You too are a part of that wealth. May you allow Jesus
to live more fully in you, and may the Passion He shares
with you be a sign of His tender love for you. Offer all
for our Society with a smile.[20]

Condolences

Your father has gone home to Jesus—to Him who loved
him first and called him into life. Now that he is with
Jesus and Jesus is in your heart, he is there too, closer to
you now than ever before, praying for you and watching
over you. Let this thought console you in your grief.
I am praying for your mother in a special way during
these days.[21]

＊

Thank you for your letter . . . and for sharing the sad
news of the death of your nephew. I offer my deep
sympathy to your brother and sister-in-law and assure
them both of my prayers that the Lord may console and
strengthen them. It must have been a big shock to all
of you, as you all had seen the child three days before
his death alive and happy. God our loving Father, who
knows us, loves us, knows the best for us, has taken [the

son] for Himself to heaven, where he is now living in full the life that God wants to give us. So it is a happy and consoling thought for the parents that [he] is not dead in sin but alive fully in heaven through God's love and mercy. And God in His own time will draw [the parents] closer to Himself with [their son] interceding for his dear parents. I am glad that you are with [the parents] at this time consoling and strengthening them in a Christian way. God, in His own time, will heal their wounds and draw out gently the good from them.[22]

※

I am sorry to learn of the death of your sister. Let us pray for her—may God grant her a share in His glory. I am praying for you, that God may give you the grace to accept your loss with courage, even joy, knowing that she has gone home to Jesus and is closer to you now than [before]. Thank God for giving you the opportunity to care for her; now God wants to use you for your family and others, especially the lonely, the unwanted. Give Him your heart to love.[23]

※

I am sorry to know your sister . . . passed away suddenly. However, I am sure your faith will help you accept it with joy, as she has gone home to Jesus and is now with Him in heaven. She must be praying for you all there. Now that she is with Jesus and Jesus is in your heart, she is there too, closer to you now than ever before.[24]

HER EXAMPLE: The Testimonies

She Listened to Everybody

I used to do the gate duty at Mother House. Each time any visitors came, I used to go to Mother's room to give her their card, and so forth, and each time Mother used to give me her blessing, and immediately [she would] get up and come to the chapel veranda or to the parlor downstairs to meet the people. She met all who came, whether rich or poor. Mother used to listen to everybody. Some came only to touch her feet, to have darshan [coming into the presence of a holy person], to take her blessing and go away. All went away from her presence with a happy smile. Mother used to pray with them, take those in trouble or distress to the chapel and pray for them.

✳

She always gave them Miraculous Medals and her "business card." She used such simple means, but people were touched. Many were also healed, because Mother was full of Jesus and radiated His peace to those who were troubled.

✳

Mother sat near him, listening and encouraging him. For Mother it was "seeing Jesus twenty-four hours a day" in the snotty, naked child, his eyes infected, or the richly clad, affluent people who flocked from all over the world to see her, sometimes from afar. Her radiant smile lit up all hearts, and while some wept at some secret touch of Jesus in the depths of their being, others experienced a release of joy within.[25]

When my brother died, I went to get a blessing from Mother. Mother gave me a blessing and embraced me and told me, "My child, Jesus loves you so much that He is sharing with you." Mother looked at me with love. Mother's tender look struck me so much, I felt real consolation, and she gave me courage and strength to go ahead.[26]

Finding Peace Again

Often I would sit with her on the bench outside her office and talk about difficulties I was having in the work or my distress over my children not practicing their faith, or my husband who is not Catholic. She assured me that Jesus loved them more than I did, and He would look after them. She took my hands in hers and giving me a rosary, told me to pray it every day and ask the Virgin Mary to intercede for them and they would come back. I have not been as faithful as I need to be, but one child has returned and is practicing his faith, and my husband has begun to inquire about prayer and God's love for him, a new concept for him.[27]

On one occasion, Mother was visiting Titagarh. There was a leper, who, though he was deformed, used to help the sisters in dressing wounds and giving food and medicine to others, just to be with the sisters. He became blind and completely lost his fingers and toes. He came close to Mother and cried, "Mother, I have become blind, I cannot see you. I have become useless, I cannot help." Mother told him, "Oh my son, don't worry. In a little while we will all go to the Other Side to our Home. Everything will be new! New eyes to see, new hands, everything new! We will see God who loves us so much!" He said, "Mother, when will it happen? Pray! I want to go soon!" This was Mother's way of inducing the desire for new life in people, not letting them get drowned in misery. From that time on [he] was sad no more. He was so happy, waiting to go Home.[28]

✳

When some relatives of a dead person were brought to her, she would console them saying . . . that we come from God and we go to God.[29]

I Felt Absolutely Loved

Mother refused to redo the interview. She said that if something did not work out, it meant that it was not God's will. I was devastated by her refusal. In that moment, as though she felt that same pain, she took off the dark glasses I was wearing and said, "——, you aren't getting enough sleep." The words were simple but the energy she emanated was immense. Time seemed to stop. My heart seemed to swell in my chest. I felt powerful love flowing from Mother through me and back to her. It was a love that I had long desired from parents, friends, and lovers but never, before that moment, experienced. In a state of heightened awareness, I suddenly knew that God existed, that God was this Love, and that Mother Teresa was a channel for that love. I felt absolutely known and loved. I said nothing but Mother seized the moment. As though she could read my heart, she said, "Let us thank God." She unhooked her rosary from her belt and began praying. I, who hadn't prayed in fourteen years, stayed on my knees and joined Mother in the Rosary, tears, once again, rolling down my face.[30]

See Him in Your Son

One day a young father of a boy appeared before the door of Mother House and asked for a "darshan" of Mother. He was accompanied by his two-year-old son. In the course of time this gentleman became Mother's co-worker. The following conversation took place at Mother House and seemed to me very touching. I jotted down their words soon after. It is now produced below:

YOUNG MAN: Mother, this is my son (showing the child). His mother is very much whimsical. Sometimes she would like this boy; otherwise, mostly he is left uncared for. I have my own job. But then again, I am made to take care of him for the whole day, nurse him, feed him, at times this child also appears unbearable! What do I do?

MOTHER: When you take care of him, say with prayers, "Lord, You in the disguise of this child, be with me now and forever. Thank You, Lord, that You are my son, as I am a son to You. Thank You, Lord, for I can serve You, as You served us all. Thank You, Lord, for I can love You as You loved us all. Thank You, for today You depend on me, as I always depend on You. Thank You, Lord,

when You keep Your sleepy head on me, for I too
rest on You forever. Thank You, Lord, when You
hold my hand, for I know You are with me. Thank
You, Lord, when You beg me to feed, as we are fed
by You. Thank You, Lord, when You grow a boy,
for I know I can depend on You. Thank You, Lord,
as so dearly You have come as my son.

The boy's father sobbed silently as Mother said this
prayer, and he left with peace on his face.[31]

Singling Out the Most Unloved

What was striking in her dealings with the poor was that
her first glance and a word of comfort went to the most poor
and dirty person in the crowd.[32]

✳

We were in Tijuana, [Mexico], visiting the fathers, at their
seminary next door to a field of slums, barrios made of trees
and huts with ten or twelve family members living in one
room. Mother saw across the way, up a very long, steep hill,
an old woman sitting outside a small hut. One afternoon she
looked at me and said, "Mother is going up the hill. We must
go see this woman. She has no one." We went up. When we
got there, this woman could not take her gaze away from
Mother. She beamed, she responded for the first time to
anyone. Mother held her hand and spoke softly. When it
came time to go back down, she called out to Mother and
said, "But what is your name?" She had no idea who Mother
was, but had been completely overwhelmed by the spirit of

Mother. Mother responded, "My name is Mother Teresa." "And where are you from?" the woman asked. "Oh, I am from Calcutta." We left. Mother never batted an eye, not a word was spoken.[33]

※

On one occasion Mother and I were waiting on a footpath for a car to pick us up. In the crowds passing by, she noticed a man who had difficulty stepping onto the footpath. She lent her hand to help him up even though she herself was failing in strength. No one else around her, including myself, had noticed the man's plight.[34]

Learn to See Jesus

I remember at one of the professions she noticed in the crowd a woman crying. She called [out to] her, talked to her, and found out that she had in the past committed an abortion. Immediately she called the priest and helped her and her husband to make [a] confession. Afterward she told us about it. "Sisters, how is it that Mother sees and you do not see? Please learn to see Jesus in the people!"[35]

Hello, My Name Is Mother Teresa

[At the airport] Mother was sitting in the lounge talking to the sisters, and this middle-aged woman walked in right past Mother to the back of this lounge. She opened a magazine. And I, who was just observing everything, found this extraordinary. Out in the airport everybody is trying to touch Mother, and this woman who could touch Mother walked right past her and she didn't even know. What struck me outside was this emptiness, this sadness in her face. Her face wasn't even alive. The lounge attendants came after a few minutes, and they said, "Mother, we are ready," and the sisters said, "Aacha," [Okay] and they got up. . . . [Mother] was the last one and I was behind her, [and just as we were leaving the lounge] Mother took my hand and said, "Father, come with me," and she went right to the back of that lounge, to that woman. Now how she had noticed that woman with all the MC confusion, I don't know. Anyway, she went to that woman and Mother reached into her own bag and she had what she called her "business cards" the Knights of Columbus [printed for] her.[36] She leaned over to the woman, and said, "Hello. My name is Mother Teresa. I just wanted to give you my card." And this woman looked up from her magazine and I heard her kind of mutter. Mother gave her the card, squeezed her hand, looked into her eyes. It was thirty seconds, no more than that, and we went. But at the door I turned and looked at this woman and she was reading that card with a smile on her face. Her face had just changed. Mother had that deep capacity to notice even the deeper pain, the loneliness, and reach out. That was extraordinary in her.[37]

Mother Was in a Hurry, When on the Way a Poor Man Stopped Her

Sister Mary was recently recalling an incident at the time of the Bangladesh riots: Two of the sisters were going in a hurry with Mother Teresa to get some urgently needed stores for the refugee camp, when on the way a poor man stopped to speak to Mother. Sister Mary said it was most edifying to see Mother, who, though she was in a hurry, gave four to five minutes listening to his worries with compassion and undivided attention. Sister Mary said that for her, that was truly the mark of a saint.[38]

※

When there was the riot between Hindus and Muslims in December 1991, Mother herself went to those areas, praying the rosary and with folded hands. She used to tell us to pray always whenever there is a problem, to trust in God and the problems would be solved.[39]

I Beg You, Be Kind

I had the privilege of going to Albania to a new foundation in Durrës. Mother was there. I could see how she suffered to see her people living in such abject misery. There was an absence of everything, material and spiritual. Mother came to our house often as we [had] the storehouse of most of our supplies that came from abroad. Mother said, "Be very kind to everyone, they have suffered so much already. I am begging you with joined hands, be kind." Mother said this over and over again. Mother also said, "Welcome everyone who comes. The priests that come have nowhere to go, look after them, feed them till they find a place." The day our house opened, Mother was overjoyed and said, "What a tremendous love Jesus has for us. This is the only tabernacle in the whole city, and Jesus has chosen us to make Him known." Mother gave us many words of love, understanding, and compassion. Mother kept saying, "Love one another and give it to others. They must see Jesus in you. They have been hurt so much already. Don't hurt them."⁴⁰

Give the Police My Umbrella

It was a monsoon evening and a heavy downpour had just stopped when Mother returned to her house. She had been terribly sick only a month ago. It had rained so much that day that the pavements of Shishu Bhavan went quite below the dirty rainwater, giving the area a [look] of Venice! Mother's car tried to pull its way through, but the driver nodded his head to say there were some troubles with the car. The accompanying sisters requested Mother to wait inside the car. But Mother had by then slipped out of the car, and [hitching] her sari [up to] her knees, she began to push through the rainwater toward Mother House. While assuring her sisters that she would safely reach home, Mother caught sight of a traffic policeman, waving both hands to manage the vehicles. The man had no umbrella with him and it was still drizzling. As Mother arrived at the entrance of Shishu Bhavan, she called for a sister and said worriedly, "Sister, give the traffic police my umbrella. He has duty tomorrow here; ask him to return my umbrella then."⁴¹

Bless This Marriage

An old Bengali Hindu Brahmin came to my office asking for some charity for the marriage of his daughter. I told him that at the most I could contribute fifty rupees. I was impressed with the outlook of this old gentleman. I told him to wait and telephoned Mother and told her that I was sending an old gentleman who was in difficulty, and I asked if Mother could help him. I did not mention anything about the marriage of his daughter. Thereafter I forgot completely about this matter. After two or three months, this old Brahmin gentleman saw me and he was so much overjoyed that he could hardly speak. He told me that Mother had helped him with everything for the marriage of his daughter. He had asked Mother to attend the marriage ceremony of his daughter and never expected Mother to come personally. But Mother did come to his house on the day of the marriage. She asked the Hindu gentleman if she could bless the couple getting married, which the Hindu gentleman gladly agreed to. Mother knelt down and prayed to the heavenly Father to bless them. Just when Mother was leaving, the groom asked Mother to pray for him as he had [taken] a competitive examination for a job. Mother simply told the young man that she would pray for him. Believe me, this young Hindu man was lucky to be successful and got the appointment for the job.[42]

A Ray of Hope at Eleven p.m.

Once one builder approached Mother and wanted to know what he could offer to her by way of service. Mother requested [that he] build a home for the prostitutes at Tangra—which he did. Years after he went bankrupt. Eventually he and his brother committed suicide. The widows were condemned by the family/priests/friends [because their] deceased husbands [had committed such sins]. They were almost outcasts. Suddenly they received a call from the MC sisters that Mother Teresa, returning from a tour abroad, had heard the news of the deaths and would like to meet the widows straight from the airport on her way home. They were once again scared of listening to some scornful remarks. At eleven p.m., Mother arrived at their house along with one more sister. [Mother] smiled at them and said [their] husbands were great men; thanks to their contribution so many prostitutes were finding shelter, and she assured them that God would definitely look after them. [For the] first time after the death [of their husbands], these widows found a ray of hope which enabled them to face the cruelty of life with renewed vigor, and today they have been able to re-establish themselves.[43]

The Beauty of All Life

Mother taught me the beauty of all life, even when disease and deformity make it hard to look at. In the midst of the greatest need, she seemed to be the most serene. She used every opportunity to help the volunteers understand that by disguising Himself in the poorest of the poor, [Jesus] was giving us an opportunity to love Him and serve Him directly. The poor are our gift, she would say.[44]

Mother Kissed Those Rough Calloused Hands

In 1970 I had the privilege of accompanying Mother Teresa to a meeting of the National Council of Catholic Women, where Mother was to be recognized for her great work among God's poor. On one of those days, Mother and I sat together in a booth on the convention floor, and all day women came and went. The women, for the most part, were very well dressed and appeared to be from families of means, but one woman stood apart from the others in her dress, which was plain and well worn, and in her shy manner of approaching us. For some time she stood off to one side looking at Mother with such longing that I walked over to see if I could be of help. She seemed to be almost afraid to ask if she could speak to Mother Teresa for just a few moments. I took her immediately to Mother, who invited her to come and sit in the booth beside her. The woman very shyly began to tell us about her husband's serious illness and that it was no longer possible for him to do the work on their farm. She begged Mother Teresa to pray for him and for his recovery. She had taken over her husband's work on the farm, and she now asked for our prayers that she could continue to do this, as well as tend to her own housework, cooking, and care of their young children.

As she spoke, the young woman held her hands tightly together on her lap, and I could see how very rough and red they were, and how cracked and sore her fingers appeared. Mother Teresa noticed the same, and just then a few tears fell from the woman's face to her poor worn hands. At that, Mother took both of those rough calloused hands into her own, and, lifting them to her lips, she kissed them and held fast to them while assuring the woman that we would pray for her husband's recovery. The woman stayed with us a little longer, telling about her family and how much it meant to all of them to be able to remain on the farm where her husband's family had lived for several generations. Then she thanked us and walked away. As Mother Teresa watched her leave, she whispered, "What great love."[45]

Badly Injured in an Explosion

Later that same week, I received a call from a woman who told me her young son had been badly injured in an explosion, and she wondered if she and her husband could bring the lad to meet Mother Teresa. That evening the family arrived at our home with their son, age eleven, who had been blinded and had both his hands blown off when he picked up a stick of dynamite and lit it, thinking it was a flare he could use for a torch. The boy's face was badly scarred, and his arms ended in stumps. It was hard to look into those sightless eyes without weeping.

I led the young boy and his parents into our living room where Mother Teresa was waiting. She seated him by her side and took his poor stumps in her hands, holding them while he talked to her. He described how he had first learned about Mother Teresa at his Catholic school, had even read about her himself before the accident. He had longed to talk to her because he knew she would tell him the truth about his appearance, and also because he wanted to ask her advice about a career, considering his terrible handicap. Mother's response was so beautiful that those of us in the room could not hold back our tears. First, she traced with a finger all the disfiguring scars on his face, telling him that in her opinion they made him look manly and strong and gave him a courageous look. Then, as he asked if his stumps were terrible looking, she took each in her hands, stroked the places where the scars were the heaviest, kissed each stump, and told him they didn't look a bit ugly, but were simply good strong-looking arms that had no hand. Then the two of them talked about his plans for the future, of one day being a counselor and using his own experiences to help others to overcome handicaps. It was a scene none of us there will forget, the young boy with all that hope being reassured by a person he had read about and admired for her own heroism, both absolutely certain that, with Jesus's help, he would someday reach his goal! I hope and pray that he did.[46]

Mother Had Time for Them All

In the last year of her life, Mother was pretty much confined to Mother House and to the second floor. In this circumstance, Mother began what I called her "balcony apostolate." She would greet all the visitors who came to see her, with warmth, kindness, and humor. Some people brought their pain, others their concerns or hopes, and Mother had time for them all and directed them to God. Once I was waiting a long time on the balcony to speak with Mother while she was greeting people. Finally Mother came over to me and began to talk. I was relieved to finally gain her attention. A poor man climbed the stairs and stood looking at us from a distance. Mother saw him and excused herself saying, "Excuse me, Father, but this man has come such a long way." And she left me to listen to him! I was frustrated, because again I had to wait, but it revealed to me that I thought I was more important than this man was. Mother obviously knew he was the more important one, because his need and pain were on his face—so she gave God's attention and concern to him first. Whomever she greeted in her wheelchair on that balcony, she would ask [them] to pray and give them a Miraculous Medal, and invite them to trust in the goodness of God. When she spoke, it was always with that purpose, to reveal the goodness of God, through some little anecdote from her life, a story about how Jesus was intimately present and involved in our lives. And she taught us that He depended on you and me to provide His care for the poor. What we saw as difficulties Mother would call "opportunities"—to look for Him in the distressing disguise. . . . She had always that positive vision.[47]

Comforting from Heaven

I was granted a grace of conversion through Blessed Teresa of Calcutta. I felt an inspiration from God to pick up the prayer booklet *Jesus Is My All in All* and pray the Novena to Blessed Teresa of Calcutta. . . . I had prayed this novena before, but felt especially drawn to one of the passages from a particular day of the novena which spoke of Jesus's love. I felt the Holy Spirit being poured into my soul, with a particular joy for loving as Christ does. The prayer that I read transformed my heart, as I had been depressed and felt little emotion or love in my heart. I had been having a hard time in trusting in Jesus's love for me. I knew that it was a miracle because it happened immediately, and I felt a newness of life in God's Spirit. I felt then called to share Christ's love and could feel the Lord working in me to show Christian love to a mother and her child. The child looked so sad, and I felt that Mother Teresa's spirit also would reach out to that child because of her love of Christ. I felt then Jesus actually calling me to help others and that my vocation would be to love Jesus. Also Mother Teresa led me back to the Blessed Virgin Mary in a special way.

REFLECTION

"Blessed be the God and Father of our Lord
Jesus Christ, the Father of mercies and God of all
comfort, who comforts us in all our affliction, so
that we may be able to comfort those who are in any
affliction, with the comfort with which we ourselves
are comforted by God." (2 Cor 1:3–4)

"Keep the joy of loving God in your heart and
share this joy with all you meet especially your
family. Be holy—let us pray."[48]

Am I afraid to get involved in other people's suffering and
thus keep my distance? Do I use the advice "not to get too
involved or too personally affected" as an excuse not to
help someone who is suffering deeply?

Can I "love until it hurts," forgoing something of my
own comfort, convenience, and enjoyment in order to help
someone in need?

How can I cultivate greater sensitivity to others' sufferings? Can I look for someone in my community or family,
among my friends, colleagues, and acquaintances, who is
afflicted in some way and offer a small gesture, a word of
comfort or a smile that will make their day brighter? Can I
do it in a way that is discreet, respectful, and nonintrusive?

PRAYER

Soul of Christ, sanctify me.
Body of Christ, save me.
Blood of Christ, inebriate me.
Water from the side of Christ, wash me.
Passion of Christ, strengthen me.
O Good Jesus, hear me.
Within Thy wounds hide me.
Suffer me not to be separated from Thee.
From the malicious enemy, defend me.
In the hour of my death, call me
and bid me come unto Thee,
that with Thy Saints, I may praise Thee
For ever and ever.
Amen.

—Prayed daily by Mother Teresa

FOURTEEN

PRAY FOR THE LIVING
AND THE DEAD

Though listed as the last work of mercy, praying for the living and the dead is not meant to be undertaken as a last resort—something to do when we have (unsuccessfully!) tried everything else. Quite the contrary, it is actually the first resort—something we should do before everything else. Prayer was probably the one essential reason that Mother Teresa could practice all the other works of mercy with such impressive fidelity and results.

Prayer as an intimate union of our heart and mind with God, a relationship with Him, held primacy of place in Mother Teresa's life. "*What blood is to the body, prayer is to the soul,*" she used to say, emphasizing the vital importance of prayer in one's life. "*We need that intimate connection with God in our everyday lives. And how do we get that? By prayer.*"[1] For Mother Teresa, prayer was communication with God: "*God talks to me and I talk to Him; as simple as that—this is prayer!*"[2] "People were fascinated just watching Mother pray. They would sit there watching her, be really drawn into this mystery."[3] She did not do anything extraordinary. "She did not spend long hours in the chapel, but she was faithful to the times of prayer," and that being so, it was obvious to those around her that "Mother lived in continual union with Jesus. A union not filled with consolations and ecstasies, but one of faith."[4]

The Church proposes prayer for the living and the dead as a work of mercy. It is therefore essential that we pray for others, and Mother Teresa's example reminds us that our prayer for others should be rooted in the intimacy of our own relationship with God. Sensing her closeness to God, many people asked Mother Teresa for prayers. She would promise to pray for them and fulfilled that commitment with great fidelity every day. Whenever there were spontaneous prayers of the faithful at Mass, she would pray loudly and clearly: "For all those who have asked our prayers and for those whom we have promised to pray." In this way, she was lifting up in prayer all those in need, placing them in God's loving care, and entrusting them to His providential love.

At times, in spite of our best efforts, we seem to be unable to help someone, and we can do nothing more than to pray for them. Praying then can become the ultimate expression of love for the person. Holding up someone in prayer before the Lord, asking His blessing and help for the living and the happiness of entering into eternal life for the dead, is a work of mercy that Mother Teresa so admirably practiced.

HER WORDS

Every Missionary of Charity will pray with absolute trust in God's loving care for us. Our prayer will be the prayer of little children, one of tender devotion, deep reverence, humility, serenity, and simplicity.[5]

Turn to Him

Bring again, I say, bring prayer in[to] your life, pray. You may not be able to make long prayers, but pray. Turn to Him: "My God, I love You." And He loves us so tenderly that it's written in the Scripture, even if a mother could forget her child, which is happening today—abortion. The mother forgets her child. "Even if a mother could forget her child, I will not forget you. I have carved you in the palm of My hand. You are precious to Me, I love you" [Is 49:15-16–43:4]. These are words in the Scripture for you and for me. So let us ask, let us ask Our Lord to keep our family together, keep the joy of loving one another, keep your heart one heart full of love in the Heart of Jesus through Mary, and who will help you best to keep your family together? Mary and Joseph. They have experienced the joy of loving one another and the peace and the tenderness of God's love.[6]

Pray and Make Sacrifice

The message of the Immaculate Heart at Fatima seems to be enfolded in this mission to Mother ("Pray, pray

very much and make sacrifices for sinners, for many
souls go to hell because there is no one to make sacrifices
[and pray] for them," Our Lady said on August 19, 1917,
in Fatima). "It was at *her* pleading that the Society was
born" are Mother's words. Mother was determined,
compelled to fulfill her call, the new step, the new way
of life.[7]

And How Does It Begin? By Praying Together

To be able to love the unloved, to be able to give [love]
in your heart to the unwanted, unloved, uncared for, [we
need to begin to love] at home. And how does it begin?
By praying together. For the fruit of prayer is deepening
of faith. Then I believe that really whatever I do, I do it
to God Himself, the deepening of faith. And the fruit of
faith is love, God loves me, I love my brother, my sister.
Doesn't matter [what] religion, doesn't matter [what]
color, doesn't matter [what] place, my brother, my sister
created by God Himself—same hand—and then the
fruit of that love must be action, must be service, I do
something. And, therefore, let us pray to bring prayer
into our family. Pray together, really have the courage to
do something beautiful for God, and whatever you do to
each other, you do it to God.[8]

Bring Prayer into Your Family

A wonderful thought to think that God loves me and
I can love you and you can love me, as He loves us.
What a wonderful gift of God. Even the poor people

are the gift of God to us. What a privilege for us, real
contemplatives in the heart of the world. So let us learn
to pray. Teach your children in your schools how to
pray. Families, teach your children to pray, for where
there is prayer, there is love; where there is love, there is
peace. And today more than ever, we need to pray for
peace. And let us remember that works of love are works
of peace, of joy, of sharing.[9]

※

And where do we begin? At home. And how do we
begin to love? By prayer. By bringing prayer into your
life, for prayer always gives us a clean heart, always.
And a clean heart can see God. And if you see God in
each other, naturally you will love [one] another. That's
why it is important to bring prayer into the family, for
the family that prays together, stays together. And if we
stay together, naturally we will love one another as God
loves each one of us. So it is very important to help each
other to pray.[10]

※

Never before has there been so much need for prayer
like today. I think that all the problems of the world
have their origin in the family that does not have time
for children, for prayer, and to be together.[11]

Take Time to Pray

I have heard that here, in families, there is much
suffering because children beat their parents and the

parents beat the children. And again I say, pray. Bring prayer into your life, into your family. Be a mother to your children. Take time for it. When the child comes back from school, are you there? Are you there to embrace your child? Are you there to love your child? Are you there to help? Or—you are so busy that you have no time even to look at your child, even to smile at your child; and the child gets hurt . . . that is the fact.[12]

Dear God, Thank You

Here is a prayer of the children for their parents and with their parents:

Dear God,

Thank You for our family, for father and mother who love us tenderly, for being able to go to school, to learn and to grow, so that we can serve people who will be needing us. Keep the joy of love in our hearts. Make us love father and mother, brothers and sisters, teachers and all our companions. For in loving them we love You, and if we love You, our hearts will remain always pure, and You will be able to dwell in our hearts. Please always keep us pure and holy, just as You have created us. Keep us always beautiful, up to the end of our lives. And bring us one day to Your home, to live with You in heaven forever.

God bless you.[13]

On Your Wedding Day

Make that resolution, that on your wedding day you can give each other something beautiful. The most beautiful thing is to give a virgin heart, a virgin body, a virgin soul. That's the greatest gift that the young man can give the young woman, and that the young woman can give the man.

✳

This is something we must all pray for our young people: that the joy of loving gives them joy in the sacrifice. It is a sacrifice that they must learn to share together. And if a mistake has been made, it has been made; have the courage to accept that child and not to destroy it. Because that's sin: it's a murder. That sin is a greater sin: to destroy the image of God, to destroy the most beautiful creation of God that is life. And so today when we are together, let us pray. Let us pray for each other that we may love God as He loved us. Because God has offered to each one of us, He offers us that lifelong, faithful, personal friendship in tenderness and love. We all experience that in our lives, how God loves us. And it is our turn to give that lifelong, that faithful, that personal friendship to Him in each other with prayer first in our own family. Bring back the child, bring back family prayer.[14]

What God Has Put Together

Dear People of Ireland, I am praying with you at this important time when your country decides on the

question of divorce. My prayer is that you be faithful
to the teaching of Jesus—"a man leaves his father and
mother and is joined to his wife and they become one
body. What God has put together, let no one divide"
[Mk 10:9]. Our hearts are made to love and be loved—
a love that is not only unconditional, but also lasting.[15]

At Least Half an Hour Every Day Alone with God

And only God has chosen you to be the leaders and to
show the way. But that way has to be shown with great
respect, with great love. And I would say, I think that if
you politicians would spend at least—at least—half an
hour every day in prayer alone with God, I think that
will show you the way; it will give you the means to
[deal] with the people.

If we spend time alone with God, then that will
purify our hearts; then we will have the light, and we
will have the means to deal with our people with love
and with respect. And we are sure the fruit of prayer is
always deep love, deep compassion; and it always brings
us close to each other. And we know exactly how to lead
our people.[16]

Kindly Build a Mosque

I remember some time ago, some years back when the
president of Yemen asked for our sisters to come to
Yemen, and I was told that for so many, many years there
has been no public chapel, public Mass, [it has not been]
publicly known that a person is a priest for many years,

many, many years. So I told the president I am most willing to give [him] the sisters but without the priests, without Jesus, we don't go. Then they must have had a consultation between them. Then they decided yes. And something struck me so much. When the priests came, there was the altar, there was the tabernacle, there was Jesus. And only [a priest] could bring Jesus there.

After that, the government built the convent for us. And so we went there to take care of the street people, the dying, and the destitute, and then they built a convent for us also. And then the governor who had sponsored the building, Sister asked him, "Can you make sure that one room is beautifully done because Jesus is going to be there?" Beautiful—our chapel. And the governor asked Sister, "Sister, show me how to build the Roman Catholic church right here." He meant "little chapel" and instead of saying *chapel,* he said "Roman Catholic church," right here.

And they built that chapel so beautifully; it is there, and the sisters are there, and then they asked us to open—they gave us a whole mountain to rehabilitate the lepers. There are many, many lepers. So we went to see the place, and I saw an open grave with the smell of the rottenness of the bodies. I cannot express what I saw. And I was thinking, "Jesus, how? How can we leave You like that?" And then I accepted that place, and if you went now, you would see quite a different place. And then I asked—being all Muslims, not a single Catholic there—and I asked one of the rich men, I said, "These are all Muslim people. They need to pray. Kindly build a mosque for them where they can pray." And the man

was surprised that I, a Catholic sister, would ask such
a thing; but he built the most beautiful mosque for the
people, and you see those lepers crawling, crawling,
going there and praying. And then when that mosque
was completely opened, he turned to me and he said,
"I give you my word, the next thing I will build here is
a Catholic church for the sisters." These are beautiful
examples of the hunger of people, of our poorest of
the poor, the ignorant, the unwanted, the unloved, the
rejected, the forgotten—they hunger for God.[17]

Pray That God Preserves the World

At my visit to Nagasaki, first of all we will pray; I'm going
there to pray with the people; and also to visit the people
there, to see the people, just as I have come here. And also
to see how much suffering there is, up to now, because
of the use of that bomb. And it can happen again. So we
must pray that God will preserve the world, will preserve
each one of us, from that terrible destruction.[18]

Today God Is Still Using Our Suffering

There must have been some reason for God to have
chosen this place specially, the Land of Martyrs; that
has been a double martyrdom. And I think today God
is still using the suffering of the people; and through
their suffering, through their prayer, peace will be
obtained. And it is for us all together to pray that God
will preserve not only Japan but the whole world from
the terrible, fearful suffering that most of the people

in Japan have already seen. So let us pray. Only prayer
can obtain the grace of preventing this terrible difficulty
from coming into the world.[19]

Great Need of Prayers and Sacrifices

I think we have also lost [our] grip on sacrifice. "Today
that man is dying. He does not want to say sorry to
God; I will pray for him and make some sacrifice for
him"—that is not there anymore.[20]

✳

Our country and our people are in great need of prayers
and sacrifices. Be generous with both. Do your penances
with greater fervor—and pray, pray much. The heads
of our country know their duty, and we have to pray for
them that they may fulfill their duty with justice and
dignity. Let us pray for all those who are facing death
that they may die in peace. Let us pray for all those who
are left behind to mourn their dead. Let us pray for all
sisters and priests who may have to face hardships—for
our sisters that they may be all brave and generous and
face all sacrifices with a smile. Teach the poor people to
do this and we will help our country most.[21]

Pray for Souls

The month of November begins with two beautiful
days: the feasts of All Saints and All Souls. Holy Mother
Church remembers all of her children, to whom she
has given the life of Jesus through baptism—and they

are now either home with Jesus in heaven or waiting to go there through purgatory. We all know that during this whole month we give them extra love and care, by praying to them and for them.

✳

On All Souls' Day we pray for those who are still suffering in purgatory and far from God. I can choose. I can go straight up or I can go down. All of us are here to love God—not only for the work. Every day should be an act of love to God.[22]

HER EXAMPLE: The Testimonies

She Prayed Constantly

She prayed constantly. You had the feeling that she was praying all the [time]—well, she was praying. She wasn't saying words, but she was praying all the time. She was always—everything that she did was measured [by] how well she was doing God's work, and she was willing to consider that [if] what she was doing was not perfectly what God wanted, He would show her by not giving her support.[23]

The Prayer of a Child, Full of Trust

Mother's prayer life was extremely simple, like that of a child, full of trust. She did not complicate it at all. She seemed to know her faith deeply and lived it with the simplicity and fidelity of children or the poor. I know that this sort of prayer life can only be acquired through asceticism, as Jesus said, "Deny yourself." Mother followed Jesus on this way through many years.

Mother was extremely conscious of the indwelling presence of God in her soul. This came out especially in the way she spontaneously taught us to pray. Her most repeated aspiration, prefixed to nearly any other, was "Jesus in my heart." "Jesus in my heart, I believe in Your tender love."[24]

She Taught Us to Pray

In the school [Entally], Mother was very strict, and at the same time she gave motherly love to us. She taught us to love Jesus, and how we could make small sacrifices and help souls to come to the Church. She taught us to have great devotion to Our Lady and the rosary, to Saint Joseph and to our guardian angel. When at night we would go to bed, she made us kneel and say three Hail Marys for a happy death and to pray to Saint Patrick to save us from the snakes, to Saint Michael to save us from the enemy, and to our guardian angel to watch over us and protect us from danger. And also for the holy souls.[25]

I Will—I Want, with God's Blessing—Be Holy

In many other ways, Mother shared with others her gift of faith. Whenever visitors came to see her, she took them to the chapel. She taught them many small ejaculations. It didn't matter to her who they were—whether they were bishops, priests, seminarians, cardinals, young people, children, poor people, presidents of countries, believers, or nonbelievers. She gave them her business card and taught them to say the following prayer, "I will—I want, with God's blessing—be holy" and "You did it to Me."

Join Prayer and Work

Sometimes she used to ask the sisters also to pray for some special intentions. Mother used to write on the blackboard near the chapel, "Please pray for so-and-so person," and so forth. Whenever anyone came, she left what she was doing and went to meet them. For her meeting each person was meeting Jesus Himself.[26]

✳

Mother in her instruction said: "If you only pray, you are not a Missionary of Charity, and if you only work, you are not a Missionary of Charity. A Missionary of Charity is one who joins prayer and work together." For her, missionary zeal came from her deep union with God. God was the source; the eucharistic Jesus was the source. It was her strong, burning love for God that led her to go all over the world, to love and serve the poorest of the poor, to labor assiduously for their salvation and sanctification, to tell them and show them God's tender love and care.[27]

Kneeling in Adoration

Even in the Active Branch, Mother gave much importance to the daily Holy Hour. So many volunteers would come to pray with Mother, and many have shared about the strength they received by seeing Mother kneeling in adoration, totally lost in Jesus. They would come for Holy Mass in the morning. They loved to pray with Mother. Even when Mother was very sick, Mother continued her apostolate with them. Mother was in the wheelchair—so the [visitors and volunteers] would come to the veranda near the chapel. Mother would listen to them and give them words of comfort.[28]

※

One of the last gifts Mother gave us was all-day Eucharistic Adoration [for the Contemplative Branch]. The main intention is to pray for the holiness of priests and the holiness of family life. We also pray for other, various intentions. I still remember the joy Mother expressed when in 1995 she came to St. John's for the inauguration of all-day Eucharistic Adoration.[29]

86,000 Priests Prayed For!

Another aspect of her zeal was praying for priests. Therefore in 1986 she began that great work of the spiritual adoption of priests by sisters of different religious congregations. Her appeal to sisters was so effective that up to [this] date we have arranged for 86,000 bishops and priests to be adopted by religious sisters, especially the MCs. Her respect for priests as other Christs was so great that you'd often see her kneel before even young priests for their blessing.[30]

Let's Make a Flying Novena

On November 9, 1975, Mother went with all the novices to the outdoor Mass at the Basilica of St. John Lateran, celebrated by His Holiness Pope Paul VI. At the time for Mass all the sky was overcast and it was raining steadily. As we sat, Mother said, "Let's make a flying novena to our Lady, thanking her for the beautiful day." We were reprimanded gently, because, Mother said, as we neared the end of the nine Memorares all the people closed their umbrellas, but the sisters did not because our faith must have been lacking.[31]

※

Mother had picked up a severely malnourished child about ten years old and brought her to Trivandrum. Then she went back to Calcutta. In the meantime, the child walked out of the house, and we did not know where she had gone. We informed Mother in Calcutta. Mother told us to keep on praying and searching for the child, and she too would pray and we would get the child back. We got the child; back from Nari Niketan—the police had found her and taken her there. Mother's prayers were very powerful.[32]

Take the Trouble to Pray

I wrote to Mother about my prayer life, and Mother told me this. "Sister . . . is often late for prayer. Ask Our Lady to help you. Prayer is the very life of our union with Jesus. Examine yourself as to why you deliberately come late for prayer." Mother in her instructions used to say, "Pray and work. You have not come only for work; otherwise pack [up] and go home." Before my final vows, I went to see Mother and I asked Mother, "Do I have a vocation?" Mother looked straight into my eyes and told me, "My child, you have a vocation. Love to pray and take trouble to pray. Ask and seek and your heart will grow big enough to receive Him and keep Him as your own. Prayer is your strength and protection. Say, 'Mother Mary, help me and guide me.'" I experienced Mother's help and protection many times.[33]

Wear the Miraculous Medal

Many sick people were also helped by praying the prayer and wearing the medal. I believe it was through Mother's prayers to Our Lady that we obtained favors when we were faithful to wearing the medal and praying as Mother taught us. When we were sick and went to Mother, Mother would give us a Miraculous Medal, bless us with it, and pray. She would ask us to keep it where we had pain. And we got better.[34]

Mary, Mother of Jesus, Be a Mother to Me Now

Though Mother herself had a profound and deep love for Our Lady, Mother used a very simple means to help us and the people to grow in our devotion. Everyone knows how Mother used to give Miraculous Medals to people and teach them to pray: "Mary, Mother of Jesus, be a Mother to me now!" Many people who had no children conceived children through this simple prayer of faith in Our Lady's intercession. Mother would give them Miraculous Medals and ask them to wear them and pray: "Mary, Mother of Jesus, give us a baby!" and they got a child! I have come across many who have told me about it. One Hindu couple in London, who was childless for fifteen years after their marriage, had a baby girl whom they named Teresa. My own niece got a child by wearing the medal Mother gave her and praying the prayer.[35]

✳

At Mass, just before it started, I leaned forward and told Mother, "Today is my sister's birthday; she has been married six years and I have been told that they do not want children—please pray for her." Mother said, "Let us both pray for her in this Mass." And eleven months later my sister gave birth to the first of her two children. . . .[36]

✳

I asked Mother to pray for an acquaintance of mine, Maria, [who had] just [been] diagnosed with AIDS four days before. Mother responded by saying, "Oh. How terrible. So many people with AIDS." Then she seemed to look past me as if in deep thought. Then Mother asked, "How did she get it?" Knowing the situation of this woman, I replied, "I think she got it from her boyfriend." Mother said, "Oh," and looked away from us again. She then repeated, "So many men, women, and children with AIDS." Mother asked how old Maria was, and I responded, "Thirty-two." Mother asked me again how Maria got the AIDS. I said, "She hasn't been living a good life." I then held Miraculous Medals in my hand in front of Mother, she blessed them and took one out and said, "This one is for Maria. Tell her to pray, 'Mary, Mother of Jesus, be a Mother to me now,' but especially 'Mary, Mother of Jesus, take away my AIDS.'"[37]

Something Was Holding Them Back

During the civil war in Jordan, when a group of army men tried to come into our tiny flat, all of us prayed together. All of a sudden they left us and went to the other flats. Much later we met some of these soldiers and asked, "Why did you leave us and go to the other flats?" They said they could not enter our flat because they felt something was holding them back. I felt it was Mother's message to us over the phone, "Do not be afraid. Jesus is always with you. Our Mother Mary will take care of you."[38]

Pray in Order Not to Become Bitter

Mother told me to say [fifty] Memorares for [fifty] days (that was how old my former husband was at the time) in order to pray for him, for me not to become bitter, and for humility. . . . She felt my prayers would be very important for him because I was the one he had hurt. She felt so strongly that I had to forgive him, and that I had to fight to keep bitterness out, and that everyone had problems, and that we had to be understanding of the weaknesses of others. Every time I saw her she would bring up the subject of me not becoming bitter about my former husband and the divorce and what he had done to me. I think she worried about that because she saw that I was pained in the years after the divorce.[39]

Cured by Mother's Prayers

When Mother came, I was having a high temperature. She came and blessed me. She prayed over me. Next day again she came near my bed and touched my cheeks and said, "Your fever is not leaving you." And she again prayed for nearly five minutes, and then and there I felt better and I became all right soon.[40]

※

First [my husband] had fever. For twenty days, throughout the day and night, the fever lasted. After taking medicines, one night at two o'clock suddenly the fever left him, but he became mentally ill. Because of his mental state, he left home at night, locking all of us inside the house. In this state he kept roaming around till nine o'clock in the morning. One of his staff who was staying opposite to our house brought him home and opened the door. When he entered the house, he beat me and the three children. It was then that I realized his mental condition. After this incident, I started hiding the children in other people's houses. The children were small, and there was no proper provision for food. I was not cooking at home. Others helped much. At home he used to beat us, and then he would run out to beat outsiders with a stick. His office staff would run away on seeing him. At night, four people would hold and feed him and then lock him in a room. This lasted for thirteen days. It was my son's First Communion. After the Holy Mass, I told one MC sister about his condition and she took us all to Mother and explained everything. Mother placed her hand on his head and prayed and then [he] was cured. Coming out of Mother House, he bought plenty of flowers to keep near Our Lady and Jesus and took us to the studio to take photographs. After which he bought mutton, and rejoicing we reached home. There he himself cooked a meal and we all ate together. Immediately after the meals, he went out to tell the neighbors and the office staff that he [had been] cured by Mother today. Others also believed that really Mother too had God's power to heal.[41]

She Prayed over Him

"Vic" was diagnosed as having terminal cancer of the colon and had one year to live. After his radical operation, I met Mother Teresa at the airport in Manila. Fortunately, I was the first to greet Mother Teresa, got her passport, and assigned an immigration person to handle her papers while we got her luggage. The first question she asked me was: "How are you, my child?" "I am well, but not my husband, for he has been diagnosed with a terminal cancer." While waiting for her luggage, she asked me to bring Vic the following day at 9:30 to the Regional House in Tayuman [Street], so she could pray over him and pin on my husband the same Miraculous Medal she had pinned on the pope when he was shot at the Vatican. I was so excited. The next day, I brought my husband to the Regional House, and exactly at 9:30 a.m. Mother Teresa came out of the chapel, and with her was the picture of a child in the palm of God's hand and a quotation from Isaiah, which she handed to my husband, praying over him for some twenty minutes and ended this with the Miraculous Medal pinned on his shirt. Tears flowed from my husband's eyes and mine too. Thereafter, Mother Teresa conversed with me about my family and even said that her own brother had died of cancer of the lungs and had it only for two years before he was called by our Lord, and that my husband should offer all his pain and sufferings to the

Lord and pray for peace in our country.[42] After three days, I brought my husband to his surgeon for his checkup, and the doctor could not believe the physical transformation of my husband.

In one week's time, Vic had become healthy. My husband's life was extended to nearly five years. Vic had all the time to prepare himself to be with the Lord, and he offered all his pains to Our Lord for His glory, became a daily communicant, and prepared the family for the eventual end, and he passed away with a smile on his lips and in peace and with apostolic blessings to meet the Creator.[43]

Thy Will Be Done

One of my officers' wives was suffering from tuberculosis of the lungs, and physicians gave her two or three weeks to live. She had two or three children. I asked Mother to pray for her, and Mother said she could only pray and beg the Almighty to spare her for a few more years. She very firmly believed that any prayer to the Merciful Father with firm faith would get God's blessings. Mother asked to call the officer, and together three of us knelt down in my office room and prayed for ten minutes. Concluding her prayer, Mother said, "Thy Will be done." After ten or twelve days, the officer told me with a strange look that his wife was improving considerably and the attending physician was pondering how this could have happened. This lady lived another twenty-five years thereafter.[44]

On hearing this, another officer approached me. His wife was very sick. I told Mother everything. I accompanied her to a village, the residence of this officer. Mother prayed for her and ended her prayer by saying, "Thy Will be done." Believe me, this lady was also restored to her own self.[45]

※

A constable working under me was very sick, suffering from epileptic disease, so much so that the authorities were thinking of getting him released from police service. I was very ill at ease as he had two or three children. One day when Mother came to my office for some registration work, I told Mother about this poor man. Mother told me to take her to his residence. The next day, I accompanied Mother in my office car to the constable's residence. Mother took with her two blankets, two saris, and a few [items of] apparel for his two children matching their age. She prayed for fifteen minutes, beseeching the God Almighty to look after the ailing person. She never prayed to completely cure the ailments of the affected person, but only repeated in her prayer to look after the sick person and also his family members. She finished her prayer by saying, "Thy Will be done." Believe me, after two or three weeks the constable met me in my office and told me that his epilepsy had not troubled him since the visit of the Holy Mother.[46]

※

I had diabetes, and one day Mother looking at me asked whether I was physically fit or not. I told her that I have high blood sugar. She gave me the locket of Mother Mary and prayed for my recovery. I am now having normal blood sugar only by some restriction of diet. My wife frequently says that since Mother has touched her, she has been able to control her temper and irritable attitude. Such was Mother's touch and blessing.[47]

They Also Need to Pray

Mother's solicitude that people be accorded their spiritual rights extended to those of all faiths. Mother herself told us about her experience when our sisters first went to Albania. In that country, no religious practice of any kind had been allowed for many years. With the change of regime, our sisters entered the country and immediately began looking for the poorest of the poor in order to care for them. Some aged and infirm women were found in what had previously been a mosque. When the sisters brought them to our house and got them settled, Mother's next concern was the mosque. She made the sisters clean it and then called the Muslim leaders to hand it over to them. In relating the story, one could see Mother's joy as she told us that by that same evening one could again hear the call to prayer from that mosque. "They also need to pray," she said.[48]

REFLECTION

"I urge that supplications, prayers, intercessions, and thanksgivings be made for all men." (1 Tm 2:1)

"Love to pray. Often during the day, feel the need to pray. For that is where your strength will come from. Jesus is always with us to love, to share, to be the joy of our lives. You are in my prayers. God bless you."

What can I do to deepen my relationship with the Lord in prayer? Do I dedicate at least a short time each day to personal prayer and reading of the Scriptures?

Do I use my busy schedule as an excuse to avoid prayer? Are there other things in my day that are less important but that I give precedence to over prayer?

Can I dedicate at least a few minutes of my time to pray for someone dear to me that has a special need at this time, perhaps a family member in difficulty, a sick friend, a discouraged colleague? What concrete prayers or small sacrifices can I offer for this person?

For which deceased person, known to me, have I never thought of praying? What prayers can I offer for them? Do I pray for my deceased family members and the souls in purgatory?

PRAYER

Remember, O most gracious Virgin Mary,
that never was it known
that anyone who fled to your protection,
implored your help,
or sought your intercession
was left unaided.

Inspired with this confidence,
I fly unto you,
O Virgin of virgins, my mother;
to you do I come;
before you I stand, sinful and sorrowful.

O Mother of the Word Incarnate,
despise not my petitions,
but in your clemency hear and answer me.
Amen.

CONCLUSION

God's mercy has a concrete countenance: the "compassionate and merciful" face of Jesus Christ that the Gospel brings close to us through the parables of the Good Samaritan, the Good Shepherd, and even more through the image of the father of the Prodigal Son. It is this countenance of God's Son that we are called to contemplate, in order that at least some of His compassion and tenderness will shine forth on our faces and in our actions.

To make this easier for us, the Church proposes to us the example of the saints, for something of God's love and compassion is also reflected on their faces. During this Jubilee of Mercy, the Church is presenting to us the person-model of Mother Teresa.

For Mother Teresa, everything began in prayer, in her relationship with God, in letting God's merciful gaze penetrate to the depths of her heart. And having experienced this gaze in prayer and contemplation, she channeled it to others.

On Divine Mercy Sunday, Pope Francis challenged the faithful to become "living writers of the Gospel" by practicing the spiritual and corporal works of mercy, which are "the hallmarks of the Christian life." In Mother Teresa's words and deeds, in particular the examples that show how she practiced works of mercy, the "Gospel became alive," as one of her followers said. She was, so to say, "writing" the Gospel by the way she lived it. This is what the Church is recognizing in her and offering to us as a model through her canonization.

Let her canonization and this book be an incentive to us to remember her love, her compassion, her soothing smile. When we see our brothers and sisters in need, let us be "apostles of mercy" by touching and healing the wounds of their bodies or of their souls, as Mother Teresa did. She keeps inviting us: "Just think for a moment, you and I have been called by our name, because He loved us. Because you and I are somebody special to Him—to be *His Heart to love Him* in the poor, *His Hands to serve Him* in the poorest of the poor . . . beginning with those around us, and even in our own families."

This is how we can be, as Pope Francis calls us to be, witnesses to mercy.

the name of the city during Mother Teresa's lifetime, and she will be known officially as Saint Teresa of Calcutta.

8. Account of Mother Teresa's Activities, December 21–23, 1948.

9. MV 15.

10. Ibid.

11. Ibid.

12. Ibid.

ONE: FEED THE HUNGRY

1. Mother Teresa's speech in Tokyo, April 26, 1981.

2. Mother Teresa's letter to the MC sisters, October 12, 1982.

3. Mother Teresa's instructions to the MC sisters, November 16, 1977.

4. Mother Teresa's address at the United Nations, October 26, 1985.

5. Mother Teresa's speech in Japan, November 24, 1984.

6. Mother Teresa's instructions to the MC sisters, April 10, 1984.

7. Translation of Mother Teresa's speech in Zagreb, Croatia, April 1978.

8. Mother Teresa's instructions to the MC sisters, September 25, 1984.

9. Mother Teresa's National Prayer Breakfast Address, February 3, 1994.

10. Mother Teresa's instructions to the MC sisters, March 7, 1979.

Notes

Note: When the citation "Testimony of an MC siste[r]
"Ibid.," it indicates that the same sister is being cited.

INTRODUCTION

1. Address of Pope Francis to the national con[gress of]
the "Misericordie" of Italy on June 14, 201[5, on oc-]
casion of the anniversary of its meeting wit[h John]
Paul II on June 14, 1986.

2. *Misericordiae Vultus,* April 11, 2015, 2; herea[fter abbrevi-]
ated as MV.

3. MV 5.

4. *Deus Caritas Est* 34.

5. Ibid., 34.

6. MV 15.

7. Throughout this work, the name Calcutta will b[e used,]
even though the city is now known as Kolkata.

11. Mother Teresa's instructions to the MC sisters, April 9, 1981.

12. Mother Teresa's instructions to the MC sisters, October 5, 1984.

13. Home of the Missionaries of Charity at Green Park, close to the airport in Calcutta.

14. Mother Teresa's instructions to the MC sisters, October 5, 1984.

15. Ibid.

16. Mother Teresa's speech in Japan, November 24, 1984.

17. Mother Teresa's speech, n.d.

18. Mother Teresa's instructions to the MC sisters, October 9, 1982.

19. Mother Teresa's speech in Tokyo, April 26, 1981.

20. Mother Teresa's interview, April 23, 1981.

21. Mother Teresa's speech in Rome, n.d.

22. Mother Teresa's address at Harvard University, Class Day Exercises, June 9, 1982.

23. Testimony of an MC sister.

24. Testimony of an MC sister.

25. Testimony of a priest who knew Mother Teresa for almost three decades until her death.

26. Testimony of an MC sister.

27. Testimony of a collaborator who knew Mother Teresa for about fifteen years and helped with various business matters.

28. Testimony of a Hindu woman co-worker in Calcutta.

29. Testimony of an MC sister.

30. Testimony of an MC priest who had frequent personal contact with Mother Teresa.

31. Testimony of an MC sister.

32. Testimony of an MC sister.

33. Testimony of a member of the Missionaries of Charity Contemplative Brothers, who had frequent personal contact with Mother Teresa.

34. Testimony of an MC sister.

35. Ibid.

36. Testimony of a co-worker of the Missionaries of Charity who knew Mother Teresa from the 1960s until the late 1980s.

37. Testimony of an MC sister.

38. Testimony of an MC sister.

39. Testimony of an MC sister.

40. Testimony of an MC sister.

41. Mother Teresa's letter to a co-worker.

42. Mother Teresa's letter to the Co-Workers, October 4, 1974.

TWO: GIVE DRINK TO THE THIRSTY

1. Mother Teresa's instructions to the MC sisters, September 29, 1977.

2. Mother Teresa's National Prayer Breakfast address, February 3, 1994.

3. Mother Teresa's address to priests, Rome, September 1990.

4. Mother Teresa's instructions to the MC sisters, June 20, 1981.

5. Mother Teresa's instructions to the MC sisters, October 14, 1977.

6. Mother Teresa's speech, n.d.

7. Mother Teresa's speech at the meeting with the Co-Workers, Tokyo, April 25, 1981.

8. Mother Teresa's address to priests, Rome, October 1984.

9. Translation of Mother Teresa's speech in Zagreb, Croatia, April 1978.

10. Testimony of an MC sister.

11. Testimony of an MC sister.

12. Testimony of an MC priest who had frequent personal contact with Mother Teresa.

13. Testimony of an MC brother.

14. Mother Teresa's letter to the MC sisters, February 25, 1979.

15. Mother Teresa's letter to the MC sisters, February 19, 1970.

THREE: CLOTHE THE NAKED

1. Mother Teresa's instructions to the MC sisters, September 15, 1976.

2. Mother Teresa's instructions to the MC sisters, June 10, 1977.

3. Mother Teresa's Nobel Peace Prize Acceptance Speech, December 11, 1979.

4. Mother Teresa's speech, December 10, 1981.

5. Mother Teresa's speech at the meeting with the Co-Workers, Minnesota, June 20–22, 1974.

6. Mother Teresa's instructions to the MC sisters, March 1993.

7. Mother Teresa's instructions to the MC sisters, September 18, 1981.

8. Mother Teresa's instructions to the MC sisters, October 12, 1977.

9. Mother Teresa's instructions to the MC sisters, September 16, 1981.

10. Mother Teresa's instructions to the MC sisters, January 16, 1983.

11. Mother Teresa's speech, December 10, 1981.

12. Mother Teresa's speech, n.d.

13. Mother Teresa, "Charity: Soul of Mission," January 23, 1991.

14. Mother Teresa's speech in Japan, November 24, 1984.

15. Mother Teresa's address at Harvard University, Class Day Exercises, June 9, 1982.

16. Mother Teresa's speech, April 25, 1982.

17. Testimony of an MC sister.

18. Testimony of a co-worker.

19. Testimony of an MC sister.

20. Testimony of an MC sister.

21. Testimony of an MC sister.

22. Testimony of an MC sister.

23. Testimony of an MC sister.

24. Mother Teresa's letter to the MC sisters, February 19, 1970.

25. Mother Teresa's letter to the Co-Workers, October 4, 1974.

FOUR: SHELTER THE HOMELESS

1. Cf. Brian Kolodiejchuk, MC, ed., *Mother Teresa: Come Be My Light* (New York: Doubleday, 2007), p. 232.

2. Mother Teresa, "Charity: Soul of Mission," January 23, 1991.

3. Shelter for men in Rome, close to the Termini train station.

4. Mother Teresa's speech in Assisi, June 6, 1986.

5. Mother Teresa's instructions to the MC sisters, Eve of Ash Wednesday, n.d.

6. Mother Teresa's speech, September 17, 1987.

7. Mother Teresa's speech in Japan, November 24, 1984.

8. Mother Teresa's instructions to the MC sisters, n.d.

9. Mother Teresa's speech in St. Louis, 1988.

10. Mother Teresa's speech at the meeting with the Co-Workers, Minnesota, June 20–22, 1974.

11. Mother Teresa's discussion with the youth, July 21–22, 1976.

12. Mother Teresa's address in Osaka, April 28, 1982.

13. Mother Teresa's address to priests, Rome, September 1990.

14. Mother Teresa's letter to a co-worker, March 11, 1961.

15. Mother Teresa's letter to a priest, July 23, 1976.

16. Mother Teresa's National Prayer Breakfast address, February 3, 1994.

17. Mother Teresa's address to priests, Rome, October 1984.

18. Mother Teresa's letter to a priest, March 4, 1991.

19. Mother Teresa's letter to the MC sisters, Easter 1995.

20. Mother Teresa's speech in Shillong, April 18, 1975.

21. Mother Teresa's talk at the Eucharistic Congress in Philadelphia, 1976.

22. Mother Teresa's letter to a co-worker, November 5, 1972.

23. Mother Teresa's speech at Marquette Discovery Awards, June 13, 1981.

24. Mother Teresa's letter to the MC sisters, February 19, 1970.

25. Mother Teresa's letter to a co-worker, October 13, 1969.

26. Testimony of an MC sister.

27. Testimony of an MC sister.

28. Testimony of an MC sister.

29. Testimony of an MC sister.

30. Testimony of an MC sister.

31. Testimony of an MC sister.

32. Testimony of an MC sister.

33. Testimony of a doctor co-worker who collaborated with Mother Teresa from the late 1950s.

34. Testimony of an MC sister.

35. Testimony of a police officer.

36. Testimony of an orphan girl.

37. Testimony of an orphan boy.

38. Testimony of a Hindu volunteer in Calcutta.

39. Testimony of an MC sister.

40. Testimony of a co-worker who had a close relationship with Mother Teresa from the 1960s onward.

41. Testimony of an MC sister.

42. Testimony of a doctor co-worker.

43. Testimony of an MC sister.

44. Testimony of a co-worker who had a close relationship with Mother Teresa from the 1960s onward.

45. Testimony of one of Mother Teresa's doctors.

46. Testimony of a co-worker who had a close relationship with Mother Teresa from the 1960s onward.

47. Testimony of an MC sister.

48. Testimony of a member of the Missionaries of Charity Contemplative Brothers who had frequent personal contact with Mother Teresa.

49. Mother Teresa's letter to the Co-Workers, October 4, 1974.

FIVE: VISIT THE SICK

1. Testimony of one of Mother Teresa's doctors.

2. Mother Teresa's Ek-Dil message, Christmas 1987.

3. Mother Teresa's letter to a layperson, April 21, 1991.

4. Mother Teresa's address at the Eucharistic Congress in Philadelphia, August 1976.

5. Ibid.

6. Mother Teresa's address to priests, Rome, October 1984.

7. Explanation of the Original Constitutions of the Missionaries of Charity.

8. Mother Teresa's speech, n.d.

9. Mother Teresa's instructions to the MC sisters, March 7, 1979.

10. Mother Teresa's address to the oblate clerics and novices, Rome, December 1979.

11. Mother Teresa's letter to the MC sisters, July 3, 1978.

12. Mother Teresa's letter to the MC sisters, Easter 1995.

13. Mother Teresa's letter to the MC superiors, November 13, 1969.

14. Mother Teresa's letter to the MC sisters, October 11, 1968.

15. Mother Teresa's letter to Jacqueline de Decker, October 20, 1952.

16. Mother Teresa's letter to Jacqueline de Decker, January 13, 1953.

17. Ibid.

18. Ibid.

19. Mother Teresa's letter to a layperson, December 22, 1989.

20. Testimony of an MC sister.

21. Testimony of a government official who knew Mother Teresa from the mid-1970s and helped her in the matters related to the Indian government.

22. Testimony of an orphan boy.

23. Testimony of an MC priest who had frequent personal contact with Mother Teresa.

24. Testimony of a collaborator who knew Mother Teresa for about fifteen years and helped with various business matters.

25. Ibid.

26. Testimony of an MC sister.

27. Testimony of an MC sister.

28. Testimony of an MC sister.

29. Testimony of a priest.

30. Testimony of a priest in Australia.

31. Testimony of a priest who helped Mother Teresa for decades in Calcutta.

32. Testimony of a priest who knew Mother Teresa from the 1980s and remained in close contact with her until her death.

33. Testimony of an MC sister.

34. Testimony of an MC sister.

35. Testimony of an MC sister.

36. Testimony of a laywoman.

37. Testimony of a doctor practicing in Calcutta.

38. Testimony of an MC sister.

39. Testimony of an MC sister.

40. Testimony of an MC sister.

41. Testimony of an MC sister.

42. Testimony of an MC sister.

43. Testimony of an MC sister.

44. Jacqueline de Decker, I need souls like you.

45. Mother Teresa's letter to the MC sisters, September 20, 1959.

46. Mother Teresa's letter to the Co-Workers, October 4, 1974.

SIX: VISIT THE IMPRISONED

1. Mother Teresa's speech, n.d.

2. Mother Teresa's instructions to the MC sisters, May 24, 1983.

3. Maximilian Kolbe (1894–1941), a Polish Franciscan who died in a concentration camp in Auschwitz, offering his life in place of that of a young father.

4. Mother Teresa's instructions to the MC sisters, May 25, 1983.

5. Mother Teresa's speech, Washington, D.C., n.d.

6. Father Joseph, co-founder of the MC fathers.

7. Mother Teresa's instructions to the MC sisters, May 21, 1986.

8. Mother Teresa's instructions to the MC sisters, March 7, 1979.

9. Mother's appeal to stop the death penalty of Joseph O'Dell, convicted and judged guilty of rape and murder. He was executed in Virginia by lethal injection on July 23, 1997, despite many appeals to save his life (Pope John Paul II also appealed). Telephone dictation by Mother Teresa, July 5, 1997.

10. Mother Teresa's speech at the meeting with the Co-Workers, Minnesota, June 20–22, 1974.

11. Testimony of an MC sister.

12. Testimony of a priest who knew Mother Teresa for almost three decades until her death.

13. Testimony of a volunteer of the Missionaries of Charity in the United States.

14. Testimony of an MC sister.

15. Testimony of a co-worker.

16. Testimony of a doctor volunteer of the Missionaries of Charity in the United States.

17. Testimony of a volunteer from the United States.

18. Testimony of an MC sister.

19. Mother Teresa's letter to the MC sisters, February 19, 1970.

SEVEN: BURY THE DEAD

1. Mother Teresa's instructions to the MC sisters, May 27, 1983.

2. Mother Teresa's discussion with the youth, July 21–22, 1976.

3. Ibid.

4. Mother Teresa's address at the meeting with the Co-Workers, Minnesota, June 20–22, 1974.

5. Mother Teresa's speech in Chicago, October 8, 1981.

6. Testimony of an MC sister.

7. Testimony of an MC sister.

8. Testimony of a collaborator who knew Mother Teresa for about fifteen years and helped with various business matters.

9. Testimony of a co-worker.

10. Testimony of an MC sister.

11. Testimony of a co-worker.

12. Testimony of an MC sister.

13. Testimony of an MC sister.

14. Testimony of a co-worker.

15. Testimony of a co-worker.

16. Testimony of a priest who helped Mother Teresa for decades.

17. Testimony of a co-worker of the Missionaries of Charity who knew Mother Teresa from the 1960s until the late 1980s.

18. Testimony of a priest who helped Mother Teresa for decades in Calcutta.

19. Testimony of an MC sister.

20. Testimony of a member of the Missionaries of Charity Contemplative Brothers who had frequent personal contact with Mother Teresa.

21. Testimony of a co-worker.

EIGHT: INSTRUCT THE IGNORANT

1. Mother Teresa to "Katoličke Misije," February 1, 1935.

2. Mother Teresa's diary, December 29, 1948.

3. Mother Teresa's letter to the MC sisters, June 3, 1964.

4. Mother Teresa's instructions to the MC sisters, n.d.

5. Mother Teresa's letter to the MC superiors, March 18, 1995.

6. Mother Teresa's instructions to the MC sisters, September 5, 1992.

7. Mother Teresa's instructions to the MC sisters, August 29, 1987.

8. Mother Teresa's instructions to the MC sisters, August 10, 1988.

9. Mother Teresa's instructions to the MC sisters, February 23, 1989.

10. Mother Teresa's instructions to the MC sisters, February 19, 1992.

11. Mother Teresa's instructions to the novice mistresses, August 7, 1993.

12. Mother Teresa's instructions to the MC sisters, January 10, 1984.

13. Mother Teresa to a journalist of Skopje (Macedonia) Television, March 28, 1978.

14. Mother Teresa's discussion with the youth, July 21–22, 1976.

15. Mother Teresa, press conference in Tokyo, April 22, 1982.

16. Mother Teresa's address in Osaka, April 28, 1982.

17. Mother Teresa's address to priests, Rome, September 1990.

18. Mother Teresa, press conference in Tokyo, April 22, 1982.

19. Mother Teresa's letter to the MC sisters, June 6, 1966.

20. Mother Teresa's instructions to the MC sisters, n.d.

21. Mother Teresa's letter to the MC sisters, June 6, 1966.

22. Mother Teresa's letter to the MC sisters, June 1974.

23. Testimony of an MC sister.

24. Testimony of an MC sister, Mother Teresa's former student in Loreto School.

25. Testimony of an MC sister.

26. Testimony of a woman whose family helped Mother Teresa when she began her work in the slums.

27. Testimony of a woman who was Mother Teresa's student in the Motijhil slum school.

28. Testimony of an MC sister.

29. Testimony of an MC sister.

30. Testimony of an MC sister.

31. Testimony of an MC sister.

32. Testimony of an MC sister.

33. Testimony of an MC sister.

34. Testimony of an MC sister.

35. Testimony of an MC sister.

36. Testimony of an MC sister.

37. Testimony of an MC sister.

38. Testimony of an MC sister.

39. Testimony of an MC sister.

40. Testimony of an Australian volunteer who helped especially in the Shishu Bhavan, the children's home in Calcutta.

41. Testimony of an MC sister.

42. Testimony of an MC sister.

NINE: COUNSEL THE DOUBTFUL

1. Mother Teresa, *Come Be My Light,* Brian Kolodiejchuk, MC, ed. (New York: Image, 2009), 209.

2. Mother Teresa, press conference in Tokyo, April 22, 1982.

3. Mother Teresa's letter to Malcolm Muggeridge, July 5, 1969.

4. Ibid., November 12, 1970.

5. Ibid., February 24, 1970.

6. Mother Teresa's letter to two co-workers, August 20, 1966.

7. Mother Teresa's letter to a co-worker, December 1, 1967.

8. Mother Teresa's letter to a co-worker, February 1992.

9. Mother Teresa's letter to a priest, September 22, 1985.

10. Testimony of a layperson.

11. Ibid.

12. Testimony of an MC contemplative brother who had frequent personal contact with Mother Teresa.

13. Testimony of an MC contemplative brother who had frequent personal contact with Mother Teresa.

14. Testimony of a priest who helped Mother Teresa for decades in Calcutta.

15. Testimony of an MC sister.

16. Ibid.

17. Testimony of a doctor.

18. Testimony of an MC sister.

19. Testimony of an MC sister.

20. Testimony of an MC sister.

21. Ibid.

22. Testimony of an MC sister.

23. Testimony of an MC sister.

24. Testimony of a priest.

25. Testimony of a layperson.

26. Testimony of an MC sister.

27. 1988 Constitutions, no. 45, no. 49.

TEN: ADMONISH SINNERS

1. Mother Teresa's instructions to the MC sisters, August 22, 1980.

2. Mother Teresa's instructions to the MC sisters, November 14, 1979.

3. Ibid.

4. Mother Teresa's letter to the MC sisters, September 29, 1981.

5. Mother Teresa's instructions to the MC sisters, 1980s.

6. Mother Teresa's instructions to the MC sisters, January 8, 1979.

7. Mother Teresa's instructions to the MC sisters, n.d.

8. Mother Teresa's instructions to the MC sisters, August 24, 1980.

9. Mother Teresa's instructions to the MC sisters, February 13, 1983.

10. Mother Teresa's instructions to the MC sisters, November 9, 1977.

11. Mother Teresa's instructions to the MC sisters, May 18, 1978.

12. Ibid.

13. Mother Teresa's instructions to the MC sisters, August 20, 1982.

14. Ibid.

15. Ibid.

16. Mother Teresa's instructions to the MC sisters, December 4, 1982.

17. Mother Teresa's instructions to the MC sisters, May 7, 1980.

18. Ibid.

19. Mother Teresa's instructions to the MC sisters, September 13, 1988.

20. Mother Teresa's instructions to the MC sisters, May 6, 1980.

21. Mother Teresa's instructions to the MC sisters, May 7, 1980.

22. Mother Teresa's instructions to the MC sisters, May 17, 1980.

23. Mother Teresa's instructions to the MC sisters, April 3, 1981.

24. Mother Teresa's instructions to the MC sisters, August 20, 1982.

25. Mother Teresa's instructions to the MC sisters, February 14, 1983.

26. Mother Teresa's instructions to the MC sisters, April 16, 1981.

27. Mother Teresa's instructions to the MC sisters, July 15, 1981.

28. Mother Teresa's instructions to the MC sisters, November 1979.

29. Mother Teresa's letter with prayer for those who have committed abortion, Japan, April 11, 1982.

30. Mother Teresa, press conference in Tokyo, April 22, 1982.

31. Mother Teresa's speech in Tokyo, April 23, 1982.

32. Mother Teresa's speech in Nagasaki, April 26, 1982.

33. Mother Teresa's instructions to the MC sisters, December 4, 1980.

34. Mother Teresa's instructions to the MC sisters, March 6, 1965.

35. Mother Teresa's instructions to the MC sisters, August 30, 1988.

36. Mother Teresa's instructions to the MC sisters, n.d. but before 1973.

37. Mother Teresa's letter to the MC superiors, June 6, 1966.

38. Mother Teresa's letter to the MC superiors, June 1962.

39. Mother Teresa's letter to the MC superiors, September 8, 1977.

40. Mother Teresa's instructions to the MC sisters, July 14, 1981.

41. Mother Teresa's instructions to the MC sisters, May 14, 1982.

42. Mother Teresa's instructions to the MC sisters, May 25, 1983.

43. Mother Teresa's open letter, October 3, 1983.

44. Testimony of an MC priest who had frequent personal contact with Mother Teresa.

45. Testimony of an MC sister.

46. Testimony of a priest from the United States.

47. Testimony of an MC sister.

48. Testimony of an MC sister.

49. Testimony of an MC sister.

50. Testimony of an MC sister.

51. Testimony of an MC brother.

52. Testimony of an MC sister.

53. Testimony of an MC priest who had frequent personal contact with Mother Teresa.

54. Ibid.

55. Testimony of a collaborator who knew Mother Teresa for about fifteen years and helped her in various business matters.

56. Testimony of an MC priest who had frequent personal contact with Mother Teresa.

57. Testimony of an MC sister.

58. Testimony of an MC sister.

59. Testimony of an MC sister.

60. Testimony of a co-worker.

61. Testimony of an MC sister.

62. Mother Teresa's instructions to the MC sisters, 1980s.

63. Mother Teresa's instructions to the MC sisters, May 10, 1986.

ELEVEN: BEAR WRONGS PATIENTLY

1. Mother Teresa's instructions to the MC sisters, n.d.

2. Mother Teresa, press conference in Chicago, 1981.

3. Mother Teresa's instructions to the MC sisters, October 5, 1984.

4. Mother Teresa's instructions to the MC sisters, March 23, 1987.

5. Mother Teresa's instructions to the MC sisters, November 19, 1979.

6. Mother Teresa's instructions to the MC sisters, April 12, 1985.

7. Mother Teresa's instructions to the MC sisters, January 10, 1984.

8. Mother Teresa's instructions to the MC sisters, April 10, 1984.

9. Mother Teresa's instructions to the MC sisters, January 15, 1981.

10. Mother Teresa's instructions to the MC sisters, n.d.

11. Mother Teresa's letter to the MC sisters, May 19, 1968.

12. Mother Teresa's letter to a co-worker, March 10, 1965.

13. Mother Teresa's instructions to the MC sisters, November 2, 1982.

14. Mother Teresa's instructions to the MC sisters, November 7, 1987.

15. Mother Teresa's instructions to the MC sisters, May 22, 1986.

16. Mother Teresa's instructions to the MC sisters, September 16, 1980.

17. Mother Teresa's instructions to the MC sisters, April 18, 1981.

18. Mother Teresa's instructions to the MC sisters, April 15, 1981.

19. Mother Teresa's instructions to the MC sisters, n.d.

20. Mother Teresa's instructions to the MC sisters, May 20, 1987.

21. Mother Teresa's instructions to the MC sisters, August 24, 1980.

22. Mother Teresa's instructions to the MC sisters, August 15, 1983.

23. Mother Teresa's instructions to the MC sisters, May 22, 1978.

24. Mother Teresa's instructions to the MC sisters, September 13, 1988.

25. Mother Teresa's instructions to the MC sisters, October 5, 1984.

26. Mother Teresa's instructions to the MC sisters, n.d.

27. Mother Teresa's instructions to the MC sisters, January 23, 1983.

28. Mother Teresa's instructions to the MC sisters, May 25, 1983.

29. Mother Teresa's instructions to the MC sisters, October 30, 1981.

30. Mother Teresa's letter to a co-worker, October 13, 1969.

31. Mother Teresa's letter to a co-worker, July 3, 1969.

32. Mother Teresa's letter to a co-worker, April 11, 1964.

33. Mother Teresa's instructions to the MC sisters, May 26, 1983.

34. Mother Teresa's instructions to the MC sisters, May 20, 1987.

35. Mother Teresa's instructions to the MC sisters, October 22, 1977.

36. Abbé Pierre (1912–2007), a French priest and founder of Emmaus communities dedicated to helping the poor and homeless people in France and throughout the world.

37. Mother Teresa's instructions to the MC sisters, October 11, 1982.

38. Testimony of an orphan boy.

39. Testimony of an MC sister.

40. Testimony of an MC sister.

41. Testimony of an MC sister.

42. Testimony of an MC sister.

43. Testimony of a priest.

44. Testimony of an MC sister.

45. Ibid.

46. Testimony of an MC sister.

47. Testimony of a co-worker.

48. Testimony of an MC sister.

49. Ibid.

50. Testimony of an MC sister.

51. Testimony of an MC sister.

52. Testimony of an MC sister.

53. Ibid.

54. Ibid.

55. Testimony of an MC sister.

56. Testimony of an MC sister.

57. Testimony of an MC sister.

58. Mother Teresa's letter to a priest, February 7, 1976.

TWELVE: FORGIVE OFFENSES WILLINGLY

1. Lk 23:34.

2. Mother Teresa's instructions to the MC sisters, April 15, 1981.

3. Mother Teresa's instructions to the MC sisters, September 18, 1981.

4. Mother Teresa's address in Nagasaki, April 26, 1982.

5. Mother Teresa, press conference in Chicago, 1981.

6. Mother Teresa's instructions to the MC sisters, June 30, 1965.

7. Mother Teresa's speech in Nagasaki, April 26, 1982.

8. Ibid.

9. Ibid.

10. Mother Teresa's talk to volunteers in Calcutta, December 21, 1995.

11. Mother Teresa, press conference in Beirut, April 1982.

12. Mother Teresa's letter to the MC sisters, May 1964.

13. Mother Teresa's letter to the MC sisters, December 14, 1973.

14. Mother Teresa's instructions to the MC sisters, February 21, 1979.

15. Ibid.

16. Mother Teresa's speech in Kentucky, June 19, 1982.

17. Mother Teresa's instructions to the MC sisters, February 21, 1981.

18. Ibid.

19. Mother Teresa's instructions to the MC sisters, August 24, 1980.

20. Mother Teresa's instructions to the MC sisters, September 12, 1980.

21. Mother Teresa's instructions to the MC sisters, February 21, 1981.

22. Mother Teresa's instructions to the MC sisters, March 27, 1981.

23. Mother Teresa's instructions to the MC sisters, December 4, 1982.

24. Ibid.

25. Mother Teresa's instructions to the MC sisters, December 6, 1982.

26. Mother Teresa's instructions to the MC sisters, October 15, 1977.

27. Mother Teresa's instructions to the MC sisters, November 7, 1977.

28. Mother Teresa's instructions to the MC sisters, February 21, 1979.

29. Ibid.

30. Mother Teresa's speech, September 17, 1987.

31. Ibid.

32. Mother Teresa's instructions to the MC sisters, January 15, 1981.

33. Mother Teresa's instructions to the MC sisters, May 14, 1982.

34. Testimony of an MC sister.

35. Testimony of an MC sister.

36. Testimony of an MC sister.

37. Testimony of an MC sister.

38. Testimony of an MC sister.

39. Testimony of an MC sister.

40. Testimony of an MC sister.

41. Testimony of a collaborator who knew Mother Teresa for more than twenty years.

42. Testimony of an MC sister.

43. Testimony of an MC sister.

44. Testimony of an MC sister.

45. Mother Teresa's instructions to the MC sisters, February 21, 1979.

46. Mother Teresa's address in Nagasaki, April 26, 1982.

THIRTEEN: COMFORT THE AFFLICTED

1. Mother Teresa's instructions to the MC sisters, May 23, 1986.

2. Mother Teresa's instructions to the MC sisters, December 24, 1988.

3. Mother Teresa's instructions to the MC sisters, February 8, 1981.

4. Mother Teresa's message at Narita Airport, Tokyo, April 22, 1981.

5. Mother Teresa's instructions to the MC sisters, December 15, 1978.

6. Mother Teresa's letter to the MC sisters, October 15, 1971.

7. Mother Teresa's letter to the MC sisters, September 20, 1959.

8. Mother Teresa's speech, n.d.

9. Mother Teresa's speech to medical personnel.

10. Mother Teresa, press conference, n.d.

11. Mother Teresa's address in Chicago, June 4, 1981.

12. Mother Teresa's speech at the meeting with the Co-Workers, Minnesota, June 20–22, 1974.

13. Ibid.

14. Ibid.

15. Mother Teresa's letter to the Co-Workers, March 1, 1995.

16. Testimony of an MC sister to a co-worker, February 12, 1981.

17. Mother Teresa's letter to a priest, February 7, 1974.

18. Mother Teresa's letter to a layperson, December 22, 1989.

19. Mother Teresa's letter to a co-worker, September 11, 1967.

20. Mother Teresa's letter to a layperson, 1992.

21. Mother Teresa's letter to a layperson, July 11, 1992.

22. Mother Teresa's letter to a laywoman, August 9, 1990.

23. Mother Teresa's letter to a layperson, March 8, 1996.

24. Mother Teresa's letter to a priest, September 7, 1991.

25. Testimony of an MC sister.

26. Testimony of an MC sister.

27. Testimony of a volunteer from the United States.

28. Testimony of an MC sister.

29. Testimony of a co-worker.

30. Testimony of a co-worker.

31. Testimony of a layperson.

32. Testimony of an MC sister.

33. Testimony of a volunteer who had a close relationship with Mother Teresa.

34. Testimony of a priest who helped Mother Teresa in Calcutta.

35. Testimony of an MC sister.

36. *Where There Is Love, There Is God*, Brian Kolodiejchuk: After Mother Teresa began receiving international recognition, she started distributing a small card. On one side were the words "God bless you" and her signature, and on the other the following saying: "The fruit of silence is prayer; the fruit of prayer is faith; the fruit of faith is love; the fruit of love is service; the fruit of service is peace." With a bit of impish humor, she referred to this card as her "business card." Unlike standard business cards, hers did not bear the name of her organization, nor her title, contact information, or phone number. Yet the sequence of phrases can be taken as the formula of the "success" of her "business." Without intending to advertise her undertakings with this well-known quote, Mother Teresa indicated that her endeavors were of a spiritual nature, focused on God, and directed toward her neighbor.

37. Testimony of a priest who had frequent contact with Mother Teresa.

38. Testimony of an MC sister.

39. Testimony of a volunteer in Calcutta.

40. Testimony of an MC sister.

41. Testimony of a layperson.

42. Testimony of a police officer who helped Mother Teresa in dealings with public authorities.

43. Testimony of a Calcutta volunteer who helped mostly in Kalighat.

44. Testimony of a volunteer.

45. Testimony of a co-worker who had a close relationship with Mother Teresa from the 1960s onward.

46. Testimony of a co-worker who had a close relationship with Mother Teresa from the 1960s onward.

47. Testimony of an MC priest who had frequent contact with Mother Teresa.

48. Mother Teresa's letter to a layperson, October 12, 1988.

FOURTEEN: PRAY FOR THE LIVING AND THE DEAD

1. Mother Teresa's letter to the Co-Workers, Lent 1996.

2. Mother Teresa's instructions to the MC sisters, n.d.

3. Testimony of an MC priest who had frequent personal contact with Mother Teresa.

4. Testimony of an MC sister.

5. Constitutions, no. 130, 1988.

6. Mother Teresa's speech at Congress of the Family, September 17, 1987.

7. Testimony of an MC sister.

8. Mother Teresa's speech in Japan, November 24, 1984.

9. Mother Teresa's speech in New York, n.d.

10. Mother Teresa's address at Harvard University, Class Day Exercises, June 9, 1982.

11. Mother Teresa to a journalist, June 1979.

12. Mother Teresa's address in Fukuoka, Japan, April 27, 1982.

13. Ibid.

14. Ibid.

15. Mother Teresa's open letter, November 7, 1995.

16. Mother Teresa's address in Tokyo, April 23, 1982.

17. Mother Teresa's speech to the International Congress for Women, Rome.

18. Mother Teresa, press conference in Tokyo, April 22, 1982.

19. Mother Teresa's address in Nagasaki, April 26, 1982.

20. Mother Teresa's instructions to the MC sisters, November 19, 1979.

21. Mother Teresa's letter to the MC sisters, September 9, 1965.

22. Mother Teresa's instructions to the MC sisters, November 4, 1965.

23. Testimony of a doctor co-worker who collaborated with Mother Teresa from the late 1950s.

24. Testimony of an MC sister.

25. Testimony of an MC sister.

26. Testimony of an MC sister.

27. Testimony of an MC sister.

28. Testimony of an MC sister.

29. Ibid.

30. Testimony of an MC sister.

31. Testimony of an MC sister.

32. Testimony of an MC sister.

33. Testimony of an MC sister.

34. Testimony of an MC sister.

35. Testimony of an MC sister.

36. Testimony of an MC sister.

37. Testimony of an MC sister.

38. Testimony of an MC sister.

39. Testimony of a volunteer who had a close relationship with Mother Teresa.

40. Testimony of an MC sister.

41. Testimony of a layperson.

42. Testimony of a laywoman.

43. Ibid.

44. Testimony of a police officer.

45. Ibid.

46. Ibid.

47. Testimony of a doctor practicing in Calcutta.

48. Testimony of an MC sister.